THE SKY BELOW

SCOTT PARAZYNSKI
WITH SUSY FLORY

THE SKY BELOW

Little a

Published by Little A, New York

www.apub.com

ISBN-13: 978-1542048507
ISBN-10: 1542048508

Cover design by Faceout Studio

Cover photo by Belief Agency

Cover composite image credits:
Gil C/Shutterstock.com
NASA ID: iss041e066940, Courtesy NASA/Alex Gerst
NASA ID: iss016e007423, Courtesy NASA
NASA ID: iss040e074785, Courtesy NASA/Reid Wiseman

Printed in the United States of America

First edition

To my parents, Ed and Linda, who inspired me to explore;
To my son, Luke, who first taught me unconditional love;
To my daughter, Jenna, who brings absolute joy and wonder;
To my magnificent wife, Mini, for the love of a lifetime.

Everything is possible until proven impossible,
and then you just need to become more creative.

CONTENTS

FOREWORD

Before I retired from NASA and moved on to other pursuits, my primary job at the space agency was to manage the training of the astronauts on science payloads, first for the *Spacelab* series of flights and then for the *International Space Station*. Although I never worked directly on a mission that included Dr. Scott Parazynski as a crewmember, I was very much aware of him almost from the beginning of his space career. His first mission was STS-66 (ATLAS-3), a *Spacelab* mission managed by my home center in Huntsville, Alabama, and stories about him bubbled up rather quickly within our training ranks. The word I received from the trainers was that Scott was supersmart, diligent, and polite. In other words, he was not only trainable but *nice*. We were later to learn he was also brave and strong and resolute but, for training folks, trainable and nice were great. As we got to know him even better, we wanted Scott on all our missions, and we let our supervisors know it. Whether that affected any of his assignments, I don't know, but I hope it did.

Another of my jobs with NASA was to work at the Marshall Space Flight Center's Neutral Buoyancy Simulator (NBS), a giant million-gallon tub of water where the astronauts practiced extravehicular activity, in other words, working in space in a pressurized suit. Although usually I worked as a safety diver in the NBS, sometimes I climbed into a spacesuit to help figure out the procedures an astronaut would need to follow while on a real space mission. Working in an inflated Extravehicular Mobility Unit (EMU) suit, as it is officially called, is like being swaddled in a dozen stiff overcoats. The gloves are also pressurized enough that they remove touch as a useful sense and require strength just to hold a wrench. Not all astronauts are good in the suit. We who worked in the NBS knew very well those who were and those who weren't. Scott was one of the good ones. In fact, he was one of the *really* good ones. He had a sixth sense on where everything was and could, without turning himself into a corkscrew, select and use the tools he needed even though his view might be obscured by his helmet or the bulkiness of the suit kept him from getting close to his work. This innate ability would come in quite handy late in Scott's NASA career when all he had to do was go outside and, without any training whatsoever, avoid getting electrocuted while saving the *International Space Station* with a flimsy, handmade tool.

There is, of course, a lot more to Scott Parazynski's life than his time as an astronaut. Simply put, I think it is fair to say Scott is a wonder, a fellow who has packed in more exploits in his lifetime than most of us can imagine or even wish upon ourselves. Although more than a few of these adventures have been dangerous with a high likelihood of failure, Scott is the kind of person who perseveres to go wherever he wants to go and somehow manages to get there. Now, with this memoir, we get to go with him, and it's a truly prodigious ride.

Homer Hickam
Author of *Rocket Boys: A Memoir*

THE INSPIRATION FOR THIS BOOK

This book was written for the women and men of Team STS-120, who worked nonstop through the nights of October 31 through November 2, 2007, to salvage the *International Space Station*'s P6-4B solar array, but who have never really been properly acknowledged or celebrated enough for their brilliant work. Their creativity, resilience, and teamwork saved the *International Space Station* solar array, and much more. Members of this remarkable team include:

The late, great Kevin Pehr

Derek Hassmann, Lead ISS Flight Director

Dina Contella, Lead Spacewalk Officer

Sarmad Aziz, Lead Robotics Officer

Allison Bolinger, EVA Task Lead

Scott Stover, Lead PHALCON Flight Controller

Rebecca Tures, NASA Mission Evaluation Room Manager

The Mission Control Team 4 Contingency Team:

Annette Hasbrook (Flight Director), John Ray, Glenda Laws, Christy Hansen, Joe Tanner, Mike Steele, Andrew Clem, Deana

Smith, Robert Pickle, Vincent LaCourt, Kauser Imtiaz, Dave McCann, Don Campilongo, Curt Carlton, Davie Moore, and Scott Keepers

Our CAPCOMs: Steve Swanson and Kevin Ford

The entire NBL dive team

The Virtual Reality Lab: Dave Homan and Evelyn Miralles

The ISS Expedition 16 Crew: Peggy, Clay, and Yuri

The STS-120 Crew: Pambo, Zambo, Flambo, Boichi, Robeau, and the Italian Stallion

CHAPTER ONE

On the Shoulders of Giants

No true adventure is fun while it's happening.

—*Dom Del Rosso*

EVEREST CAMP 2, 2008

It's well before sunup on the south side of Mount Everest, and I'm in my tent at Camp 2, twenty-one thousand feet up in the sky, on my way to the summit. The jet stream tears at the thin ripstop nylon walls as it has all night long, but it's not the bone-chilling cold or shrieking winds driving away any chance of sleep. It's the searing pain in my back.

My wristwatch alarm chirps at 3:00 a.m. and I struggle out of my bag, determined to ignore my condition. After pulling on my boots and crampons, I cinch down my waist harness until it is vise-tight, like a weight-lifting belt. The pressure helps, and my back feels a little better as we set off in the frigid predawn.

Climbing from Camp 2 to Camp 3 today means over three thousand staggering vertical feet of hard, blue ice, including the Bergschrund, a massive crevasse formed by a migrating glacier separated from the ice on the mountain above. My team includes Kami Sherpa, Ang Namya Sherpa, Chip Popoviciu, Vance Cook, and Adam Janikowski, a good friend I attempted Denali with a few years ago.

After we cross down into the crevasse via fixed lines, we climb up a short, near-vertical pitch of ice to get on the Lhotse Face itself, a long, very steep slope of unforgiving ice leading up to Camp 3 at 24,500 feet. I make it to camp in a very respectable time of four hours, strained back and all.

Camp 3 is the next-to-last waypoint on the route to the top and by far the least comfortable, situated on a few small platforms etched out of the very steep incline of the mountain's face. Climbers typically confine themselves to their tents except to answer the cold call of nature because it is dangerous to get out and move around without being roped up. There is potential, and historical precedent, for a fatal slip and fall with a catastrophic slide down the Lhotse Face, ending in a 2,500-foot abrupt splatter at the Bergschrund and the Western Cwm below. If we want to make a successful push for the summit, then getting as much rest as possible here and throwing some food down our necks is crucial.

Upon arrival at Camp 3, my tent mate, Adam, and I hurry to settle in well before sunset. When I eventually release the tension in my waist harness to climb into my sleeping bag, I know it isn't good. The pain and stiffness come back with a fury, and then some. I just need to get some sleep, I keep telling myself. Then I can give it a go and head for the summit in the morning. It feels like someone is hacking away at my lower vertebrae with a Rambo knife. I writhe in my sleeping bag as the pain comes in waves, then recedes. Again and again. It's tough to breathe.

I work hard to keep myself in great physical shape, but the reality is I'm an aging astronaut, and space missions aren't kind to the back. I picture my spine like a game of Jenga blocks slowly growing unstable as the game progresses. The average human back's vertebrae, and the cushioning discs in between, take a real beating from the rigors of a life of upright, bipedal locomotion. These incredible loads on the spine cause disc pressures as high as 230 pounds per square inch.[1]

But I'm a perfect candidate for serious back problems and not just because I'm oldish and getting older. Add in height, six foot three when I'm not slouching, and then factor in the high-g exposures I experienced competing in luge and flying in high-performance aircraft.

Finally, and probably even more important, my multiple spaceflights and spacewalks mean the likelihood of spinal trouble is almost as inevitable as an overloaded, rickety Jenga tower toppling over into a ragged heap. In space, the spine straightens and the intervertebral discs swell when not being compressed by gravity, so my height in space would increase to an impressive six foot, five and a half inches in the absence of gravity—almost worthy of the NBA (regrettably minus the talent). But a return to gravity always meant a return to my original height, or less.

For most astronauts, this zero-g spinal growth is part of the routine, so spacewalking suits are size-adjusted to account for the temporary increase in height. That's the theory anyway. NASA engineers add about an inch to the spacesuit's torso, but since it never seems to be quite enough, initially you feel a sense of compression from the slightly too small suit. But after a few minutes your body adjusts, the suit presumably overpressurizing your poor intervertebral discs and squeezing away the excess height.

I know my back pain is a big problem here on the mountain. But my time is running out, and there is a lot at stake. Climbing Everest is all about stacking the cards in your favor, and most climbers aim for the premonsoon season in the Himalayas, before the summer snows arrive, because temperatures are generally a bit warmer. The month of May typically offers a one- or two-week weather window when conditions are at their absolute best. Even so, temperatures average minus 13 degrees Fahrenheit with winds that can crest to 50 miles an hour on a bad day.

Most people don't know the top of the mountain is so high that it almost penetrates into the stratosphere. The summit feels the full brunt of the jet stream, which can hammer the mountain at speeds approaching 175 miles an hour. By comparison, a tropical storm is considered a hurricane when winds reach just 74 miles per hour, and the winds of a Category 5 hurricane, the most severe, top out at 156 miles per hour. That means these Everest megawinds would be rated as a Category 6 hurricane, or stronger, if there even were such a thing, and temperatures can drop to minus 73 degrees Celsius (or, in Fahrenheit, about 100 degrees below zero).

I am already at Day 59 of my expedition to the top of the world. I've planned and plotted with my patented extreme focus, hoping for success but preparing for serious kinks in the road. I've made four trips[2] up the harrowing, near-vertical, and not infrequently fatal Khumbu Icefall, a frozen river of jumbled snow and icy cliffs interspersed with dizzying crevasses opening up beneath my feet, sometimes 150 gnarly feet down. I've front-pointed my crampons up the hard blue ice of the Lhotse Face higher than I'd ever been before, as the lactic acid burns in my legs and my heaving lungs warn me I am working right up at redline. I've fought hard to get up here, where people were really never meant to tread, and I can't wait around for my back to feel better. With experts recommending spending no more than forty-eight hours at that altitude else your body begins to degrade on its way to death, I have a short window of time. More than anything, I need to rest at Camp 3 and give my back a chance to heal. If that's even possible.

Adam is asleep in the tent before sunset, a bandana over his eyes and an oxygen mask over his face. He immediately starts snoring, deep gulps of air interspersed with periods of silent apnea. It's frightening and sounds like a death rattle, but the rational part of my brain tells me it's just a physiologic condition known as Cheyne-Stokes respiration,[3] normal at these extreme altitudes.

I'd give anything to settle into my own blissful pattern of snores, but instead I spend the next twelve hours tossing and turning in my sleeping bag, trying in vain to reposition my body to something approaching comfort, or at least bring my pain level down a notch or two. I have a few tablets of oxycodone in my medical kit for team emergencies, but at that altitude even a small amount of narcotic medication can suppress respiratory drive, and I reason that breathing is more important than blunting the pain. So I rely on ice, awkward stretches in my sleeping bag, and high hopes of healing through a very long night.

It's my worst possible nightmare coming to life. At just twenty-four hours from the summit of my dreams, searing pain has kept me up all night, and this morning it's much worse. *How the hell can this be?* I writhe in my sleeping bag as the pain comes and goes again. It's even tougher to breathe now that we're above twenty-four thousand feet, where the oxygen level is only 40 percent of what you get at sea level. Even though I've been on the mountain for almost eight weeks and feel acclimatized to the thin air, it's still like being slowly choked. But when the pain plunges me into a cold sweat, my thirst for oxygen is of secondary importance.

Every thirty seconds all through the night, I thrash around and instead of recharging, I feel myself sinking down into complete and utter exhaustion. It's like the worst night on-call I'd ever had in the hospital, racing for my patients all night long, except this time I have a touch of hypoxia, some dehydration and malnutrition, plus a healthy dose of pain. This is not what I planned.

I'm clearly not ready to climb, but at 5:30 sharp, Kami Sherpa and Ang Namya Sherpa unzip the tent flap, pop their heads in, and hand us hot water so we can make tea and eat some oatmeal. They're anxious to get up onto the upper Lhotse Face in position for a run at the summit from Camp 4, also known as the South Col, our next destination.

Will I make it?

Adam peels off his bandana, sits up, and looks over at me. He frowns, mirroring my own grimace as he looks into my bloodshot eyes, staring back at him over my oxygen mask.

"I feel like shit, but I've gotta try," I say, loud enough so he can hear me through the mask.

He nods knowingly, climbs out of his bag and gets ready, then turns to help me. This time, I cannot get ready on my own. I slept in my thick, insulated suit, and now I need help getting into my harness and the bulky, rated-to-minus-60-degree boots. I have to stop Adam several times to let the spasms in my lower back subside before we can continue. I try not to scream or cry.

An hour later, at 6:30, we're almost ready and I force myself outside. The team takes turns helping me get my crampons installed as a radio transmits the sounds of our teammates Casey and Ari celebrating from the summit. There is joy in their voices, but I feel ashamed when I realize I'm flooded with envy more than happiness. How shallow can I be? Snap out of it, just be happy for them, and forget this freakin' pain! My friends are standing on the top of the tallest mountain in the world, and if my back calms down and cooperates, I'll be there, too, in just twenty-four short hours.

The weather up top today is excellent, minus 25 Celsius and the winds are less than 15 miles per hour. Before we depart, I want to sit and try to stretch out my back, but there isn't room. It's difficult to even turn while Kami changes out my oxygen cylinder for the upcoming ascent. The distraction camouflages the pain for a few moments, but now that I'm geared up, the spasms return with a vengeance. I cannot stay upright any longer. As the pain overwhelms me, I more or less collapse between the tents and consider my plight.

I've taken two months' vacation from work, left my (unhappy) wife and two wonderful kids at home, and signed on the dotted line for a $40,000 home equity loan to finance my quest. As I wallow in the misery of possibly never living out my dream while wasting so much time, energy, and money, I can clearly see the South Summit up over my shoulder to the right, tantalizingly close both in time and distance. Hope stirs again. Maybe I can do this. Maybe I'm just being a wimp. Can't I suck it up and push through this?

I know I don't have much time to figure out if I can do it or not. I can see and hear the others tightening up harnesses and hoisting packs. It's now or never, but I'm in an agony of indecision, not sure if I should go with my team. My mind is racing. If I turn my back on the summit this day, will I ever be able to take another shot? Will I be able to afford a second shot? Will my wife agree? Will I even have a wife to come home to?

If I go for it and press on, what will it mean for the summit chances of my teammates? They'll most likely stick with me, especially if my back gets worse or I get into a difficult situation. Is that fair to them? I'm not the only one who has sacrificed to be here. If the pain gets worse and I collapse, will I die? Will my teammates end up in a life-or-death situation, risking their lives, too?

"You try go up, yes?" It's Kami Sherpa, his voice snapping me out of my fretting as I look up at this perpetually smiling Iron Man of the Himalayas. He looks down at me with grave concern.

I'm not sure what to do, and even though I'm lacking in both conviction and energy, I decide to give it a test. My lower back now locked in full spasm, I force myself up into a very feeble standing position. I hold my breath while my back punishes me for moving, then after a few seconds I slowly begin to work my way toward the main fixed lines of the steep face, just fifty feet away. I'm walking like Frankenstein on crack, but it's the best I've got. Maybe, just maybe, my back will loosen up once I get going.

It's not the first time I've faced this kind of dilemma. Sometimes, there's nowhere to go but up.

CHAPTER TWO

Cliffhanger

A good face climber plans ahead.

—*John Long,* How to Rock Climb!

SOUTH PLATTE, COLORADO, 1992

I'm way the hell up and gone here with no hardware between me and John. Just a scattering of jagged boulders to cushion my fall at the base of the route.

The rest of the world evaporates, and it's just me and a face full of near flawless rock. I scan the steep, sun-drenched granite for potential cracks to insert a small camming device or wired hexentric nut.[4] I'd give just about anything for an anchor and a carabiner on this wall. A thirty- or forty-foot fall will really, really hurt. I'm in trouble.

Like a gecko, I have my hands spread out, pressing in and down and gripping at the rough granite face. I'm feeling for tiny imperfections in the rock, but there's nothing resembling a handhold.

I spot a crack way to the left. Can I make it? Too far.

But there is something to the right. A small overhang, if I can work my way up another ten feet or so. Maybe more like a bump. Can I inch over? No. Can't make that, either. Nothing solid to step on, just microscopic imperfections in the tan granite for my fingers to call home. I'll have to lunge for it, and the bump doesn't project out enough for my hands to lock in, so I'm stuck, frozen in place, soles smeared against the rock and staying there through sheer friction, determination, and a rapidly building fear.

I breathe in the scent of sunbaked rock and pine trees while my hands sweat through the chalk. I can feel my heart beginning to thump. My calves start to burn and then shake uncontrollably as if in a myoclonic seizure. *Sewing machine legs*. This is really bad. It means I'm reaching exhaustion and a state of panic. I look down because now John knows I'm in trouble, too.

"I can't put in any pro," I call down to John, trying as hard as I can to keep my voice calm and even. "Hey"—my voice cracks just a bit—"where's the next spot where I can put in some protection?"

"Keep climbing." John is a man of few words, and always cool.

Shit.

This would be a terrible time to die because I'm about to leave for Houston. I've been chosen from among thousands for astronaut training, and I'm about to go live out my childhood dream. I can just imagine the embarrassing headlines: "Rookie Astronaut Craters after a 30-Foot Fall Off Cliff." *Thud.* What a pathetic way to go.

My buddy John McGoldrick and I had raced out of Denver early that morning after tossing our climbing gear into the back of my dusty blue Jeep Wrangler. Belting out riffs from a scratchy cassette tape of Dire Straits, I hadn't yet realized how apt the group's name would be for the upcoming climb. We'd headed for the South Platte near Colorado Springs and Pine Junction, an extensive region of granite domes, crags, and cliffs with over two thousand routes spread out over hundreds of square miles. We were planning to climb a face route called Left Out on the attractively named Bucksnort Slab, an area with several classic climbs on beautiful granite. The infamous Sphinx Crack, one of the most challenging technical climbs in America, lurks across the road. We had arrived late morning and immediately racked up, preparing for the first climb of the day.

John and I are in an emergency medicine residency training program together. Lean and weathered, John is a few years older than me and he had enjoyed *the life* in Alaska for several years as a clam digger, carpenter, gold miner, and mountaineering guide. After living in the back of his truck, a broken-down school bus, and then a house he built himself, he sold everything and moved back down to the lower 48 to go to medical school. You know, the usual linear career path for a medical professional. John is currently Chief Resident in the ER program, a damn fine climber, and my rock climbing mentor.

Since John is more experienced and a few years older, he often leads. We've even climbed Left Out before, with John leading. We had set up what's called a top rope, where we could scramble to the top of the cliff from the left side and then set up an anchor or pulley system at the apex of the route. The beauty of top-roping is if you fall, your climbing buddy controlling the rope won't let you fall more than a couple of feet. Tackling more ambitious routes requires the lead climber to put in protection as he or she ascends, which means there can be significant gaps in safety and potentially very long falls. If you're ten feet above your last anchor point and you fall, you will endure a very rapid descent of at least twenty feet before coming to an abrupt stop. Assuming your climbing partner has lightning quick reaction times, that is.

I'd started the morning reasonably strong and ready for the exciting challenge of lead climbing, eager to take my turn at the front of the rope. I was ready to leave the comfortable and pursue the challenges, excitement, and danger of lead climbing. Exchanging leads on a climb is a very special bond and hard to explain to people who've never experienced it.

But now, as I cling to the wall in an adrenaline-fueled moment of clarity, I realize I've neglected to check the rating on this particular face climb. If I had, I would have realized it's a particularly sheer granite face with very little in the way of anchor points—no cracks, no jugs, no ledges, no bolts. Without a top rope to save my soul, this is a whole different climb.

All I see around me are a few rough spots, along with some shallow indentations and ripples. That's it. And it's not enough. I'm carrying plenty of carabiners, wires, nuts, and rope. But they're dead weight. As the lead, I am all dressed up for climbing with nothing to clip into. A lifeline means nothing when it's not anchored to something.

Survival depends on choosing the right place to step and calmly planning ahead as you look for irregularities in the rock face to plant your foot. Small footholds and steep faces mean less contact, less friction, and less purchase on the rock, putting incredible strain on your legs. Maintaining balance over your feet with such limited friction requires exquisite concentration and control. I should know better.

My love affair with climbing started a long time ago in Greece. When the wind wasn't scouring the scarred brown mountains above the seaside town of Glyfada, a suburb of Athens, the sun baked everything else stubborn enough to hang on. But those bald hills were a place where a fifteen-year-old novice rock scrambler could run free.

On weekends I'd sprint up the slopes, avoiding ankle-twisting potholes by opting to go up and over choice boulders. I'd imagine pulling off impossible rock moves on the frightening North Face of the Eiger or kicking in crampons up the final steps to the lofty summit of Everest. My heart racing and my lungs huffing with excitement and adrenaline, I was transported to the mythical mountains I'd read about so often. I imagined climbing with those in the pantheon of exploration—Herzog, Harlin, Harrer, Mallory, Irvine, Hillary, Norgay, Bonington, Messner. Sometimes, when I recited the list in my head like a mantra, I'd even dare to add *Parazynski.*

There were no mysterious gaping crevasses or skyscraping towers of ice in Athens, though. Just scruffy wild onions and scattered weeds between the knee-high boulders and talus. But squinting through my wild imagination, and fueled by the classic books of mountain exploration I'd devoured as a boy, I could see the precipitous drop-offs around me, the majestic views that only a few had ever truly experienced before. I yearned to one day climb into the rarified, magical air I'd read about that I was still so far away from in time, distance, and technical skill.

Among the rocks I'd discovered a teenage scavenger's gold mine, left over from a violent conflict decades earlier as Greek forces fought off World War II aggressors. Old bullet shells, rusted ammo boxes, and the occasional mortar casing littered the ground. On one occasion a buddy and I stumbled across a slightly dented and pitted but otherwise intact mortar. It's a good thing we were young and immortal back in those days, since hunting for decades-old unexploded ordnance doesn't always end well. Thankfully, those scavenging efforts never earned me a Darwin Award.

As I got older, I kept hiking and rock climbing wherever I could. Eventually I graduated from rock scrambling to climbing ribbons of waterfall ice with steel crampons extending from my boots and ice axes leashed to my arms, kind of like a wintertime Spiderman. My love of the mountains eventually led me to the emergency medicine residency training program in Colorado so I could spend even more time in the lofty air, picking my way along rugged ridgelines where few others would dare tread. I found an amazing freedom up there, surrounded by aerial views that quickly became one of my life's greatest passions.

I yell down to John, "What's this thing rated?"

"5.10X."

What? Not what I wanted to hear. With the Yosemite Decimal rating system in place at that time, a 5.10X basically meant if you make a mistake, it's all over. If you fall, you die.

"I'm going to kill you," I yell down to John, not convinced I'll ever get the chance.

Now I'm not only scared, I'm raging mad. I'm in way over my head, and I'm definitely thinking bad thoughts. John always seems to know what he's doing and never outwardly gets scared. He usually leads, I follow, and the climbs come easy. He has plenty of confidence and extensive experience. He's never led me wrong before, and therefore I trust him to know my skills and make sure we're on a climb I can lead. But I am clearly in over my head. What the hell was he thinking? But to be fair, what is happening isn't John's fault. The climb didn't look life-threatening from the bottom as I adjusted my harness and looked up at the route I'd top-roped several times before.

Since the rock face is smooth and there's nothing on either side to help me out, I can either try to slither down the rock—and probably fall and break some bones—or I can go up using my technical abilities. There are no other options.

I've been clinging to the rock with my knees locked for what seems like about ten hours, although it's really only been ten minutes. I look up, neck straining, and finally spot a small ledge several feet up. Above the ledge, the rock falls slightly away, meaning the grade up above relaxes, making it a little easier to navigate. That fact alone helps me relax a little and breathe a bit deeper. But I have to overcome the leg seizures if I'm going to survive this.

I slow down my breathing, then slow it down some more.

You've done this climb before. There is no other way down. You have to go for it.

I look up again, plan where to put my hands and feet, and start. Ten minutes later I'm at the top of the pitch, clipped into the anchor chain. Done.

There's no warm, fuzzy feeling of success or achievement with this one. I'm just glad to be alive. Looking back, it's the scariest thing I've ever done in space, sky, land, or sea. Including venturing into a couple of volcanoes.

I didn't fall, so I didn't die.

With those first few steps on the rock, I'd gone into a very familiar hyper-focused state, where I'm attacking a physical puzzle that needs to be solved. The rest of the world simply vanishes, and I'm immersed in the smooth face of the rock in front of me.

Over time, I've learned to go into a zone or flow state where I can tune out extraneous things not contributing to success. I'll call it up when it matters most, although I'm not quite sure how. That high performance edge where you're at your peak and can do no wrong relies on previsualization, which means research and rigorous preparation. But at the first major challenge on this lead climb, I'd fallen into a fear state instead of a flow state. Pucker factor over performance, and it could have killed me. Shallow, panicked breathing and a lack of focus are a prelude to disaster.

As relief starts to flow through my lactic acid–laced body, clearing my head of the smell of fear, earth, and sweat, I let fly a few more expletives when I realize it's me, not John, who failed. I'd been overly confident, let down my guard, and allowed myself to get into a risky situation. I'd been too trusting and too comfortable and I hadn't asked enough questions. It had come down to just me and the rock and the rock had almost won. Too unaware, too casual. Too stupid.

Next time will be different. If I'm lucky enough to make it through astronaut training, get assigned to a shuttle mission, and maybe, if I am really lucky, I get a spacewalk, there will be no repeat of this. The stakes are too high with no second chances in space. And no shaky legs.

CHAPTER THREE

Rocket Boy

It's the possibility of having a dream
come true that makes life interesting.

—Paulo Coelho

OLYMPUS MONS, MARS, 1979

When I was a kid, whenever I wanted to fly to Mars, I'd close my eyes and hear, "Houston, the *Odyssey* has landed." A few minutes later I'm in my spacesuit, out of the hatch, and climbing down the ladder toward the Red Planet.

I look down at my feet, strapped into big white boots with gray rubber toes. I'm slowly working my way down the ladder now, my gold visor shielding my eyes from the bright sunlight. I hold tight with my space gloves, and my breathing is noisy inside the bubble helmet.

I step down the final rung very carefully, remembering the millions of people probably watching on television. With an American flag on my shoulder and a NASA patch on my chest, the stakes are high and I want to make my country proud.

Just before stepping off the landing pad, I rehearse what I'm going to say. Then I'm off, planting my boots onto rusty Martian soil. I stop and look around at the piles of rocks, the rugged mountains, and the yellow and white clouds in the sky.

Are there any living things here? If there are Martians living behind those mountains, I wonder what they look like. I hope they're friendly and know that we humans come in peace. I'll be leaving a carved plaque: *Here people from the planet Earth first set foot upon the planet Mars, July 1979.* (Kennedy had sent a man to the moon in 1969, so I estimated we'd need about ten more years to send someone, hopefully me, to Mars.)

But first, I have an important message for everyone on Earth. I clear my throat and take a deep breath. "That's one small step for a man, one giant leap for mankind and for the universe." Neil Armstrong is about the coolest human being ever, so I don't need to add much.

Although I haven't made it to Mars (yet), I inherited my wanderlust genes from my parents, who probably would have purchased their own tickets to Mars by now if they could have. My mom, Linda Marsh Gaillard, was born in 1937, in Mineola, New York, and was brought up on Long Island by her ophthalmologist father and nurse mother, along with a younger sister, Stephany.

Petite and blonde with a flair for fashion, Mom was captain of her high school cheerleading squad, then studied French at Keuka College in upstate New York. Midway through her college years, shortly before the unexpected death of her father, she sailed away one summer to work at a YMCA refugee camp in Austria for children fleeing the Hungarian Revolution. When she had time, she toured Europe, and during that summer, she made up her mind travel was going to be her primary avocation in life. When she graduated from college, she became an Eastern Air Lines flight attendant.

My dad, John "Ed" Edward Parazynski, was born in 1935 in Ballston Spa, New York. He grew up an only child in Saratoga Springs, where the town revolved around the horse track, the oldest in the nation. Tall and lanky with a quick and sometimes offbeat sense of humor, Dad went to Cornell on scholarships, including an Air Force ROTC scholarship, earning a degree in engineering and an MBA in just six years. A descendant of Polish immigrants who came through Ellis Island, he was the first in his family to go to college. He played saxophone in a Dixieland jazz band and always says if he'd used the time he spent on social activities to study, he could have had another degree.

Mom and Dad met at a fraternity party on a spring weekend at Cornell. Her stint as a flight attendant turned out to be a brief one when Ed proposed and they got married on Long Island. With a shared sense of adventure, they splurged on a three-week honeymoon in Europe.

Dad began his ROTC commission with the Air Force as a lieutenant in engineering assignments. Step one: a cross-country drive to his first assignment at McClellan Air Force Base in Sacramento, California, where Mom took a job as a junior high school French and Spanish teacher.

Step two was Little Rock, Arkansas, where Dad worked with USAF Missile Command on Titan ICBM (Intercontinental Ballistic Missile) site activation. The Titan II Missile program was a Cold War weapons system featuring fifty-four launch complexes in three states. The Titan II missiles carried nine-megaton nuclear warheads each and could be launched to strike targets thousands of miles away, including China and the Soviet Union.

When Mom was six months pregnant with yours truly, my parents boarded a military flight to Rio for a vacation. The flight was delayed due to the Bay of Pigs invasion that week, but undeterred, they had a great time in Brazil. The family joke was that I was a world traveler before I ever emerged, inheriting the wanderlust of a young couple that was adventurous as can be.

I was born on July 28, 1961, in Little Rock, just three months after Russian cosmonaut Yuri Alexeyevich Gagarin's pioneering orbital spaceflight. Mom says I was the happiest little guy you'd ever want to see, a tall and skinny baby with a bouncy personality. As soon as I learned to stand up in my crib, I also learned how to scoot it across the floor to the window of our apartment complex, where I waved at the other residents on their way to work. Every day. I couldn't wait to get out of the apartment and go somewhere, too.

When I am a year old, we relocate to New Orleans. Dad leaves the Air Force and joins Boeing for the Apollo lunar program. Boeing has the NASA contract to develop and build the first stage of the Apollo launch vehicle, the mighty *Saturn V*. The work will be exciting and the hours long. Shortly thereafter, halfway through first grade, we end up moving east, so Dad can continue to work for Boeing in Washington, DC, at NASA headquarters.

I love the basement workshop in Arlington where Dad lets me tinker with his tools. I learn to anticipate what he's doing and jump in to help when I can. I love the process of creation—designing, planning, and buying materials, then cutting, drilling, hammering, and bolting. Dad helps me build model rockets, including one called *Big Bertha*. Start with a huge plain-Jane tube of cardboard, like a toilet paper roll made for giants. Add on a balsa wood nose cone connected to the tube with a shock cord, which is a fancy name for a rubber band. Then, cut four tail fins out of sheet balsa wood and glue them into place. Finally, finish off the assembly by adding an engine packed with solid rocket propellant and a parachute, and you've got pyrotechnics that can pack a punch. My astronaut crews are typically ants and spiders, and I swear I never lose a single one.

I'm lucky to be at the Apollo 9 launch with my family on March 3, 1969, at the Kennedy Space Center (KSC) in Florida, savoring the thundering roar of the rocket launch from a nearby beach, perhaps ten miles away. I feel the power of the ship reverberating through my chest as Commander Jim McDivitt, Command Module Pilot Dave Scott, and Lunar Module Pilot Rusty Schweickart launch into low Earth orbit to spend ten days testing several aspects critical to landing on the moon.

The crew performs the first manned flight of a Lunar Excursion Module (LEM), including docking and extraction, and the first spacewalk in an Apollo spacewalking suit, just two months after the Soviets performed a spacewalk crew transfer between *Soyuz 4* and *Soyuz 5*. The US-Soviet space race is at its peak. Apollo 9 proves the LEM worthy of manned spaceflight and paves the way for the ultimate goal, landing Americans on the moon.

I'm in awe and decide that's what I'm going to do. From that moment, everything I do on the surface, in the sky, or in the sea is going to be part of my program to someday walk in space. It's in my DNA—at Boeing, my dad is helping to design and test a rocket ship that first takes men to the moon.

The *Saturn V* is a three-stage, liquid-fueled rocket that launches thirteen times from Kennedy Space Center in Florida in the late '60s and early '70s. Not only does it carry twenty-seven astronauts to the moon, but it's later used to launch *Skylab*, the first American space station. *Saturn V* is the tallest, heaviest, and most powerful rocket ever brought to operational status. It is also reliable and never loses a crew or a payload in flight.[5] It was designed under the direction of Wernher von Braun and Arthur Rudolph at the Marshall Space Flight

Center in Huntsville, Alabama, along with several aerospace contractors, including Boeing, where my dad works.

Dad invites one of the original German rocket scientists home for dinner one night. Hermann Lange, one of von Braun's brilliant deputies, has a thick accent. Mom sets the table with her best china and crystal, and his presence has a profound effect on me. The talk of sending astronauts to the moon and Mars is mind-boggling.

I never grow out of that boyhood dream of the red planet. I have a deep natural curiosity about the world around me, and it isn't easy for me to sit still. Going to a restaurant with my parents is pure torture. I learn to escape by excusing myself to go to the restroom, sometimes within minutes of sitting down, and then blasting out the back door. I don't care if it's a pier or a parking lot; I just know there is something to see on the other side.

Some of my first explorations involve a withering streambed behind our house, and I follow it for miles and miles through the nearby woods and neighborhoods. One time I find a snake and proudly carry it back to our aquarium, reveling in Mom's terror. But sometimes I'm stuck in a boring classroom or on a tedious car ride with no chance to get out and look around. That's when I go inside my head and back to climbing down that ladder onto Mars. All I need is a spacesuit and a spaceship. I already have the long vision.

As the Apollo program begins to wind down in 1972, after six successful lunar landing missions and other technological successes too numerous to count, for some reason America seems to lose interest in moon exploration. My folks see what is happening and begin to plan a new adventure. One location where Boeing really needs help is in Dakar, Senegal, the westernmost point of the African continent. They want to open up a field office to build a major tourist resort complex on the sandy Atlantic coastline south of Dakar. The idea is that European tourists who want to tan their pasty bodies in the middle of winter might be more likely to buy a plane ticket on a Boeing 747 to someplace like Dakar if they know there is a beautiful new resort they can check into. New resorts mean more Boeing airplanes will be needed.

The capital of Senegal, Dakar is located on the Cap Vert Peninsula between the mouths of the Gambia and Sénégal Rivers. Its location on the western edge of Africa made it an advantageous departure point for transatlantic and European trade, and the city grew into a major regional port. Mom is happy the

Senegalese speak French, as the city had once been one of the major outposts of the French colonial empire. I'm about to start junior high, and although I know nothing about Dakar, my heart is literally racing for this huge adventure. My well-intentioned but geographically challenged Grammy Parazynski, however, is much less enthused. In an effort to dissuade us from moving to Africa, she mails us a newspaper clipping: "Great white shark sighted off Puerto Rico."

We pack up our belongings, say goodbye to friends and family, and depart in high spirits until a stopover in Paris, where we lose most of our luggage in a car burglary near the summit of Montmartre. Adding insult to injury, what is left of our luggage is lost on our Air Afrique flight into Dakar. We've moved half a world away and arrive without even a change of underwear.

Not to be deterred from my trademark optimism, I am immediately enamored with the friendly Senegalese, the warm air, and the clear water, which I can't wait to jump into. My parents enroll me in the only English-speaking school available, Dakar Academy, a Baptist school with kids whose missionary parents are off in the wilds of Mauritania, Mali, and beyond. My multicultural classmates include South Korean, Nigerian, Vietnamese, Cuban, Senegalese, Spanish, and American kids. I've been raised a low-key Roman Catholic, so I'm a little in shock at the intensity of their religiosity. The Baptists are hard core, requiring an hour or two a day of biblical studies and singing hymns, plus the usual academic subjects, including PE and French. I start speaking French pretty quickly, along with some very basic Wolof, the local tribal language. *Nanga def?*

My favorite instructor is also my basketball coach, an energetic and warm guy. He perishes in a tragic moped accident in the crazy traffic flow of Dakar when he veers to avoid a stopped truck and is crushed by oncoming traffic. I am already traumatized by the loss, as this is the first death of someone close to me. But the funeral compounds my sorrow when no one seems to be crying. I seem to be the only one choked up, and I wonder why he had to die. Happy talk flows around me about what a wonderful life Coach had lived and how he was going to be in heaven now, so we should be rejoicing in his life and be happy for him. I'm sure heaven is amazing, but I just can't relate. At my core, I know life on Earth is a miracle, too, a celebration to be pursued and savored.

But life gets pretty awesome after school when I head outside to explore. My parents hire an English-speaking Gambian named Dembo, in his early twenties, to help us out around the house, and he becomes a good buddy. We wash our big black, gray, and white sheepdog, Arachide (French for "Peanut"), and I learn how to play soccer, or what the rest of the world calls football. Dembo also teaches me how to drive my parents' British Ford station wagon at an abandoned French air base nearby. Domestic help is very affordable, and there are many, many people in need of jobs. As a result, we also hire affable Dialo as a somewhat hapless cook, and sleepy-eyed Mr. Sanou as a night watchman. I'm not sure we really need all that support, but my parents say if you are in a position to help, you should.

For a few West African francs, our family often takes the ferry on weekends to beautiful Gorée Island, a place with a dark past as the major slave-trading center on the African coast. My parents also rent a primitive cottage on nearby N'gor Island, right on a small bluff a few feet from the water's edge. Most weekends we float out there in a colorful pirogue with an outboard motor, and we spend Saturdays and Sundays relaxing and swimming and snorkeling with friends. I love jumping off a rickety three-meter springboard into the protected bay right in front of the house. Although the bay is small, it's deep, and underneath the surface, I swim through jumbled rocks full of sea urchins, puffer fish, and moray eels. I learn how to reach into the rocks, carefully timing my approach with the surge of the waves, and retrieve sea urchins. We chop them in half and eat them, raw and barely dead, with a spoon. A bit slimy and salty, but I quickly acquire the taste.

Before long, I can dive down twenty-five or thirty feet, holding my breath and slithering in between rock outcroppings. The locals do it all the time for spearfishing and to harvest sea urchins, so I don't think it's that big a deal. I learn how to spearfish and snorkel with a baited hook on a line so I can see what's biting. Luckily, I never become prey. As I get better at free diving, I begin to bring back treasures from the bottom—old castoffs from fishing boats like pulleys, tackle, and anchors. I start my own little museum in an attached shed at the beach house and stash my finds there.

I feel at home underwater, calm and at peace, a master of this strange environment. The whole ocean seems to open up beneath me, calling me even deeper. Free diving has its limits, so when some older French kids offer to teach me how to scuba dive, I am more than game. I read everything I can about the exploits of Captain Jacques-Yves Cousteau and his *Calypso* and watch his documentaries.

The totality of my scuba diving instruction consists of the kids strapping twin 80s[6] on my back, with just this: "Come back up when you run out of air." The rubber regulator smells old and tastes salty, but I imagine myself as Jacques Cousteau and plunge thirty feet beneath the surface. I'm surprised how loud my breathing sounds, punctuated by the gurgling of rising bubbles. I savor the time under the water and the feeling of not having to hurry back up as when I free dive. I cheat death on that first unsanctioned and unprepared-for scuba dive and I'm hooked, exhilarated from my very first breath. I decide then and there I'll learn how to scuba the right way, although I'm not quite ready to let my parents in on the ultimate plan.

After a couple idyllic years in Dakar, Dad has a surprise for us. "We're moving to Beirut," he says, breaking the news about his next Boeing assignment. I love my life in Dakar and don't want to leave the school, Dembo, my treasure hoard, or Arachide. I don't even know anything about the Middle East. Once again, we pack up our stuff, say our goodbyes, and board another plane to points east.

On the way, we stop off for a Christmas safari in Kenya and Tanzania. The wildlife is beyond amazing, with graceful gazelles, families of elephants, zebras, giraffes, wildebeest, hyenas, cheetahs, and lions roaming the wide expanses. My eyes gravitate away from the wildlife and toward the snowcapped summit of Kilimanjaro as I daydream about what it would really look like and feel like to actually stand up there.

On a guided tour of the preserve, we happen upon a small group of lions. Our Kenyan guide stops the car and announces, "Lions meeting!"

I snap on my telephoto lens and get ready, popping my head out of the Land Rover. My Canon FTb with a 200mm ought to do the trick. Alas, the lions meeting turns out to be "lions mating." *Ahem.* Biology in action. Some of life's greatest lessons are learned outside the classroom.

Beirut, Lebanon, is an elegant and sophisticated five-thousand-year-old city on the Mediterranean coast. The banking capital of the Middle East at the time, it is flush with oil money and a rich cultural life. Beirut is also home to the Boeing Middle East office. We land in January 1975 and find a really nice apartment near the center of the city, just a block off the main avenue called Hamra Street. It looks like Paris, vibrant and bustling with shawarma stands instead of creperies. My favorite destination, with friends or solo, is the souk, or Arab marketplace, overwhelming my senses with spices, food, gold, carpets, brass, and the haunting calls to prayer.

I can walk to my school, the academically renowned American Community School (ACS) of Beirut, where I soon find out I am more than a little behind. I've had lots of Bible study and music training at the missionary school, but I'm not up to code in English and math. With the school year already half over, I have to work hard to catch up with my new peers. With the help of a tutor and my teachers, I am soon holding my own in advanced algebra and playing basketball, too. With my shaggy long blond hair and rangy build, I am clearly an outsider, and I have to put up with some bullying.

We've only been in Beirut for a few months when the Lebanese Civil War breaks out. The war will last about fifteen years, with Beirut divided between the majority Muslims, who are the have-nots, and the Christians, the minority, ruling class. The downtown area becomes a no-man's-land known as the Green Line, with much of the area ultimately destroyed. Thousands of people die and many others flee the country. Refugee camps pop up around the city, along with checkpoints on the highways.

I spend many restless days closed up in our apartment, with the neighboring businesses shut down, no cars on the road, and periodic sniper fire and explosions booming in the distance. On one occasion my mom and I join a friend's pool party at the glamorous St. Georges Hotel, the place where diplomats and movie stars used to hang out. A sniper from one of the tall neighboring buildings begins targeting the hotel. Either he's a lousy shot or just trying to spook the Westerners around the pool, but he successfully clears the area of Speedos with a few crackling rifle shots. I'm not overly scared, just focused on getting everyone inside for cover.

More and more, Mom tries to keep me inside as the conflict grows increasingly violent. One morning at two o'clock, Smith's Supermarket explodes just two doors away. The windows of the buildings around us blow out in a cacophony of shattering glass. I look out the window and watch hundreds of people milling around the burning building, crunching through the glittering shards as police arrive. I insist on going out to explore, wandering about with the other startled and frightened residents in the middle of the night, the firefighters and police still busy.

I wonder if whoever did this is walking in our midst, or maybe even standing right next to me. The shop is owned by an Englishman and his Lebanese wife, and they primarily cater to the many Western shoppers of Beirut. To our surprise, they reopen their store the very next day. My mom asks Mrs. Smith, "When did you reopen?"

"My dear, we never closed." The store is delivering milk and newspapers the next day like nothing ever happened.

Almost immediately after the bombing, Boeing decides to temporarily move its staff to Athens, Greece, to wait for things to settle down in Lebanon. Although the warfare is sporadic, it is too close and deadly. We pack up what we can and buckle in for a fast taxi ride to the Beirut airport. On the way I spot ad hoc roadblocks made of burning tires, hear widespread gunfire, and see smoke from artillery in the mountains outside of town. I also spot a few dusty tanks on city streets.

I'm not overly disappointed to be leaving. I'm learning how to always be ready for the next adventure, and I have a feeling Greece might be a great place to learn how to scuba dive, this time the right way.

CHAPTER FOUR

Wanderlust

Only those who risk going too far can possibly
find out how far they can go.

—*T. S. Eliot*

ATHENS, GREECE, 1975

On rare occasion I wonder what a white-picket-fence life might have been like had we stayed in American suburbia. I'd be at Yorktown High, chasing the same girls who'd once had toxic elementary school cooties and leading the life of a so-called typical American youth. There are occasional pangs of longing for consistency and predictability, and certainly anxiety with the awkwardness of relocating and making new friends every couple of years. But I mostly revel in regularly establishing a new base camp in a new country and in a new culture.

Greeks savor life, and they never sweat the small stuff. *Ola Einai Endaxi*, or "everything is all right!" For my mom, the laid-back Mediterranean lifestyle melts away the tensions of Beirut, and I soon find my footing in high school life at the American Community School of Athens, one of two English-speaking schools in town. Many of my classmates come over from Beirut, too, and it feels good to transition with a few friends to my new school. In Beirut I learned enough Arabic to swear like a drunken sailor on shore leave, though not in front of my parents, especially my mom. In my new host country of Greece, I rapidly acquire the most important vulgar expressions with matching hand gestures as I master the art of expletive fluency.

Dad's job, marketing jets and services throughout the Middle East, doesn't really change other than his office address. But Mom faces new challenges as she sets out both to find a place for us to live and to build a social circle. After a couple of months living in the Athens Hilton, we settle in Glyfada, a sleepy beachside suburb of Athens across town from my high school. Hellenikon Air Base, a joint Greek-US facility, is nearby so there are lots of other American kids to pal around with on the weekends, along with other American expatriate adults for my folks to get to know.

Family wanderlust continues to propel us to places like Egypt, the Soviet Union, Austria, Belgium, Poland, Turkey, Hungary, Romania, India, Thailand, Singapore, Hong Kong, and Japan. I also begin curating a truly impressive collection of airline barf bags, furnished through my travels and our frequent-flying family friends. A hand-painted Royal Nepal Airlines barf bag is my coveted favorite, while on the other end of the spectrum, TWA allows you to use their plain paper barf bag in the traditional sense, or to deposit your camera rolls into this unlikely container for photo processing.

As a freshman, I decide to leave my lackadaisical study habits behind. It is almost like a neural switch flips, prompting me to make a conscious decision to do my very best in high school. To continue to live a life of adventure and travel like the one my parents are sharing with me, I'll need to go to a top-tier college. Almost overnight, I go from a B-minus, back-of-the-classroom student to straight A's in the toughest classes. I've somehow found my inner student. It helps that when we study the literary classics or the geography of the ancient world, I can actually visit the Roman Colosseum or the Greek Acropolis. And I love heading out to the Greek islands on weekends with my friends.

Alas, my Greek idyll ends abruptly at the end of my junior year when my dad is reassigned again, this time to Tehran, Iran. The news hits me hard. My parents have always tried to include me in the decision making—not in any structured way, but they let me know well in advance when and where we'll be moving and then listen to my concerns. This time, I can't seem to scrounge up much enthusiasm. I have put down deep roots in Athens and do not want to leave my school, my buddies, my basketball teammates, the cute cheerleaders, or my burgeoning diving adventures. My dad says we can always go back to Boeing's home base of Seattle, but I can't get excited about moving to cold, wet Washington after living in Greece for three years. Unfortunately, however, staying behind is not an option, so as hard as it is, we pack everything up for our impending move to the capital city of Iran.

At four thousand feet, Tehran lies near the Caspian Sea at a strategic crossroads between Turkey, Afghanistan, and Iraq, with the surrounding countryside a mix of deserts and mountains. The snowcapped Alborz Mountains loom over the city and I hope maybe I'll get a chance to explore them. But three days after we arrive, the country erupts in revolution. September 8, 1978, marks Black Friday, a massacre in the capital city's Jaleh Square.

After checking into the Tehran Sheraton, we become front-row witnesses to the beginning of the Iranian revolution, loudspeakers blaring from rooftops and calling for mass demonstrations. The Iranian people are angry: Mohammad Reza Shah Pahlavi, the self-proclaimed Shahanshah (Emperor, or King of Kings), has abolished Iran's multiparty political system in favor of his own Rastakhiz, or Resurrection, Party and declared martial law. During the protest in Jaleh Square, where the crowds demand Islamic rule, the military opens fire and the Western media reports up to fifteen thousand dead, fanning the flames of revolution. In reality, deaths add up to less than a hundred, but the rising emotions push the country toward a full-blown revolution in an attempt to remove the Shah from power and replace him with an ultra-conservative Islamic cleric.

Optimistically betting on a quick and peaceful end to the protests, Dad goes to work at the Boeing office selling aircraft in the Middle East and I enroll in the twelfth grade at the Tehran American School, home to 1,059 high schoolers. I enroll in four Advanced Placement courses and end up the second-string center for the mighty Vikings football team, with extreme workouts every day after school. My mom faithfully washes my #74 jersey every evening in the hotel sink with the local detergent called Barf, or *snow* in Farsi.

What the Vikings lack in talent and physical dominance on the field is compensated for by the most enthusiastic spirit, with us winning the coveted spirit stick at every pregame pep rally. For my part, all I do is snap the ball and blindly push during my limited playing minutes, along with serving as a mediocre placekicker. At the start of the season I'm told I'll make a great wide receiver since I'm tall and fast, but not having grown up playing contact football, I turn out to be worse than horrible. I suppose my instincts for self-preservation are just too strong. I don't enjoy the feeling of guys running straight at me to smack the crap out of me. But even though I really stink at the sport, being part of the team helps me find my place in my new school's social realm.

I also begin college applications, and since we don't have a typewriter at the hotel, in the evenings we go to Dad's office to fill out and mail the forms. I apply to a place called Stanford University, even though I've never been there before.

The atmosphere around the city remains tense, with furious speeches blaring from the minarets. Shops are frequently closed, there are shortages of food and fuel, and an eight o'clock curfew means the streets are deserted at night. I begin to notice more people in black robes and more women in burqas. My height and blonder-than-blond hair seem to elicit overt hatred, and I can't walk to school like in Beirut. I feel the intense animosity of the locals toward anything Western, with riots, bonfires, and gunfire commonplace.

In December we receive notice that our 5,500 pounds of household goods have finally arrived from Athens, and Dad arranges for delivery on December 23. We move into a nice but compact rental house in a walled compound, but sometime that month, Dad finds a note on his car.

Die, imperialist pig.
You have one month to leave the country or we'll kill you.

Mom is beside herself, and after that I am not allowed to leave the house, except for busing to and from school each day.

Dad feels sure the Shah can put down the insurrection with his substantial army, and he wants to go back and do his job, looking to the promise of a bright future. But right after we return from a Christmas holiday, we get word Boeing has decided to close their regional office in Tehran. My school closes, and my parents agree to let me finish up my senior year in Athens with my friends. We flee. Later I find out the superintendent of the Tehran American School, William Keough, a huge bear of a man, was one of the hostages held for 444 days. It's hard to believe what is happening as we watch a once-prosperous country with such a rich history descend into chaos and oppression.

One memory still haunts me. A month before we evacuate, we decide to leave Tehran for a quick Thanksgiving visit to Athens to get away from the terror and unrest for a few days. When we return at the end of November, things are worse. At the airport I am frisked, more like being groped. The Tehran airport is packed with people frantically trying to get out of the country while crazies like us are going back in. The customs people yell at me in Farsi. There is jeering, and I feel seething rage being directed toward me, the tall, scared blond kid in the blue knit ski cap. When we finally leave the airport, we climb into a decrepit diesel Mercedes taxicab and putter back toward the rental house. The car's heat is on full blast but I'm shivering, arms wrapped across my chest. I lean forward to try to capture whatever warmth I can from the vent while my parents huddle together in the back seat, their breath visible in the headlights of oncoming traffic.

The taxi slows as we round a corner and approach a barricade ringed by floodlights. An Imperial Guard officer in fatigues strides to the driver's window, then begins waving his rifle and shouting in Farsi. He wants our passports. The driver collects them from us and hands them over. The soldier peers into the cab, shines his flashlight on each of us, stares at our passports.

While I wait, shivering, something makes me turn and look out the window to the right. Behind a pile of sandbags stands a kid. He looks to be about fifteen or sixteen years old, just a little younger than me, and he is holding a machine gun trained directly on my forehead.

I can tell he is even colder than me. Each time his body jerks with the cold, his gun twitches, his finger on the trigger. My heart racing in sensory overload, I stare, and I can't stop. I look directly into his eyes for what seems like forever, and I see a fear and uncertainty that mirrors my own.

Finally, the cabdriver revs the engine and breaks the spell as our papers finally clear, and we roll forward through the checkpoint. I look back and the boy's face dematerializes into shadow, although I can still see the light playing on the barrel of his rifle as he shivers.

Will he survive the revolution and find a fulfilling future? Will he get married someday and have a family? Does he want to explore, too? Will any of his dreams ever come true, or will conflict and revolution derail him? I will never know, but I still think of him every once in a while.

The flight from Tehran to Athens is a quick four hours, but it feels like a different planet as we trade the riots, incendiary cries from atop the minarets, and nightly curfews for the sunshine, bouzouki music, and ouzo (with no drinking age) of Greece. After getting us settled into the Greek equivalent of a Residence Inn, Dad continues on to Seattle, Washington, to work at Boeing headquarters. It's not an easy time for him, with Mom and me across the world in sunny Athens while he toils away in rainy Seattle. I'm grateful to my parents for enabling me to finish high school with my buddies in Athens, returning to ACS for the spring of senior year like the prodigal son. I even get my varsity basketball number back.

The kids and teachers at the American school are used to students coming and going, so midyear I revert right back to my life of Advanced Placement courses, sports, and exploring with friends, and it feels like I've never been away. Although still a bit shy, I manage to make friends in the many overlapping cliques of the school. As a senior with my dad thousands of miles away, I test the boundaries of independence with my mom and certainly provide her with a few gray hairs in the process. For the most part, my buddies and I are responsible and do the right thing, but there is that one night in a Greek jail.

Remember *Midnight Express*, the film about the young American arrested by Turkish police for trying to smuggle hashish out of Istanbul? Based on a true story, it is a sweat-inducing, harrowing story with Billy Hayes being tortured and then sentenced to thirty years in prison. The movie has just come out, and my friends and I have all seen it together. Not long after, a bunch of us decide to play hooky from school one Friday and take a ferry over to an island called Spetses. Our backpacks are stuffed with shorts, T-shirts, and some food, and we plan to camp out on one of the beautiful beaches, with a number of others arriving the next day.

The *Flying Dolphin* is a brand-new hydrofoil that takes about two hours to ferry us to the island. There are eight or nine of us aboard with enough Amstel in our systems to lose primary inhibitions and volume control. We get more than a little rowdy on the boat, and in my adolescent mind, we're holding it together and not drawing too much attention. Then I look out the window and see my wild-man buddy John, and his Cheshire Cat grin, as he climbs around like a death-defying spider on the outside of the speeding, bucking boat.

When we arrive, a welcoming committee of stern Greek police greets us on the pier. The captain must have called ahead to complain about the noise and our unruly behavior. At first, I'm not too worried, and I anticipate a slap on the hand from the cops for being brash, embarrassingly ugly Americans, but what I don't know is that some of the guys with us have something more than trail mix in their backpacks.

The police haul us over to the police station, strip-search us, rifle through our backpacks, and find marijuana and related paraphernalia in four of them. Although I'm far from a choir boy, and had tried, and even inhaled, a couple of times in the past, my backpack is clean. I can act goofy enough without such things in my system, and I was never drawn into any serious misuse.

Mark Wolper has a package of marshmallows in his backpack, intended to become gooey s'mores over our campfire on the beach, and the police are very suspicious, thinking they've discovered an exotic new form of drug. Luckily, Mark had spent his childhood in Athens and is fluent in Greek, so he convinces the police to taste them. When they finally realized the marshmallows are just marshmallows, he is off the hook. The police keep the marshmallows, though.

Those of us who clear the backpack and body search are released the next morning after some tense moments and not much sleep. At one point they make us do push-ups—I guess to exact some sort of punishment. When we get out, we call our parents, something we had not been allowed to do the night before. I'm worried about my mom's reaction, but I want to let her know I'm okay. Mom is with some family friends in Karpenisi, a small ski town north of Athens, but she is reassuring and understanding while I am nearly in tears, still quite afraid of the possible consequences.

The next day we say goodbye to our four felonious friends on the pier. They are being sent to an Athenian prison on the same boat we came in on. Without much discussion or a better idea, we head to the beach to continue our camping trip, worried about our friends. All our food has been confiscated, so we are hungry and close to broke. We decide to chase some of the local, semi-wild island chickens to cook over a fire. We eventually catch one or two, and someone breaks their necks. We then have to figure out how to pluck and skin them, which I'm pretty sure we don't get quite right. We end up cooking them, but it is the worst chicken ever, and it barely dents my hunger. I can't wait to get back home and recuperate. I am so grateful to be free.

The following Monday, I'm called into the Vice Principal's office for two very different, conflicting messages: I, along with the others, will be suspended for two days as a result of skipping school. Okay, I anticipated something like that.

Secondly, will I be willing to serve as co-captain of the ACS track team, about to travel to Cairo for our annual meet? Vice Principal Derry is also the track coach. Apparently he still trusts and values me, but it definitely sends mixed messages.

The four kids caught with the contraband end up being sentenced to life in prison. The US embassy asks for their release, but the Greek government is adamant that they have broken the law and will be facing the consequences. Eventually, they are released on bail, and soon thereafter all four skip the country.

After the dust settles from the *Midnight Express* escapade, I renew my quest to get properly scuba certified. Mom cleverly sets a seemingly impossible challenge to recruit two other buddies and their parents to carpool across town for scuba lessons. I meet the challenge, and within two hours I recruit a couple of neighborhood friends to commit to the long trek and lessons three evenings a week. We dunk in a pool cold as hell, do our "ditch and don" exercises, and drive home over mountain roads, dodging the occasional flock of sheep to get back home by about midnight, utterly exhausted. Diving in Greece is even better than in Dakar, with antiquities scattered almost everywhere on the sea floor. The Mediterranean is fished out and visibly polluted, but everywhere I dive I see pottery shards. One time I even spot a complete, intact amphora, a huge clay urn with a pointy bottom probably used for olive oil or wine. It is three to four feet long with a big mouth and curved handles, partially buried on its side. It's perhaps two thousand years old and had probably come off a trade ship that met some unfortunate fate. Treasure hunting is highly illegal, though, so I leave it in place. I won't be taking any chances. I learned my lesson on Spetses.

Graduation is coming up soon, and I'm waiting to hear back on my twenty college applications. I really don't know if any of the most competitive colleges I want to go to will take me seriously, coming from an unknown high school overseas. Sure enough, Harvard quickly makes it clear I am not worthy, but since my folks will be in Seattle on the West Coast, I rationalize that Stanford will be a better option anyway. Then, a fat envelope from Stanford finally comes. They want me!

Dad flies to Athens for my graduation, and as we pack everything up and prepare to move back to the States, I consider my future. My dream of being an astronaut is still very much alive, even though I never talk about it. For the moment, I decide to pursue becoming a doctor like my grandfather. I research the early Space Shuttle recruits and realize three members out of the 1978 astronaut class of thirty-five, nicknamed the TFNGs[7] for the "Thirty Five New Guys" (or unofficially and more improperly "The F*cking New Guys"), were physicians.

In Seattle, I find a summer job as an orderly at the Kirkland Convalescent Center. I'm hired muscle, but my new job quickly becomes more than just a paycheck. Although my minimum-wage job involves much cleaning up of bodily fluids, I find out I really like getting to know the elderly patients and helping them in tangible ways. My all-time favorite patient is Alice. Affectionately known to the staff as Alice in Wonderland, the sweet older woman shuffles down the corridors all day long and tells soft-spoken stories to anyone she comes in contact with.

The summer flies by, and before I know it, I am on my way down to Stanford University, an immaculate, leafy campus with Spanish-style sandstone buildings crowned with red tile roofs, on the peninsula just south of San Francisco. It's beyond perfect for me with so many great outdoor adventures nearby. It's also one short flight away from home, but not too close.

During my summers, I work as a lab tech at the Issaquah Health Research Institute. It's the very beginning of the recombinant DNA era and the quest to unlock the secrets of the genome. The lab focuses on finding a cure for African sleeping sickness, transmitted by the tsetse fly and wreaking havoc in many of the areas where I'd lived and traveled as a kid. In my spare time, I work with Dad rebuilding a fire-engine red 1964 convertible, which becomes my first car. It's been a while since Dad and I built model rockets, and it's great to be tinkering with him again in his workshop.

Toward the end of my four years of college, in the spring of 1983, it's time to make some decisions about medical school. I love Stanford and want to be near my current girlfriend, who will be going to med school somewhere in the state. Although I apply to several schools around the country, when I am finally accepted to Stanford's med school, my decision is made. I also apply for and win a National Institutes of Health MD/PhD fellowship in cancer biology, starting on a track to be a physician-scientist in biomedical research.

Medical school is an assault to the memory banks, an overwhelming deluge of factoids that might or might not be critical to saving your patient someday. You just don't know enough starting out to ascertain what is critical and what is trivial, so you begin by trying to memorize absolutely everything. Quickly coming to your senses, obscure biochemical pathways and "zebra" orphan diseases are strategically placed into short-term memory, hopefully available for the final exam but unlikely to stick for life. Thankfully Stanford's School of Medicine is pass or fail, no letter grades, so the adage is "P equals MD."

One of the core fundamentals of medical school is anatomy lab, understanding the intricate plumbing, wiring, and framing of the miraculous human body, as developed through eons of evolution. Thanks to unknown donors, my classmates and I use the brownish-gray, formalin-treated cadavers to study the body's extraordinary complexity. Thankfully, we eventually grow immune to the pungent odor.

A real live patient named George reminds me, however, that the stakes are high. As a first-year medical student, I'm rotating with an ambulance crew when we go out on a call in the middle of the night. A man is on the floor in his house, sweaty and pale, his wife hovering above. The paramedics intubate him; I help with chest compressions and shock his heart back into rhythm. We lose him again, then get him back. Finally, he stabilizes, and we take him with sirens blazing to the Stanford Emergency Room. He codes again, and I spend another couple of hours with him that evening, helping to keep him alive and hoping he'll make it through the night.

I go home exhausted, sleep a little, then head back to school the next morning. I am scheduled to lead a tour of prospective medical students. We walk by George's intensive care room and the drapes are closed. He is inside, but he is not alive. Apparently, he died early in the morning, and his wife hasn't arrived yet.

I am stunned. I automatically explain to the students what happened and then do my best to hide my shock, but I am devastated. Last night, we'd saved a man's life. Just hours later, he is gone. I go home after and to my surprise burst out weeping. I realize there are problems medicine cannot fix. The shock of seeing George's lifeless body stays with me. He is my very first patient, and I've lost him. Life suddenly seems tenuous, and it makes me want to really live my life full out and to maximize the value of every moment.

CHAPTER FIVE

Dr. Luge

Luge is the only sliding sport measured
to the thousandth of a second.

—*Team USA Luge*

PALO ALTO, CALIFORNIA, 1985

A poster catches my eye one day when I'm at the gym—something about luge. A Stanford student named Bonny Warner, a member of the 1984 US Olympic luge team, is holding one-day summer tryouts around the country, looking for athletes from other sports who might be interested in competing in luge.

I'd been mesmerized by the sport since the last Winter Olympics. Shooting down an ice track on a sled the size of a cafeteria tray at up to ninety miles an hour, with extreme g-forces on crazy tight turns? Yes, please. So, in 1985 I spend my twenty-fourth birthday with seventy-five complete strangers, not far from the Stanford Linear Accelerator and the epicenter of venture capital, on my back dodging traffic cones on a steep slope off of Sand Hill Road.

Enthusiastic, powerful Bonny sets up a nearly impossible slalom course and shows us how to carve turns on the crude training sled, complete with shopping cart wheels. She demonstrates steering by applying pressure through the shoulder and pulling in with the opposite calf. It requires extreme focus, finesse, and quick reactions, coupled with a love of adrenaline. As an astronaut wannabe, I figure this high-adrenaline adventure might help me learn how to master another challenging environment.

By the end of the day, sweating under my helmet in the summer sun, I am one of just a handful who make it through the course unscathed, and I realize I have an insatiable need for speed. Even more than driving my roadster or flying a Cessna, luge makes me feel alive. I can't wait to get out on the ice for real at the Olympic Training Center in Lake Placid, New York. I'm invited out for three weeks of training—and to get hooked on the sport for life.

Luge only formally became an Olympic sport in 1964 when the games visited Innsbruck, Austria. Although I am a reasonably skilled and fearless skier, I never imagined I would find myself feet-first on a sled traveling at warp speeds and maybe even having a shot at Olympic glory. *Olympic Dreams Can Come True,* the flyer at the gym promises. I'm about to go chase that dream.

A luge run takes less than a minute to transition from shivering cold in the start house to panting for breath as you slam into the foam padding in the out run at the bottom of the track. Seated upright on your sled in a rubberized Lycra speed suit and wearing toe-pointing booties, you carefully lower your visor with your spiked gloves, literally becoming an aerodynamic human bullet. You are in another world, listening to your breath echo inside the hush of your helmet. With your heels locked into the curve of the sled's runners, you forcefully rock back and forth from a sitting position, and then, with an explosive pelvic thrust and a ripping tug through your shoulders, you push off the handles at your side.

With two or three rapid, violent paddles into the hard ice with your spiked gloves, it's time to quickly find your inner peace and somehow become graceful. After launch, you smoothly lie down on your back on the fifty-pound sled and aim for that perfect, imaginary fastest-line-down-the-track. You use the pressure of your legs and shoulders to change the point of ice contact on the steel runners. If done well, you steer by slight shifts of weight and tensing of muscles without oversteering, which shaves ice and adds to your time. It's an extraordinary challenge to relax when the world is whizzing past you at mind-numbing speeds, but it is a sport often won in milliseconds. The more subtle and fluid your inputs, and the less overcorrection, the faster you will go.

A helmet and visor shields your head and face from a dreaded face plow, while a neck strap keeps your head from bouncing on the ice, with your body experiencing as many as six g's during the tightest luge turns. Very thin thermoplastic pads molded to the profile of your wrists, elbows, knees, and shoulders will take some of the sting out of accidentally skimming a side wall, but nothing really helps if you dramatically lose control and ricochet like a pocket full of coins in a washing machine spin cycle.

To be competitive, you have to keep your body stretched out flat and relaxed, absorbing the micro-imperfections of the icy track as you thunder downhill. One of our coaches, Soviet defector Dmitri Feld, used to tell me in his thick *Amerikanski* dialect, "Keep your head back or I'll chop it off like in Bolshevik Revolution."

Excellent advice, as craning your neck up to look around creates huge amounts of aerodynamic drag, so you must rely on peripheral vision to the extent you can, but most everything is a blur. Ideally you'll only briefly look down past your armpit to enter a curve, anticipating one or two turns down the track, but for the most part your head should be far back in the slipstream, relying upon limited peripheral vision to judge your progress down the track.

Through trial-by-bruise I soon learn that the key to managing the dynamic forces of luge is the carefully timed application of power with finesse. I learn how to channel my energy and anxiety while accelerating down the Lake Placid track, the steel runners whirring, shaving ice crystals off the almost perpendicular walls. I hurtle past the sometimes-terrified faces of my peers at fifty, sixty, and later over seventy and even eighty miles an hour. Each run lasts between forty-five and fifty seconds, but by the time I cross the finish line I'm typically drenched in sweat, out of breath, sometimes bruised, and always high on adrenaline as I come out of what feels like a trance, or flow state.

With that kind of intensity and strain, I can only manage between four and six runs a day, with overall time spent on the ice totaling less than six minutes. The rest of the time it's physical and mental preparation, and recovery.

But it's perhaps not as dangerous as it sounds. While people have seriously injured themselves, and two Olympians have died in precompetition training, most luge injuries are more on the order of bumps and bruises, sometimes from head to toe. In spite of the speed and the adrenaline rush, which I will admit can be addicting, luge is not a sport for a reckless speed junkie or daredevil. It takes disciplined calm to safely negotiate your sled down the track.

The short stint in Lake Placid serves to lure us neophytes into getting serious about the sport, and for me, it works. I am hooked. My scheduled three weeks turns into staying for the whole winter as I get serious about vying for Calgary in 1988. Bonny Warner tells us it typically takes four years to get enough training and experience to become competitive, as other sliders often start the sport as kids. I'll be competing for one of only four spots with guys who were already experts, so I have a lot of catching up to do, with just over two years until the US trials for the 1988 Olympic Winter Games in Calgary. I'll never forget driving out to the luge track with long-haired Joel Peskin in his Chevy El Camino, our sleds and his purple speed suit in the back, screaming along to AC/DC's *Highway to Hell* blaring on the stereo.

At the end of three months, I take full runs on the men's course, a rare achievement for beginning sliders. Lake Placid is known among seasoned competitors as the toughest track in the world from the men's start house. According to Coach Dmitri, "at Curve 3, instead of looking forward, you were looking into the eyes of God."[8] The mental preparation turns out to be just as important as the physical training, and it all just seems to click. Plus, it's understanding the dangers in a given situation, and then creating a strategy to overcome those dangers. Failure means massive bruises and excruciating pain in your joints from ricocheting like a little steel ball in an icy pinball game. But I can't believe how alive it makes me feel, and subconsciously I'm learning lessons that will last a lifetime. I begin to truly study the challenges in front of me, and I'm able to come up with tangible physical and mental solutions, then methodically approach my most daunting challenges with a degree of confidence.

Mom is cautious by nature and maternally concerned for me, so I work hard to remind her that I'm not looking to get hurt. Believe it or not, I am actually a very safety-conscious person. Adrenaline junkies are not my heroes or role models. Italian Paul Hildgartner, who'd won three Olympic luge medals with his tenacity and consistency, is the obscure exemplar I aspire to.

I begin to practice previsualization, lying down on the floor or a bench at the start house, physically and mentally taking myself through the run in advance. I become good at moving my body exactly as it will be moving on the track in exactly the same time it will take for the run. I later use this skill in many life challenges, from surgical procedures to scuba diving and from spacewalking to high-altitude mountaineering. I learn that if you can't previsualize success, it's much less likely to happen.

Back in California, I talk Stanford into allowing me a new kind of med school curriculum—five months of all-out luge training and competition from November to March, followed by seven months of medical school clinical rotations and staying in shape. Intense weight lifting, sprinting, running up and down the Stanford stadium steps, and biking become part of my off-season training regimen when I'm not cruising on a wheeled sled, dodging orange cones, joggers, and dogs at forty miles per hour down a makeshift slalom course off of Sand Hill Road. Stanford turns out to be tremendously supportive of my quest, and I am often proudly introduced by faculty as the medical student luger on rounds in the hospital.

"Please, we prefer to be called sliders," I protest, to no avail.

My frequent off-season practice partner is a guy named Ray Ocampo. We hit it off, as we'd both competed in basketball. Plus, his father had been in the Navy, so he'd also moved around while growing up. Ray is the most likable, engaging soul you'd ever meet and works as an in-house attorney for a small but fast growing IT company, Oracle (where he would later become its General Counsel), when not getting beat up on a luge sled. Even though he's been in the United States for most of his life, he was born in the Philippines. He plans to compete for a spot on the US Olympic team, but in case he doesn't make it, he's started formulating a Walter Mitty–inspired backup plan to compete for the Philippines.

Since I am taller than most luge athletes, with long arms and legs, I have to customize my sled to fit my large body type. Lake Placid's Olympic Training Center has a small workshop downstairs where we work on our sleds. I buy a stock sled and then modify the pod (where my torso will lie) along with the kufens (*Kufen* is the German word for "runners") that my legs will push against. Fiberglass cloth and tape are cut to size, dunked in smelly resin, and contoured to the hockey stick–curved form of the kufens, with lots of residue left on my hands and clothing. Once the sled is dry and sanded, its name will be painted on the front of the runners: *Rosebud*, for the most famous sled I know. Ray also tweaks his sled and christens it the *Cory Aquino Express*, celebrating the downfall of the Philippines' dictator, Ferdinand Marcos.

I compete first in Lake Placid and then in Europe, both in singles and doubles, on my way to the Olympic trials. But it is a doubles run that almost ends my luge career, and perhaps my future in space as well. Leading up to the 1987 National Luge Championship, with the Winter Olympics less than a year away, I look at my odds and it is clear that competing in doubles luge will be a slightly easier pathway to an Olympic berth. *Rosebud* won't work for two people, so I borrow an old doubles luge and prepare to take to the ice with Rick Frye, a wiry former competitive wrestler who will be in the bottom position on the sled. I'll be in the top position as the driver, belted to the upper deck of the sled, while Rick will have to help relay inputs and signals from me to the runners on the ice below.

In the final heat, we get off to a good start, accelerating through the upper turns, but at the transition from curve ten to eleven we hit trouble. We exit very late from a huge curve in the shape of the Greek letter omega (Ω), with a serious price to pay. Roughly four hundred pounds of steel, wood, fiberglass, and us, traveling at perhaps sixty miles per hour, begins to ping and then pong. We enter the next curve really late, and before I know it, we flip upside down and into midair, with my right shin somehow riding on the far lip of the track.

The accident happens so quickly, at such incredible speed, that it is hard to understand what is really happening as I stare straight down at solid ice, four feet below. I am still strapped to a projectile that seems like it will never find grounding again. But somehow we end up sideways on our shoulders, the breath completely knocked out of us. With some sort of divine intervention, we are able to right the sled and coast across the finish line. Miraculously, after taking a deep breath and checking all body parts for damage, we both walk slowly away as onlookers cheer—a standing ovation—with a mixture of fright and relief.

From that day forward, I concentrate on becoming the very best singles slider I can be, with the goal of peaking at the Olympic trials the following winter. The ride from the top of the Lake Placid men's singles start house is still considered so dangerous that some international competitors refuse to compete on the course, but to make the US squad there is no alternative. Not infrequently, sliders get injured, face-planting into the ice or ricocheting off the sides in the horrific transition between curves two and three, an aggressive right to left combination that takes place in less than the blink of an eye.

I manage to put together the best runs of my life in the Olympic trials competition, a three-race series, with each race comprised of four runs apiece. I put down my personal best finishes, including two seventh-place race finishes and a thirteenth-place finish. Since the scoreboard at the bottom of the track has seven places for competitors' names, it's exhilarating to see "PARAZYNSKI" in lights.

As much as I've trained and worked out and competed, including endless hours of nighttime training at Lake Placid in as low as minus-sixty-degree windchill, I finish ninth overall in the 1988 US Olympic trials. Only the top three can go on to compete, with the fourth man an alternate. I am twenty-six years old, and my Olympic dream is abruptly over. All that time and all that pain—along with the shivering, sweat, bruises, and hours of previsualization—have not been enough. I have given it my all but, sadly, it is time to retire *Rosebud*.

Then Ray Ocampo calls. "Hey, why don't you come to Alberta and help me out?"

Alberta? Calgary? What??

I haven't seen Ray much lately (he's been training and racing on other tracks when he's not regularly working sixteen-hour days at Oracle), and it turns out the Philippine Olympic Committee is going to accept his dual citizenship and allow him to compete in the 1988 Olympic Winter Games. Ray is a luge team of one, and he needs a coach. Me. I am going to the Olympics!

Ray tells me he's asked me for several reasons. First, he likes me. Second, he knows I've built my own sled and can fix anything wrong with his. Third, I'm almost a medical doctor and have lifesaving skills we both hope won't be necessary. Last, he suspects we'll have a great time together in the Olympic Village. Plus, he recalls that one of my personal goals is to meet the glamorous East German figure skater Katarina Witt.

I've failed at my own Olympic dream, but my friendship with Ray leads to something even greater—supporting a friend with an Olympic dream. I am learning failures mean I need to be open to new ideas and different models of success. As Ray's coach and the head of the Philippine delegation to the Winter Olympics (the latter a promotion since no one from the Philippine Olympic Committee shows up in Calgary), I have the privilege of staying in the Olympic Village with the other athletes, including Eddie the Eagle and the Jamaican bobsled team. And, yes, Ray introduces me to Katarina Witt! I attend daily meetings with the heads of the Olympic committees. I play games in the video arcade, work out in the gym, dance in the disco, and down carb-heavy meals with the other athletes.

The best moment of all is walking in the opening ceremony. We are by far the smallest delegation on parade. Ray calls us "the blond and the Filipino," and I'll never forget him proudly bearing the flag as we enter the stadium to thunderous cheers. Even though it's a frigid and brain-numbing minus ten degrees, we decide not to wear our hats so we can show off the contrast of my golden locks and Ray's jet-black hair. Our navy-blue and red ski parkas with yellow embroidery vaguely match the colors of the Philippine flag. The crowds seem to really root for us, even though ABC disappointingly times their commercial break as we are formally announced to the crowd, and we gleefully embrace our role as the lovable underdogs. Ray still swears we got the loudest cheers, louder even than for the Canadian home team. I'm not quite so sure, but my ears have yet to thaw from that hatless night.

I have to work my tail off when Ray shatters one of his sled's kufens, the runners used for steering, just two days before the opening ceremony. He'll have to have a clean run the next day if he wants a chance to officially compete. In a MacGyver moment, I rebuild the runner, visualizing a femur fracture completely snapped through and I'm the orthopedic surgeon putting the bone back together, then wrapping it with fiberglass and sealing it with resin. I sand it down, then paint it in an all-night marathon in the basement workshop of the Olympic Village. The *Express* looks good as new. And the next day Ray does indeed qualify to compete, representing the country of his birth. To say that we are both elated is the understatement of the year.

When Ray slides down the ice in his fourth and final run of the Olympic men's luge competition, he finishes thirty-fifth and out of the medals. But Ray's Olympic moment means racing over the ice to a personal record against multi-year veterans on a sled cobbled together by a late-night emergency repair. And to top it all off, every Olympian, including the coach, gets a special bronze medal, minus the ribbon. It may sound silly, but being Ray's proud friend and pit crew, I feel like it is my moment, too.

CHAPTER SIX

You Sleep When You Die

Drench yourself in words unspoken
Live your life with arms wide open
Today is where your book begins
The rest is still unwritten

—*Natasha Bedingfield*

MOFFETT FIELD, CALIFORNIA, 1988

Even though I never talk openly about it, even to my parents or any of the girls I date, my dream of becoming an astronaut is still very much alive, still burning in my gut. I'm a secret ASHO (pronounced *az-ho*), short for Astronaut Hopeful, the flattering nickname real astronauts use for wannabe astronauts like me. My luge adventure is just that, an adventure, and when Coach Dmitri and others urge me to continue training for the 1992 Winter Olympics in Albertville, France, I know it is time for me to move on. I need to put all of my energies back into med school, put aside my dream of flying down the ice, and instead chase my dream of flying up into space.

Right after coming home from the Calgary Olympics, I apply for a NASA Graduate Student Fellowship at NASA Ames Research Center, just down Highway 101 from Stanford. In return for my work and help with research, NASA will pay for a year of my med school tuition, and I'll get to be a small part of the actual space program. I work in the physiology lab of Dr. Alan Hargens, Chief of the Space Physiology Branch. A PhD with Danish roots, Alan is world-renowned for his pioneering experiments in gravitational biology, and is one of the most clever scientists I've ever met. He has a terrific wit, with dozens of racy limericks committed to his memory, and he's been known to spontaneously create an original limerick for particularly special occasions.

Dr. Hargens is widely known for a paper he published on how the physiology of giraffes prevents swelling in their extremities and in their brains. He's done adaptive physiology animal studies all over the world, including Antarctica. At NASA Ames, he is trying to determine why astronauts get facial edema in space. My project in his lab is especially audacious, as we aim to measure the four so-called Starling fluid pressures by placing a human subject in a bed, head down, with cinder blocks under the front to effect a six-degree tilt. This fluid redistribution mimics what happens in the weightlessness of space. Tests afterward entail the use of a barber's chair, a surgical microscope, and micropipettes drawn to such a fine point we can stick a needle into a beating capillary blood vessel and record the pulsatile pressure within. It will become a well-known and referenced study and will eventually be published in the *Journal of Applied Physiology*.[9]

In space, astronauts often develop facial edema or swelling, associated with a mild runny nose and headache, because gravity no longer pulls blood and interstitial fluid into the legs as it does on Earth. Conversely, astronauts appear to have "bird legs" with this redistribution of fluid into the central blood circulation, accompanied by a 10 to 30 percent decrease in leg circumference.[10]

After a few days in space, a new fluid balance is established and the facial fullness resolves, although in some long-duration astronauts, we're seeing significant, potentially irreversible visual acuity changes now known to be as a result of mild, chronic elevation of intracranial pressure. It's an important issue for medical scientists to understand and address for future long-duration astronauts, especially those who will someday undertake a two- or three-year mission to Mars.

I also have the opportunity to work with another world-class scientist at NASA, Dr. Emily Morey-Holton. She is a pioneer in bone physiology and has invented a technique called hindlimb suspension to simulate the physiologic effects of weightlessness in rats. While the rats move about in their cages by pulling along with their forepaws, their hindlimbs are kept off the floor by a rig that attaches their tail to an overhead trolley of sorts. This allows scientists to look at bone health at the cellular level in order to understand how bone is shaped and formed over time based on a person's level of physical activity, including astronauts in space.

A few of us working together come up with a compact, lightweight exercise device for possible use up in space, enabling an astronaut to work one side of their body against the other at very high workloads. A stack of weights up in zero gravity would have little value for resistance exercise, so we call ours the Inter-Limb Resistance Device, or ILRD in NASA-speak. I get my first taste of zero-g by trying out the device along with my co-inventors, Alan Hargens, Doug Schwandt, and Mike Aratow on the KC-135, NASA's infamous Vomit Comet. The KC-135 aircraft is specially modified to do parabolic arcs, treating passengers to several twenty-five- to thirty-five-second periods of weightlessness. My face hurts from smiling so much, getting to do five consecutive spins in one parabola.

Our efforts are successful enough to publish some of our results in respected scientific journals and get me to the podium for the first time to nervously deliver our results at scientific conferences. More than anything, I love tinkering in the NASA lab. It's intellectually consuming and takes me back to the fun I had in our basement workshop with my dad, building rockets to launch those friendly neighborhood insects into space.

But it's almost too much fun, and I delay taking my board entrance exams until the very last moment. I also need to apply for specialty training, called residency training, the next phase of my medical evolution involving on-the-job clinical experiences. My top choice is a first-year internship program in Boston at the famed Brigham and Women's Hospital, affiliated with Harvard. I then aim to complete a second program in emergency medicine at Denver General Hospital. Both of them are the most competitive in their categories to get into, so I have several backup applications lined up just in case.

I travel to Boston to interview for the Brigham and Women's Hospital internship with Dr. Marshall Wolf, a brilliant, bow tie–adorned physician with extremely high standards. He's known as a warm and compassionate mentor with the doctors trained in his program, many of whom are making a profound global impact, including Dr. Paul Farmer with his humanitarian work in Haiti.[11]

"What do you think you'll be doing in ten years?" asks Dr. Wolf.

"I can't tell you." I manage to produce a small, nervous grin.

"Why?"

"If I tell you, you won't take me."

He smiles back a little and straightens his bow tie. "Well, just so you know, I won't be taking you. So tell me."

Is he joking? I'm not sure, and I have no idea how he will respond. This could be the end of the line for me. I swallow hard and take the plunge, unfurling my deepest and most closely held dream. I have rarely said it out loud before.

"I want to be an astronaut."

He looks at me, smile gone.

I wait.

He smiles again. "Why would you think I wouldn't take you for wanting to be an astronaut? If you're an astronaut, you'll make the program and the Brigham famous."

Whew.

He tells me later it wasn't my cutting edge space research or my luge adventures that sway him. Or that I pass his sandbox test, convincing him I can work and play well with others. Instead, he thinks I'm interesting and unique. It's sort of like saying I am special, or have a good personality (when you'd rather be called really ridiculously good-looking). But I love that Dr. Wolf takes me seriously, and he seems to believe I can do it. This is a group of people convinced they will change the face of medicine. When Match Day comes, I open the envelope revealing my medical training destiny. I feel an amazing euphoria, combined with a tinge of disbelief. I've been selected by my two first choices against very long odds. Another leap toward my ambition to become a physician-astronaut.

Before I can start my internship in Boston, I have to pass an intense, multipart professional exam called the United States Medical Licensing Examination. I am still working in the lab when I sign up for the test, and I don't take much time to study. How hard can it be? After all, I'm conducting boots-on-the-ground research in extreme human and animal physiology. But as soon as I begin the eight-hour exam, I realize I haven't done any basic science stuff in two or three years, and the exam covers a wide range of subjects, including pathology, pharmacology, microbiology, biochemistry, behavioral sciences, nutrition, aging, and genetics.

I try to stay busy as I wait on the test results, checking the mailbox every day or two with a big lump in my throat. Finally, the envelope arrives. This time, I tear it open with trepidation, hoping somehow I've scored the golden ticket. But it isn't quite golden. I have failed two of the six subsections. Until I pass, my entire future will be in limbo. I'm overcome with sheer terror, and I feel physically sick, my heart thumping in my chest every time I think of it. More than that, I am embarrassed. I have never truly failed at anything of such significance before, with the possible exception of choir class in seventh grade, when I cratered spectacularly on account of my lip-synching.

I am facing a test of what I am truly made of, with an opportunity to retake the two sections of the test I've botched; if I pass, I'll be on my way to Harvard and beyond. If I fail, I might as well be flipping burgers at McDonald's (not that there's anything wrong with that profession, but it's in stark contrast to where I think I am meant to be, and I'm not much of a cook). I dust off my review guides, which are essentially brand new, and study pharmacology and pathology with a vengeance. I take it again and pass, but I've cut it way too close. I learn it's better to temper my confidence and overprepare, and that I need to constantly assess my priorities. I've been too focused on my lab work.

Dr. Wolf's program is hard, with lots of sleepless nights, but during the year in Boston my interest in the impact of space on the human body, and the physiology of extremes, only grows. I feel like an Eagle Scout again, adding another important merit badge in my long quest for space.

After the year in Boston, I pack up my blue Jeep Wrangler, my first new car, and head across the country to the Colorado Rockies. I can't wait to climb some mountains. I know Colorado has fifty-nine fourteeners (peaks with an elevation of at least fourteen thousand feet), and as I bounce along in the Jeep, I'm already hoping I can find the time to bag some.

I find a small mountain cabin to rent in Evergreen, Colorado, about a forty-five-minute drive in to Denver. But the commute is worth it to live at 7,500 feet, where I can walk out the front door and take off on my mountain bike or hop in my Jeep and explore. And I need that serenity with the intense energy and drama of my training program in emergency medicine. There's a dark and intense photographic book of life in the Denver General ER called *The Knife and Gun Club*. It's a hopping urban hospital and trauma center, and the nonstop energy and life-and-death decisions make it the perfect place to learn the trade. The faculty aren't a warm and cuddly bunch, but I know what is expected, and I generally have a blast.

Emergency medicine is shift work with long hours, and whenever I get off work, I head home to the mountains. My best friend in the program is Mark Radlauer, a New Yorker with sandy brown hair and a wise-guy smile. He isn't your typical MIT grad, at least in the tightly wound way I imagine. Instead, he has a very strong command of irony and the absurd, and he's always up for a rock climb, a fourteener hike, or a ski trip if we aren't on call.

Our motto is "You sleep when you die," and in spite of perpetual near-exhaustion we force ourselves to get outside and do stuff, even though our bodies want to sleep. We often work through the night, clock out, jump in the car, and head up to the slopes for a day of skiing.

Priorities being priorities, I also find the time for a relationship with a very sweet woman in my residency training program. When we eventually break up, she calls me a "restless soul" in an effort to get me to see I'm making a big mistake. To her dismay, the description resonates positively with me; I am restless, as there is much to do in this life. Living in the heart of the Colorado Rockies, surrounded by towering peaks, stirs up my explorer's soul, and I want to climb every last mountain, running along the knife-blade ridgelines and scaling the sheer faces. Mornings usually go like this: I breathe in the thin, crisp morning air, savoring the evergreen scent and filling in the alveolar voids all the way down to my diaphragm. *Ahhh.* Full of clean air and appreciation, I'm just a little smug. Life does *not* suck!

CHAPTER SEVEN

Say Cheese

> If at first you don't succeed, then
> skydiving definitely isn't for you.
>
> —*Steven Wright*

COLORADO ROCKIES, 1991

By this time, I'm a very experienced mountain hiker and backpacker, but still a bit new to hard-core mountaineering and rock climbing. I have no idea how long it will take me to conquer every last fourteener, but I resolve to try. Back in my undergrad years at Stanford, I'd done some backpacking in the Sierra Nevadas with another adventurous buddy, Don Clark. An engineering major from Sacramento, Don would go on to lead his family's large construction company after graduation. He was always full of enthusiasm and energy, although our collective planning and judgment was often lacking in those early years.

Don is pretty excited when I move to Colorado, and he soon joins me for a winter climb on Longs Peak up in Rocky Mountain National Park. It can be a serious climb even in sunny summer months, and downright desperate up high when the weather turns. Unfortunately, we get caught in blizzard conditions and have to hole up in a tent for two nights at eleven thousand feet above sea level—two big guys with full winter gear in a tiny tent—hoping the weather clears so we can catch some fresh air and hopefully move upward. One of the unfortunate side effects of going to higher altitudes with lower atmospheric pressure is that all gases must adhere to Boyle's law; gas must expand the higher we go, including the gas contained within our gastrointestinal tracts. The condition remarkably even has a clinical name: HAFE, or High Altitude Flatus Expulsion. Imagine how grateful we are when the wind and weather break.

Looking for our next big challenge, I call Don and Mark up with a less-than-half-baked plan. "Let's go climb Stettner's Ledges on Longs Peak this summer." That means rock climbing, instead of just rock scrambling at altitude. I've been doing some lead climbing on local crags with more experienced rock climbers, and I think I'm ready to lead the multipitch route to the summit of the 14,259-foot peak. Mark isn't yet doing much lead climbing, while Don has to go out and take a quick lesson in basic rock climbing. What can possibly go wrong?

We hike up to Chasm Lake the night before, just below Mill's Glacier with the ominous, towering Diamond Face of Longs Peak lurking overhead. We arrive just as it's getting dark, and we trudge across an unstable, blocky boulder field using our headlamps, eventually setting up a makeshift camp under a rock outcropping at lake's edge. It's a terrible night, wind and rain lashing us for hours, and I long for first light and a reprieve in the weather to make our move.

Cold, anxious, and stiff, we get up early and rack up for the climb ahead. I keep a fast pace, knowing Mark has to be back at the hospital by 11:00 p.m. for his ER shift, a two-hour drive away, not including a most necessary shower and change of clothes. With me as the sole lead climber, and just three of us on the route, we have to inchworm our way up the six pitches of technical rock climbing. I lead a section of 150 feet or so of ledges and features known as dihedrals, resembling an open book that can be scaled by stemming your feet and hands across the pages of opposing rock walls. Then I belay, or take up rope for Don as he climbs toward my position, the rope coursing through a Figure 8 friction device, enabling me to quickly lock off the rope and prevent him from falling more than a few inches, should he slip.

Don's job on the way up, besides not looking down too often, is to remove the fall protection gear, or pro, that I've put in on my way up. These include mechanical camming devices and other chocks that could be wedged into cracks to support me if I inadvertently fell. Then we have to belay Mark up to our position before I can set out again on the next section of the rock wall. It is hurry up and wait, and overall very slow going.

By early evening we arrive at a prominent, cross-cutting feature on the Diamond Face of Longs Peak called Broadway. While this is the end of the technical challenges, there are still a few hundred breath-stealing feet to continue up to the true summit. Given the late hour and Mark's impending ER shift, it's time to bail out. We traverse to the left on Broadway to reach Lamb's Slide, the upper portion of Mill's Glacier often used to descend from the route.

As it begins to get dark, I realize we are going to have another epic challenge on our hands. We don't have a single ice axe or pair of crampons between us to descend the snowy, icy bowling alley of a glacier. We rope up, switch on our headlamps, and slowly rappel down the glacier from makeshift anchor points through the middle of the night. Occasionally we hear a whooshing, thundering sound as a rock breaks free overhead, building up frightening momentum as it accelerates past us.

We finally make it back to last night's base camp around two in the morning, physically exhausted but with a strong sense of relief. Because we have just cheated death. However, Mark really is going to catch hell for missing his shift and we have no way of letting anyone know we are okay. We get up well before dawn, and as we trudge toward our car, we're met by two of our ER residency buddies who've come out looking for us. Our girlfriends are understandably spooked by our absence and have called for reinforcements to check on us. We vow to return at a later date, so we can check the box on a successful summit.

Another night, after hiking in from the trailhead toward Little Bear Peak, Mark and I debate which direction to go in the morning. We make camp in the dense woods just below tree line, nine thousand feet above sea level. The next morning, as we struggle out of our sleeping bags and carry over the debate of last night into the frigid predawn air, my exhaled breath forms huge clouds of condensation as I hurry to answer the call of nature and empty my bladder onto a nearby bush.

"Hey, Scott! Why don't you make yourself useful and run down and get us a couple lattes?!" Mark yells from his sleeping bag.

"Excuse the Polish, but f*%k you very much!" is my retort.

As my technical skills expand, I become a better expedition planner, leader, and teammate. Moreover, my mountain classroom teaches me many things beyond the usual technical skills and judgment that will eventually transfer to the other extraordinary worlds I yearn to inhabit: teamwork, resourcefulness, and resilience.

I love overcoming the obstacles and detours of the mountains and savor sharing the intense challenge with great friends. I love my life of adventure, and even the occasional moments of suffering as I master these new skills, including on rare occasion being benighted and having to bivouac out under the stars with limited gear until descending in the next day's light. No matter what goes wrong, and even as the routes get more difficult, we find the best solutions, oftentimes learning an important lesson or two, and then laugh it all off as we head back to civilization for a big, hot breakfast.

I'm also finding many parallels between emergency medicine and climbing. At Denver General's ER, there are no shortages of focused adrenaline and trauma. I am learning to carefully observe my patients, calmly assess what is going on, and work with the limited amount of data I have in the midst of incredible chaos. I then have to make critical decisions with the ER team on how to treat the patient based on my assessments and acquired clinical judgment. And live with those decisions.

I learn to subconsciously anticipate the problems coming toward me, even though I don't know for sure when or how they will manifest. Working the ER and climbing both sometimes require a leap of faith, where you take a deep breath, don't look down, and make a quick decision as to what next step you need to take. You stay completely in the moment, with the next few moves becoming your entire world, an all-absorbing mental and physical puzzle requiring your full cognition. You lean up the route and act with confidence that your feet will hold and your fingers will be able to grab something you can't yet see.

As I finish my first year in Colorado, NASA opens up the selection process for a new group of astronauts, the news thundering through the ASHO community like an avalanche. I send off for an application form and as soon as it arrives, crank up my trusty electric typewriter to fill it out. I attack the application with off-the-charts energy and excitement. The application is exhaustive, however, and includes requests for references along with an application for security clearance that requires information about every single place I've ever lived. My list is long and sometimes exotic: Arkansas, Louisiana, Virginia, Senegal, Lebanon, Greece, Iran, Greece again, Washington, California, Massachusetts, and now Colorado.

I don't really expect to get an actual astronaut interview the first time around, or possibly even the second or third. Everything feels so out of reach. I am still an astro-fanboy, wondering if I will ever be able to reach up into the NASA stratosphere. But then I rally. Astronauts are just people with really cool business travel, and I'm going to give it a shot. If I can just make the cut and get to Houston for a first interview, maybe a few years down the road I might have a shot at the job.

I get a friendly phone call from Teresa Gomez in the Astronaut Selection Office a couple of months after I send my application off into the ether, and to my great surprise, they want to see me in Houston for an interview. My application has miraculously made it to the top of the keeper pile. My schedule at Denver General Hospital is so tight, I can't take the first week of interviews they offer me, and that is torture. It's difficult to break free for a whole week; I have to do some schedule gymnastics with my kind fellow residents to swap shifts and make the trip.

After a month of restless waiting, I'm on my way to the NASA Johnson Space Center with a chance to become a real astronaut. When I report to NASA, I find out I am part of a group of twenty-two other astronaut hopefuls. *Holy crap, I'm here!* This is beyond cool.

I am in awe of my impressive competition—fighter test pilots, accomplished scientists, and impressive engineers—and I immediately recognize it's going to be a long shot. All of them would probably make outstanding astronauts (except for one ubernerdy guy who is smart but is trying too hard to impress everyone with his knowledge—beyond eccentric—the kind of guy you might not want to spend six months in a tin can with). They are experienced, accomplished, smart, funny, and engaging. I don't really have a snowball's chance in hell with this. But I'm just going to have fun with it and learn as much as I can so I can come back with a vengeance next time and land the job.

NASA puts us up in a dumpy little hotel right by the front gate of the Johnson Space Center. Every morning, they send a van for us and chaperone everything we're doing. Our first meeting is with Dan Brandenstein, a veteran Space Shuttle Commander and current Chief of the Astronaut Office, along with John Young, who flew on the first manned Gemini mission and was the first person to orbit the Moon solo during Apollo 10 (later walking on the Moon when he was Commander of Apollo 16). Young also later commanded two Space Shuttle flights, including the audacious first flight of the Space Shuttle Program. These guys are legends, and I am starstruck.

I soak in the sights—the sleek T-38 jets parked in the Ellington Field hangar; the giant indoor swimming pool where astronauts suit up, get neutrally buoyant, and practice for their spacewalks; and actual real-life astronauts walking the halls and occasionally talking to us. I remember seeing Kathy Sullivan, from the Hubble Space Telescope deployment mission, and the first American female to do a spacewalk. I spot her from across the Ellington Field hangar, smiling knowingly, perhaps recalling her own first awestruck visit to this place as an astronaut hopeful. I quickly go over and say hello. She is very gracious to this random, unknown ASHO, and it makes me feel like the stars are somehow getting closer.

In between the informational briefings and sightseeing are myriad medical procedures, including medical and psychological exams, endless scans, giving up gallons of blood, and the dreaded proctosigmoidoscopy. Mona was my affable and aptly named nurse for the procedure. "Say cheese," she teases me as I eye the impossibly long hose that she is prepping to pass upwards and through my innards.

I reply with trepidation to Dr. Hine (also his real name), the physician performing the procedure, "Make sure to stop before you see the backs of my teeth."

I'm sweating and hoping they won't find anything disqualifying, and I try to stay my coolest. It costs millions of dollars to train an astronaut, so NASA performs all these tests to make sure they only hire astronauts who are likely to remain healthy for many years and many missions.

One test involves a large, round, inflatable object that looks something like a white beach ball. The Personal Rescue Enclosure was ostensibly invented to transport astronauts from one Space Shuttle to another in case of emergency. Just thirty-four inches in diameter, the ball enabled one crewmember to curl up inside in pitch blackness and thoughtfully provided an air supply. I'm hooked up to an EKG and told to climb inside so they can monitor my ability to handle the claustrophobic environment.

"Jump in and let us know what you think," the technician says.

I scrunch up my large frame into fetal position. "Can you pipe in some MTV?" I ask.

It's hard to know how you will react in new, extreme situations but this one is easy for me. It feels comfortable and certainly cozy, and even though I'm stuck inside something about the size of an exercise ball for an indeterminate period of time, I quickly relax and fall asleep. Instead of my heart accelerating with the stress, mine goes down into the low forties, and I can't tell you how long I spend inside because of my slumber. Finally, they unzip the ball, reach in, and shake me awake. Their smiles tell me I've passed. No claustrophobia here.

The interviews are the all-important crux, though. It's all well and good to be able to relax in the rescue ball, and to be medically and psychologically cleared, but the selection committee wants to assess us in person. To keep calm and at ease, I keep telling myself this is just a practice run. The interviews are held in an unimposing, single-story, standard-issue government building, built onto the astronaut gym and crew quarters at the back of the space center. As I push through a set of double glass doors, it's great to see the smiling face of Teresa, who reigns over a small reception area covered in gray government carpet and furnished with a couple of sofas. No windows. A few pamphlets on astronaut selection and the space center are strewn on the coffee table in the waiting area to help us bide the time.

We are called one at a time into a tiny, windowless conference room paneled in blue-gray cubicle fabric, with a few small Space Shuttle launch photos on the walls. Two long tables are arranged in the shape of a T. Seated around the table are men and women I recognize immediately and hold in the highest regard, including Carolyn Huntoon (JSC Director of Space Life Sciences), Duane Ross (who runs the selection office), and astronauts John Young, Rhea Seddon, Hoot Gibson, Jeff Hoffman, and Dick Covey. I am directed to sit in an empty chair with interviewers all around me.

Hoot asks me about my recent flying experiences. Flying had been a dream of mine since childhood, and I'd first learned to fly in medical school, so with great excitement I recount a fantastic cross-country trip I've just taken with a couple of buddies of mine from Denver to Telluride, the Grand Canyon, Death

Valley, and back. When asked about achieving success, I emphasize my belief in the importance of hard work, perseverance, teamwork, and a touch of luck. Dick asks me about my near miss at becoming a Rhodes scholar.

"I was proud to be there then, and I'm very proud to be here today," I say. "Judging from the incredible pool of folks here this week, most any of them would probably become great astronaut candidates."

I've had a lot of help from incredible, generous people on my journey to this moment, and I am grateful for the opportunity to sit in that tiny dark conference room for ninety minutes to take a big shot on goal. I've been waiting for this moment since I was a little boy, and I leave Houston feeling like I've given it my best. I have no idea if I am a real contender, but I am grateful to be part of a group of really impressive people, all of whom want their own spacesuits. Now it's time to wait. And daydream.

CHAPTER EIGHT

Hogs in Houston

The only way to do great work is to love what you do.
If you haven't found it yet, keep looking. Don't settle. As with
all matters of the heart, you'll know when you find it.

—*Steve Jobs*

DENVER, COLORADO, 1992

Every time the phone rings, I think, *This could be the call.*

Due to the demanding patient load, some of my shifts at Denver General are thirty-six hours, sometimes even forty-eight by the time I can sign out and jump in my Jeep for the long ride home. I fret during extra-long shifts. *Maybe they're trying to call me right this second.* Every time I drive home, I feel anxious as I roll up the steep and narrow dirt driveway. *I. Am. Not. Running,* I say to myself as I run-walk inside to check the answering machine.

I stay busy with work, climbing, skiing, and spending time with my new girlfriend, Gail, a pediatric ER nurse. We meet on a blind date, and I learn she moved from Boston to Colorado to learn how to ski. I like how she is very calm and low-key, with a sarcastic sense of humor. On our first date, we go out for sushi and talk for hours.

"What do you want to do with your life?" she asks.

I pause. *Should I tell her?* I'm still not used to casually talking about my lifelong dream. Maybe it's the beer talking, but I decide to blurt it out. "I want to get through the emergency medicine program, but what I really want to do is fly in space."

Gail looks at me but doesn't say anything. Later, I find out she went home and called her mom about our first date.

"You'll never believe what this guy wants to do."

"What?"

"He wants to be an astronaut!"

"You meet the funniest people!" her mom says.

But even though Gail helps to keep me distracted, I still wait. And wait. And wait some more. I've never been very good at waiting. January. February. March is well under way, without even a clue as to when we'll all get the verdict: Astronaut, or Astro-Not?

A few encouraging reports trickle in from friends and family who hear from the government's Office of Personnel Management (OPM) as it snoops around and asks questions about me to determine if I've told the truth on my application and if I can be trusted with a security clearance and the keys to a Space Shuttle. They are beyond thorough in their quest, even talking to long-since-ex-girlfriends whom I've strategically not offered up as references. But OPM cleverly digs up more connections by interviewing friends, coworkers, and family. I also hear from Dr. Emily Morey-Holton, my mentor from NASA Ames, when an OPM agent comes to her office to interview her about my application.

OPM agent: "Do you think we should hire him?"

Emily: "Absolutely not!"

"Why not?"

"He's too good for NASA."

Awkward silence. Then a laugh.

Emily tells me she bragged on me, telling the agent I am bright enough and creative enough to set the medical world on fire. I don't think I quite merit that sort of praise, but I am so grateful for her friendship and guidance.

One morning I am catatonic at home after a long overnight shift in the ER. It had been one of those nonstop, hair-on-fire, never-sit-down-or-get-to-the-bathroom shifts, so I'd even had to stop on the side of the I-70 for a quick fifteen-minute nap on what should have been just a forty-five minute drive up to Evergreen. I'd eventually made it home and fell on top of my bed with my scrubs still on, covered in Betadine and sweat. I've probably been asleep for about an hour when the phone startles me awake.

"Hello?" I hear scratchy REM sleep in my voice.

"Hey, Scott. This is Don Puddy at NASA. How ya' doin'?" Don's voice is quiet, slow, and low, probably sensing I'm not yet fully awake. And maybe wondering why I am less than alert at 10:15 in the morning. But when I hear that Oklahoma drawl, a rush of adrenaline shoots through my body, and I bolt upright in bed at full attention, like a lottery-ticket holder waiting for the sixth and final number to match.

Wait. This is the right time and the right person. Don Puddy is NASA's Director of Flight Crew Operations. This could be it!

ASCAN (meaning Astronaut Candidate, pronounced *az-can*) wisdom says a call from Puddy probably means good news, but a call from his cohort, Duane Ross, Manager of the Astronaut Selection Office, usually means bad news. Ross is an exceptionally nice guy, probably why he is tasked with the rejection calls.

Don and Duane have been known to pull cruel practical jokes on astronaut wannabes holding their breath for some good news. I've heard that occasionally Duane places the call, and when the recipient is beginning to digest the fact that he is not going to be accepted into the astronaut program, he then hands the phone over to Don for a casual we're-wondering-if-you'd-still-like-to-come-to-work-for-us question. So you really never know what's going to happen with these two jokers until you hear the actual magic words.

Puddy joined NASA back in 1964 and served as the agency's tenth Flight Director, following NASA legends like Chris Kraft and Gene Kranz. He led teams during the Apollo Program, as well as the three long-duration *Skylab* missions in 1973 and 1974. He was Flight Director on the very first shuttle mission, STS-1, with Space Shuttle *Columbia*. He is a humble legend, and he is on the line with me.

I take a deep breath, hold it, and feel like my entire body becomes one giant ear, waiting on Don's voice to say the words I've been yearning to hear since I was a kid.

"I'm wondering if you'd still like to come work for us?" Puddy is still not in a hurry. "We're really excited to have you as part of our team."

"Yes, sir. I would really, really like that." I can't believe what I'm hearing, nor that I don't have anything more profound to say right now.

"Great to hear. Please be aware a press release isn't going out until tomorrow, so please don't tell anyone. This is strictly confidential."

"Oh, no, sir. I won't tell anyone," I quickly agree as an absolute condition for the job. We chat a few more minutes about something, but I have not a single recollection because I am going to be a freakin' astronaut! My mind is rushing at supersonic speeds, thinking about all the calls I am going to make in the next ten minutes to tell my family the incredible news.

After a polite goodbye, I scream with joy at the top of my lungs, literally hooting and hollering, jumping around the cabin and punching the air in a cosmic touchdown end zone dance for an audience of none. The date is March 31, 1992, and I feel like my life is on the launch pad to extraordinary.

I place an illegal phone call to my parents, probably setting a new world record for breaking confidentiality. But there is no way I can't *not* tell my parents first and foremost.

I swear them to secrecy, but can neither confirm nor deny whether they subsequently keep their vow of silence. Mom's voice quivers, and I can almost hear the tears streaming from her eyes before she starts sobbing. Dad does most of the talking. "I can't believe it. I didn't think you had a chance first time around. This is going to be amazing!"

Next I call Gail and my best friends. I pace back and forth, as far as my phone cord will let me go, while I share the unbelievable news and my heart takes luge runs around the inside of my chest. My dream is coming true! I replay the call in my head over and over, and I can't sleep much for the next few nights. *This is happening,* I keep thinking. *I'm really going to do this.*

I won't be reporting to Johnson Space Center until August 3, so I have plenty of time to find a place to live in Houston and prepare for the move. And Gail and I need to talk. We've been spending more time together. Over the next few months we realize we don't want to be apart, so Gail decides to move with me. We are excited to start a new life together in Houston.

I'm still in the middle of my emergency medicine residency program, with a bit more than a year to go until graduation, so the program directors are the next folks to share the news with. They are well aware of my goal to become an astronaut, but like me, they didn't really think I'd have an honest shot at the job until I completed my residency training and began clinical practice. They'd noticed how zealous I was about a space medicine presentation I had delivered as a residency program assignment. I'd researched the hell out of it, although it was way too detailed and way too long as I tried to pack every detail of space medicine into a forty-five-minute lecture. A few of the other residents nodded off—they preferred presentations with copious amounts of blood and guts—but I was talking about the coolest subject in the known universe. "That was pretty good," one of my instructors said, trying to be nice. "I can tell you're passionate about it."

When it comes time to turn in my official resignation from the ER program, it doesn't go over too well. In a way, the aggressive nature of the program mirrors the intense nature of the emergency room at Denver General, and not much emotional support is directed my way as I prepare for NASA.

But it's more than understandable—there are just twelve residents per class, so if someone leaves, it creates an unexpected hole in staffing at the local emergency rooms. My closest friends are ecstatic, but it stings that some people I've worked with and laughed and sweated alongside aren't at least a bit happy for me. I didn't expect a ticker tape parade, but it's a surprising letdown.

During the summer, as I begin preparing to move, I spend as much free time in the mountains as I can in an effort to top out on as many fourteeners as possible in preparation for the flatlands. My astronaut training will be all-consuming, and there won't be much free time, nor are there many substantial mountains in the state of Texas, as far as I know. I also do as much rock climbing as I can with John McGoldrick and other buddies.

Left Out, the granite face climb where I almost killed myself (and was subsequently almost left out of the space program), was no big deal for John. He told me later he didn't think I was quite ready to lead on that particular climb, but he felt it wasn't his place to hold me back. John wasn't one to get excited or offer effusive praise, so when I told him about the call from NASA, he simply said, "That's pretty cool." But he didn't try to talk me out of it, either. I learned a lot about both being a partner and a leader from John.

With our households packed up and en route to Houston, Gail and I decide to make a road trip out of it and caravan in my well-worn Jeep and her Ford Bronco. My parents fly down to join us on a portion of the drive. Before we leave Colorado, we stop at Handies Peak near Telluride, and Gail climbs to the top with me as I bag one last fourteener.

You can't see any signs of civilization from the rounded, rocky summit, and it feels like you're at the top of the world, with 360 degrees of snow-tinged peaks all around. The exhilaration of the hike coupled with the big move and my transition to my dream job give me an idea. At the summit, I impulsively decide to pop the question to Gail. I don't have a ring, but I can't think of a better place to ask her to marry me.

The weather isn't great: storm clouds are on the horizon, and it's sleeting by the time we get back to our vehicles at the trailhead. The greatest weather danger on a Colorado peak is lightning, with climbers killed almost every summer in Colorado by lightning strikes, mostly in July. But we survive the weather, Gail says yes, and we head down the mountain cold and wet but feeling happy and excited to begin our new life together.

A week later, after a very anxious night, I show up for work at the Johnson Space Center and am officially sworn in as a government employee. I wear a light-brown suit and a tie for my first day, thankfully one of the very few times I ever have to wear a necktie as an astronaut.

I am as excited as a five-year-old on his first day of kindergarten. Most of the day is taken up by introductory briefings. NASA Astronaut Group 14 is later nicknamed "the Hogs" by the rest of the Astronaut Office (since pigs can't fly, and therefore won't scoop up any coveted flight assignments). Our class is made up of three women and twenty-one men. We have four Pilot-Astronauts, five international Mission Specialists (one from Italy, one from France, one from Japan, and two from Canada), and fifteen NASA Mission Specialists, including me.

John Young welcomes us, along with some senior astronauts including my new boss, Dan Brandenstein, the Chief of the Astronaut Office, whom I also met during interview week. We get up and introduce ourselves to our new colleagues, then attend a quick press conference in front of a mock-up of a very-distant-future *International Space Station*. With nervous energy and enthusiasm I give my name, a brief bio, and a short reflection on making it to NASA, comprising my first official words as an astronaut. It's all a blur, but I do blurt out something about how I can't wait to fly.

While the press conference is plain vanilla, and almost all the media attention focuses on the international partner astronauts, I feel an incredible sense of elation. I am walking off into the unknown. How do you mentally prepare for something so exciting when you don't fully understand where you're headed? Along with every other person in our passel of Hogs, I hope and believe my ultimate destiny will be a trip into space. But I am also overwhelmed by all the things I'll have to learn, and the unknown and daunting experiences yet to come before I can ever hope to ride a rocket.

I think back to the syllabus I received in the mail a few weeks earlier on water and land survival training, T-38 jet training, and Space Shuttle simulations, and I anticipate the substantial blocks of time I'll be spending in classrooms alongside an incredibly select group of people. They are extraordinary, and I wonder how I will measure up. Will I be able to perform at their level? Will I be able to keep up? I'm brimming with uncertainties, and I'm not sure how to deal with those. I certainly don't want to make them public in any way. Astronauts are known for their stoicism, and I have to fit in.

Another worry is my looks. Even though I'm thirty-one, I still have the baby face of a twelve-year-old, and I am afraid no one will take me seriously, especially when it comes to getting tapped for a flight assignment. Within a few days, one of my classmates, a decorated and jocose Navy test pilot named Kent Rominger, decides I need a proper aviation call sign. In tribute to my youthful good looks, height, blond hair, and medical training, he dubs me "Doogie Howser."

You probably remember the television program; *Doogie Howser, M.D.* aired from 1989 to 1993 and starred Neil Patrick Harris as a precocious teenager who became a licensed physician at the age of fourteen. Although I'm more than twice that, I have to admit I look the part. The nickname catches like wildfire doused with kerosene, and much to my chagrin pretty soon everyone is calling me Doogie.

I don't know anything about the time-honored tradition in military aviation circles wherein senior squadron mates scope out how best to tweak you through a funny or embarrassing nickname. I wish I could pretend I love the name, because then maybe they'd keep hunting and eventually find one I dislike a bit less. Among pilots, if you cringe at your new call sign, you'll surely be stuck with it for life. So, even though I can't stop myself from observing a pregnant, annoyed pause before responding to Doogie, I more or less take it in stride. Until the next nickname comes along.

CHAPTER NINE

Doogie Begins

Flying a plane is no different than riding a bicycle. It's just a lot harder to put baseball cards in the spokes.

—*Captain Rex Kramer, in the movie* Airplane

HOUSTON, TEXAS, 1992

Although I wear a necktie for my NASA photo ID on my first day of work, my uniform thereafter will be astronaut-casual, meaning khaki pants and a collared, short-sleeve polo shirt. What quickly separates us lowlife ASCANs out from *real* astronauts like Bernard Harris and Rhea Seddon, physician-astronauts I'd long looked up to, is a shirt monogrammed with a mission logo and an STS number.

STS stands for Space Transportation System, a nondescriptive acronym referring to a Space Shuttle mission. Each shuttle mission receives an STS number, commencing with STS-1, which had been an audacious two-day test flight on Space Shuttle *Columbia*. Gemini and Apollo veteran John Young commanded that first shuttle mission, which launched April 12, 1981, from Cape Canaveral in Florida and landed fifty-five hours later at Edwards Air Force Base on a dry lake bed in the high desert near Lancaster, California. With Bob Crippen in the Pilot's seat, they flew the most complex spacecraft ever assembled into space, and they bravely did so without the benefit of an unmanned test flight beforehand. By the time I arrived for my training in August of 1992, the STS mission numbers were up into the high forties and low fifties.

I settle in for months of lectures, memorizing training manuals and spacecraft systems schematics, visiting all of our NASA field centers, and becoming conversant in the many languages of space science we'll eventually be responsible for on orbit. We delve into material science, combustion physics, meteorology, oceanography, geology, biochemistry, and celestial navigation. Space celebrity guest lecturers include legendary Apollo 13 Flight Director Gene Kranz and astronauts Neil Armstrong, Alan Bean, and Charlie Duke, with stories about walking on the moon and the harrowing near miss of Apollo 13.

Participating in simulations prepares me to manage the Space Shuttle's many subsystems, operate the robotic arm, conduct spacewalks or EVAs (Extravehicular Activity), run through prelaunch and launch sequences, fly a space rendezvous, and deorbit and land the shuttle.[12] I especially love the Shuttle Motion Simulator, or SMS, where you climb into a cabin outfitted with functional displays and controls just like our actual shuttles. We strap in for a shake-rattle-roll similar to launch, just minus the actual g-forces (which I experience later in a centrifuge at Brooks Air Force Base in San Antonio, Texas). Pitched on our backs, we run through multiple launch sequences, and all hell invariably breaks loose. Our clever instructors introduce failure after failure to our poor shuttle just trying to make it to orbit. With audible and visual alarms going off like an out-of-control Fourth of July show, stacked failures in one system compound and cause failures in other systems. Losing a computer, then an electrical power bus or a main engine, is completely overwhelming as you scramble to diagnose and repair those problems before they escalate into massive, compound failures. Certain conditions are not survivable, and it's not a good feeling when the simulator shudders, then pitches, rolls, and shuts down while lowering itself into a neutral position. This is not a good day at the office. The instructors mercilessly try to stress us to our limits every day in the simulator, so on a real mission we'll have the knowledge and confidence to make it on a round-trip to space and back.

At first I feel overwhelmed, wondering if I will match up to expectations, a throwback to the feeling of trying to process the onslaught of information back in medical school. Out of necessity, I'd taught myself, or perhaps unlocked, the skill of photographic memorization. Unfortunately the biochemical pathways and pharmacologic interactions I memorized for my medical school finals had a brief retention life, probably because of the mnemonic methods I'd used to quickly latch onto the facts. To fly in space, I need to learn and retain vast amounts of systems knowledge. Our lives and mission success just might depend on it someday.

Looking in the mirror each morning provides an added incentive to really know my stuff. I see the reflected visage of a kid who is physically incapable of growing a realistic mustache or beard (a two-month superblond mustache simply looks like I haven't washed my face). I don't want the Chief over in the corner office to dismiss the young "space camper" when it comes to flight assignments. My best defense is therefore a strong offense: being well prepared. If you aren't prepared for a class or a sim, it's generally pretty obvious. I certainly don't ever want to repeat my Left Out rock climb or my med school exam debacles.

Just like mastering the sport of luge or learning a new medical or surgical procedure, I know how important it is to study and practice well beyond the minimum. In the unforgiving world of spaceflight, I must know in detail how things function, understand how they could break, and have an idea of how I might respond if plan A and plan B don't work. In medicine, it's *primum non nocere*, or "first, do no harm." It's the same when facing a problem in the simulator or up in space—don't make things any worse.

Another pressure point is how astronauts are unofficially but continually evaluated by our instructors, flight controllers, peers, and even the public. I feel a responsibility to uphold the professional integrity of the Astronaut Office for the taxpayer who supports us. I always think about the possibility that I might be the only astronaut a person ever comes across, and as such they might form a lasting impression of our entire office on an N=1 basis. For that reason, I think we all work to uphold the values of the office. We want to represent NASA, our country, and our vocation well.

Although I care for my wife, I fall in love all over again—this time with the sleek T-38 jets hangared at Ellington Field, a short drive from the Johnson Space Center. The Northrop T-38 Talon is a two-seat, delta wing, twin-engine supersonic jet used by NASA to train and transport astronauts around the nation. It looks like an airborne sports car breaking the speed limit, even when parked on the ramp. My first T-38 flight is with Stephanie Wells, a terrific and very trusting NASA flight instructor who gives me the controls right after pulling off the runway and then coaches me to accelerate and climb at blinding speeds. Going from the Cessna to the T-38 is like graduating from an arthritic pony to a thoroughbred racehorse in its prime.

The T-38s fly supersonic up to about Mach 1.3 in a dive and easily soar into the mid-40,000s, about 10,000 feet higher than commercial airliners typically cruise. The plane can wrench its pilots through more than six g's, or six times the force of gravity, enough to make it difficult to lift a little finger and cause the average person to black out. As a Mission Specialist astronaut, I'm relegated to flying the jet from the back cockpit. Only military-trained pilots are checked out as first pilots up front, but the back seat is still the coolest rocket ride within the atmosphere. You have to pay close attention—nothing is automated on these high-performance aircraft, and you'll veer off correct altitude and ground track in a heartbeat if you're not careful. But what fun, strapped into a rocket-propelled ejection seat and flying in formation, aerobatic maneuvers upside down and backward—I'd put it right up there with climbing a frozen waterfall.

As a kid, I had loved all sorts of flying machines, an interest certainly inherited from my dad. While in the Air Force, he had wanted to become a pilot, but his eyesight prevented him from achieving that dream. With an ongoing passion for anything that flies, he enjoyed working on model rockets and model planes with me in the basement workshop. When I subsequently learned to fly a claustrophobia-inducing Cessna 152 in medical school, I was hooked from the very first lap around the pattern. I kept my pilot's rating top secret from my parents until graduation weekend, when I drove them onto the flight line and took them flying (Mom first) as a huge surprise.

When I was in Colorado, flying in the mountains at altitudes up to fourteen thousand feet, eye to eye with major mountain summits, took a lot of discipline in a single-engine, unpressurized aircraft. High-altitude flight was something I pursued and became quite adept at. I would approach mountain passes at a forty-five-degree angle, and I had to be ready to quickly retreat if I detected a strong downdraft on the far side of a ridgeline. It required a clear-cut plan, solid training, and constant monitoring of fuel and weather conditions. I was always thinking about the possibility of engine failure and where I could glide down and land on a mesa or even on Interstate 70.

If we ever have to bail out from our T-38s, the Hogs need to know how to survive and thrive, so NASA sends us on a three-day land survival training exercise to Fairchild Air Force Base in Washington State. We'll be going through a very civilized version of the Air Force's SERE school, otherwise known as Survival, Evasion, Resistance and Escape training. As NASA flyers anticipating just T-38 flights over a peaceful continental United States, it's mostly a class team-building camping trip featuring some helpful survival skills, minus the hard-core resistance and evasion hazing.

I know it will be pretty easy when the instructors let us stop at the Safeway on the way to the field exercise to pick up Silver Bullets (also known as cans of Coors Light) and s'mores supplies. We learn how to survive ejection (keep our eyes on the horizon and perform proper Parachute Landing Fall or PLF), how to get the attention of rescue crews (use flares and mirrors), and how to trap food (this was the worst—due to my medical training, I am tapped to butcher a cute, white bunny rabbit to barbecue for dinner over an open fire).

As we wrap up our training, it's clear my Hog classmate John Grunsfeld will handily win the facial-hair competition with his mountain man beard. While John could now potentially join ZZ Top, I am decidedly at the other end of the spectrum. My smooth-as-a-baby's-butt face renders Doogie Howser my official, undeniable, and painfully eternal call sign.

After a year of astronaut training, I graduate and earn my silver astronaut wings, a small lapel pin of a shooting star flying through a halo, designed by the original Mercury astronauts. The silver pin means I have officially completed ASCAN training, and I am technically a full-fledged astronaut, eligible to be assigned to my first shuttle mission. I know I won't feel like a real astronaut until I've flown a mission, though, and I am dying to take that next step.

An interesting, subtle transformation occurs once you begin astronaut training in earnest. I'd always placed astronauts up on a high pedestal as an ASHO, but despite the intimidating accomplishments of my ASCAN classmates and the grizzled veteran astronauts in the office, I come to realize they are very real people, just like me, with strengths, accomplishments, weaknesses, and even an occasional fear. One exception is John Young. This guy had walked on the moon and flown that outrageous first shuttle mission, and much more. You were always treated like a prime crewmember when you were slated to fly with John, with the flight line crew carrying your parachute and bag out for you. When I flew in the back seat of John's T-38 to El Paso for Shuttle Training Aircraft sessions at dusk, I got to listen to him describe, in his humble, Southern cadence, how he bunny-hopped in the one-sixth gravity of the moon, or how he prepped for STS-1. He will always stand tall on a pedestal and deserves a cape, too.

A few months before I graduate, Gail and I get married in Chatham, Massachusetts, and set up house in a little townhome with a marina in Clear Lake, a suburb of Houston. We happily live on water that is anything but clear, overlooking the expensive homes across the way. We have a kayak and a windsurfer at hand, as well as classmate Chris Hadfield's sailboat tied up in our slip.

Training continues and late in '93 I get the call to report to the corner office with two other Hogs, Jean-François Clervoy (of the European Space Agency) and Joe Tanner. Hoot Gibson is Chief Astronaut, and as a plebeian ASCAN, it is both surprising and intimidating to be asked to step into his office. A highly decorated and accomplished Navy fighter and test pilot, Hoot is also a really warm, charming, and funny guy. But the three of us don't know what to expect, and as we settle into our chairs, it feels a little like we've been called to the principal's office.

CHAPTER TEN

Rookie Rocket Ride

I wish that being famous helped prevent
me from being constipated.

—Marvin Gaye

KENNEDY SPACE CENTER, 1994

"Doogie, you've been doing such a crappy job in the EVA branch, we're going to have to assign you to a flight. And you guys are going to have to go with him," Hoot says, smiling at all of us.

The three of us erupt in cheers and high fives, startling the hell out of the admins just outside his office door.

"You can't tell anyone until the press release goes out tomorrow," says Hoot.

I've heard that one before, and it will be next to impossible for the three of us to be discreet, having just heard the best news in the universe. We file out of the room, trying to act cool, but as soon as the door shuts behind us, we give each other high fives and share hugs, smiles, and a couple of low *woot-woots!*

Within a microsecond the boss pops his head out of his office: "Didn't I tell you guys to keep it down?!"

"Rookies . . . !" he mutters as he shuts the door.

I'll have some great crewmates to fly with on STS-66, slated to launch on the Space Shuttle *Atlantis* in November of 1994. Jean-François, Joe, and I, all first-timers, will serve as Mission Specialists. Our easygoing yet highly accomplished Commander is Don McMonagle, an Air Force F-16 test pilot and veteran of two prior shuttle flights. Our sharp-as-a-whip Payload Commander is veteran Mission Specialist Ellen Ochoa, with a PhD in electrical engineering from Stanford, although I hadn't met her there.

On STS-66, we'll be flying the third in a series of science flights called ATLAS (Atmospheric Laboratory for Applications and Science) to study the energy of the Sun and, more importantly, to learn how changes in the Sun's irradiance affect the Earth's climate and environment. We'll fly with a suite of sophisticated instruments in *Atlantis*'s payload bay, along with a small science satellite carrying a payload from Germany called CRISTA (Cryogenic Infrared Spectrometers and Telescopes), for observing the atmosphere, and MAHRSI (Middle Atmospheric High Resolution Spectrograph Investigation) from the US Naval Research Laboratory, for dayglow studies. In short, we'll be flying an alphabet soup of instruments studying climate change, including ozone mapping and characterization of the Antarctic ozone hole. Studying the ozone layer is important for us all. If we continue to produce chlorofluorocarbons (CFCs) widely used as refrigerants, the resultant decrease in this protective atmospheric layer could result in widespread death of plankton in our oceans, adverse impacts to our crops, and a higher incidence of skin cancers. The Montreal Protocol of 1987 had successfully brokered a global agreement to phase out the use of CFCs, and our mission will be taking a detailed look at how Patient Earth is recovering. Another objective is to help us prepare for future *Mir* and ISS rendezvous missions, where the shuttle will be approaching the station from below.

"Planning on success, but preparing for failure" permeates the way we train for every mission. It's impossible to anticipate each and every failure or combination of failures that might happen on orbit, but by really understanding how the hardware (our spacecraft and payloads) works you can often have some "hip-pocket procedures" for a really bad day. One such contingency plan develops when we are in Germany studying our CRISTA-SPAS scientific satellite. If for some reason we are unable to latch the satellite back down into the shuttle after nine days of free flight, priceless ozone distribution and atmospheric data would be lost forever. None of the data can be beamed to the shuttle or down to the ground in real time. I note that the data processing unit, where a detailed snapshot of our planet's upper atmosphere will be recorded, is held in place by a series of special Torx-tip bolts. Although they can be difficult to remove, and we don't have any special spacewalking tools to turn them, we come up with a plan to slightly modify a Torx bit we have inside the shuttle and remove the data processing unit in the event of such a contingency.

It will be an intense, round-the-clock mission conducting experiments in the payload bay, with Ellen and Jean-François using the shuttle's robotic arm to pluck the CRISTA-SPAS satellite out of the payload bay and set it loose to gather data; then we come back nine days later to pick it up. During free flight, the battery-powered satellite will gather enormous amounts of data and record it on board for later analysis on the ground. I'll also be taking up one of my own experiments, the ILRD exercise equipment I co-invented in Alan Hargen's lab at NASA Ames. The year of mission training includes trips for satellite payload training in Germany, science instrument operations at the Marshall Space Flight Center in Huntsville, Alabama, and other prelaunch preparations at the Kennedy Space Center in Florida. Most of our domestic travel involves formation flights across the country in our T-38s, faster and much more exhilarating than commercial flight.

Launch morning is November 3, 1994, but I'm wide awake well before the alarm goes off, as anxious as a little kid on Christmas morning hoping to find a Red Ryder BB gun under the tree. Astronaut Crew Quarters are located on the third floor of the Operations and Checkout Building of the Kennedy Space Center. All of our rooms lack windows, since we have to "sleep-shift" our internal body clocks to match our launch window. The only way I can tell it's nearing time to wake up is by the inviting smell of bacon frying at the very far end of the facility, wafting to my room through crew quarters' closed air-circulation system.

As I get ready, I feel more alive than I ever have. Today is the day I've been dreaming of for most of my life. Even more than getting the call from Don Puddy, this is a dream-come-true day. I've been exhaustively trained in simulators and the centrifuge, and I've talked to so many other astronauts who've been there and done it that I feel like I know what it will be like. But today

I'll be suiting up for real, adult pull-up diaper and all. I'm also carrying aboard something special from one of my heroes—I'd invited undersea explorer Jacques Cousteau to observe the launch, and he'd even brought me one of his famous red caps. I hope to return it to him in person some day!

The simulations and dress rehearsals are over, and I am about to strap into a rocket ship loaded with over seven million pounds of gravity-busting thrust. Crawling through the side hatch on my hands and knees, I'm able to enter the middeck of the shuttle and then pivot around to the right and drop my feet into the flight deck. It's slightly disorienting, but the closeout crew helps me get settled onto my seat, right below the Pilot, Curt Brown. Lying on my back with my feet and legs above heart level for the next couple of hours before launch, I'll soon fully comprehend the importance of that diaper.

Nine minutes before launch things get pretty serious inside. The Launch Director has polled all of his engineers, and the weather is looking good, so unless someone throws an inadvertent switch or a critical system fails in these last minutes on Earth, we are about to lurch off the planet on a column of vapor and flames.

I wonder for a millisecond what would happen if I start yelling, "Lemme outta here!"

Ten seconds before launch, an enormous deluge of water releases below the shuttle, dissipating both heat and sound waves as the three main engines on the tail of the ship throttle up. With my visor down and breathing ship's oxygen, I can hear a low, gentle rumble beneath me. No big deal—just like the sim.

The energy of the solid rocket boosters (SRBs) creates an instantaneous, incredible acceleration, quickly approaching three times my body weight, and it almost feels like one of my most exhilarating luge runs, times a googol (ten to the one-hundredth power, or 10^{100}). And then there is the vibration, like an unbalanced washing machine banging and shaking itself across the floor, making it difficult to read the cathode ray tube displays in the cockpit.

Over the next eight and a half minutes of outrageous power and up to three g's pushing me back into my seat is the ultimate amusement park ride, and my face hurts from my huge grin. As *Atlantis* does a nice roll onto its back during our climb to space, I look down at the mirror positioned on my knee and see the waves on the beach below, as well as the scattered cloud deck receding beneath me.

Two minutes into the launch, I have a brief moment of panic when the SRBs separate. I'd expected the bright flash of light through the front windows, representing the separation motors of the SRBs firing toward us after they'd done their part of the job. But for an instant it becomes very quiet and silky smooth as the rockets drop away. It actually feels like we were decelerating. *Oh, my god. We just lost all three engines and we're dropping back to Earth like a falling leaf.*

I look around the cockpit and no one else seems alarmed in the least. The front-seaters and Joe Tanner to my left are just going about their business without a look of terror on their faces. I quickly realize all is well, just the normal transition to second stage, when SRB vibration and acceleration abruptly disappear. I wish I'd anticipated that.

I thankfully don't have a whole lot to do during our perfectly nominal launch. As Mission Specialist 1 (MS1), I am supposed to serve as a backup, a reference on all orbiter systems, keeping global situational awareness. If some sort of failure does occur, I can assist, especially in cases of multiple, compounding failures.

Main Engine Cut-Off. MECO. Zero-g and I feel fine! With the acceleration gone in an instant, I feel as if I am lurching out of my seat, as comm and power cables begin to float at my side. I look out the forward windows of *Atlantis* and see both the deep black of space and the brilliant blue curvature of home below. We are already zooming across Europe, and it will be an image etched in my mind for all eternity.

The ten-day mission goes almost without a hitch, gathering enough data for hundreds of PhD students and postdocs. Ellen and Jean-François retrieve the CRISTA-SPAS satellite, although there is a short period when it isn't clear whether it will latch properly in the payload bay for a return trip home. Joe and I have a brief moment of exultation when we think we might get a chance to go play hero and latch the SPAS down by performing a contingency EVA, but the two robot arm operators skillfully solve the problem. Damn them!

Before flight, I'd decided I really wanted to spot and photograph Everest from "upstairs." I studied maps that showed our anticipated flight tracks over the ground, in particular the prominent landmarks in Tibet to the west of the mountain, including aptly nicknamed Bowtie Lake and Champagne Glass Lake. Even though we'll be zooming by at orbital velocity, they should guide me to major Himalayan glacial features including the Rongbuk Glacier, which in turn will point me right to the mountain's summit. Sure enough, I'm able to spot it through my telephoto lens on the first opportunity, and I feverishly snap some of the very best Everest photos ever acquired on a perfectly cloud-free day. These include some amazing stereo pairs, two images taken a few seconds apart, creating almost a topographic view of the various routes to the top. What would it really feel like to stand there someday and look back up into space?

On the half day off provided to our crew, I want to set (or at least tie) an audacious feat: cycling around the planet, in space. We have our cycle ergometer beautifully situated up on the flight deck, right beneath our overhead windows. Since we are flying with those windows facing directly down to Earth, optimized for all of the science in our payload bay, I'm treated to a ninety-minute glass-bottom boat's perspective of one full revolution at the equivalent of Mach 25, zipping over the Himalayas, coral atolls in the Pacific, and the great Andes while sweating to the likes of Eric Clapton, Al Jarreau, and Paula Abdul. Up-tempo music inspires me to pedal fast and "uphill" with friction, perspiration accumulating on my skin in a glistening, Jell-O-like blanket. Any sudden change of movement or momentum might result in a slosh of salty sweat breaking free and anointing my nearby crewmates or the cockpit panels. A towel is always close at hand.

Also on that half day off, I have some fun with Jean-François, aka "Billy Bob," so-named because our North Carolinian Pilot couldn't quite articulate his French name. Billy Bob is of medium height, with dark hair and a wiry build, always ready with a quick smile and a joke. We all lose it when he tries to muster up expressions like "I reckon we oughta go over yonder, y'all" in his thick French accent. Maybe he's from the south of France? He and I create perhaps the world's first zero-g sport: space tennis. Both of us like to play tennis under the constraints of gravity, but taking it to weightlessness adds a huge degree of strategic opportunity as well as potential for bodily injury. With a couple of magazine-sized procedure manuals as our rackets and a ball of wadded-up duct tape as our makeshift tennis ball, we set up court in the middeck of the shuttle. We line up on either side and try to get the ball past each other: the walls, the floor, and the ceiling are all inbounds. Our spins, ricochets, and spectacular gymnastics as we dive for the ball often result in complete LOC, or loss of control.

My exercise device, the ILRD I had worked on when I was in medical school, works like a champ up in space. I set it up in the middeck along with a video recorder and film myself pumping iron without the iron; with a series of pulleys and a harness, I work one side of my body against the other, generating tremendous forces and rapid exhaustion in less than fifteen minutes.

I learn the ins and outs of eating, sleeping, flying around, and exercising in microgravity. I operate dozens of experiments, doctor some minor ailments of my crewmates, and take hundreds of photographs, including those stunning cloud-free shots directly over Mount Everest, to kindle my imagination for years to come.

The only thing I don't quite master is the bathroom situation. I end up getting really constipated, probably because of dehydration and the lack of a gravity vector. In space, your bowels have no "gravity assist," and instead depend completely on what is called peristalsis, the smooth muscle contraction that forces contents through your GI tract. After a couple of days on orbit, I become bloated and uncomfortably distended when things aren't starting to happen down below. It's not polite conversation, but thank god for a propulsive medicine called Dulcolax, or bisacodyl, if you're a pharmacologist.

The whole toilet experience is not fun, either. The space potty requires a lot of rigmarole to first position the privacy curtain, insert a urination adapter onto the drainage hose, and get situated on the throne, feet strapped in and legs restrained with your cheeks properly aligned for a good vacuum seal.

Then you have to open up the aperture in the vacuum system by pushing on something that looks like a Ford Model A stick shift, listen to it start drawing down, and then realize you aren't going to be able to produce anything. As a rookie, it takes three to five minutes to set up and take down. The many false alarms waste a lot of my energy and time, and only through the miracle of pharmacy do I eventually find true relief by flight day 8 or 9.

I've been in all sorts of challenging bathroom situations while climbing, on multipitch rock climbs and snow-covered peaks, but this is the most straining, and I end up having to confess my problem to the flight surgeon on the ground.

The satellite works great. My plumbing? Not so much.

CHAPTER ELEVEN

Cosmobutts

> If you aren't in over your head, how do
> you know how tall you are?
>
> —*T. S. Eliot*

STAR CITY, RUSSIA, 1995

I feel like I've won a dozen successive Lotto jackpots with my first taste of spaceflight. Once my internal plumbing starts working again with an assist from Earth's gravity and I no longer feel like I'm carrying a nine-course French dinner around in my guts, I begin to process the fulfillment of such an enormous childhood dream. I often look up into the night sky and think, *Holy crap, I've actually been up there!*

Before that first mission, I'd almost been embarrassed to do any public speaking as an astronaut, a core requirement of the job. Audiences of kids were always impressed by my blue flight suit and colorful patches suggesting that I was a real astronaut, but I had often felt like an imposter, like I was letting them down when I confessed that I hadn't actually been-there-done-that yet. But now I feel like a card-carrying astronaut and can go out and represent NASA, proudly able to wear a gold version of the astronaut pin.

Burning inside me, however, is the desire to get back in line and do it all again as soon as possible. Then, in a routine Monday briefing, our Chief asks—or perhaps it's better described as begs—for volunteers to live aboard Russia's space station *Mir*. Only a handful of flown astronauts had stepped forward to volunteer because the assignment requires relocating to Russia, learning to speak and read Russian, and flying in a completely foreign spacecraft and operational culture.

The Space Shuttle is flying six or seven flights a year, and those missions are a known, exhilarating opportunity that will avail itself to me again in a couple of years, based on the way flights are being rotated among eligible flyers. But the opportunity to step back into training almost immediately, and the potential for an international adventure, is really tempting.

Will it ruin my career to get out of line for the shuttle mission training flow, or possibly jeopardize my marriage to drag Gail over to Russia? That evening I talk it over with her, and she seems to be up for a Russian trek. The next day, I walk into Hoot Gibson's office and enthusiastically offer to go to Russia to become a long-duration flyer. My gut (now fully recovered) tells me this is going to be something extraordinary.

"You've got it, Doogie," Hoot says with his typical beaming grin. With a simple handshake the job is mine. One less *Mir* billet for him to fill.

My EVA Branch Chief, Mark Lee, comes to see me that very same afternoon, asking me if I'm ready to do some Hubble Space Telescope (HST) spacesuited runs in the training pool in two weeks' time. He has already been assigned as the lead spacewalker for the second HST servicing mission, and he says I am penciled in as a spacewalker on one of the most coveted of flight assignments. The revelation hits me like an icy Siberian snowball direct to the face. Have I just given up the greatest assignment of my life because I am impatient to get back up into space? Will the inevitable suffering away from home and the mainstream Astronaut Office be worth it in the long haul? Why can't I be a bit more patient?!

Almost immediately I'm swept up into intensive, immersive language training at the Defense Language Institute (DLI) in Monterey, California, for a jump start on the Russian language. For eight-plus hours a day I am partnered with an instructor who is a native Russian speaker. Every word spoken is Russian, and new words are picked up only by context. There is no asking for an English translation or surreptitious peeks at a dictionary. It is mentally exhausting and sometimes frustrating work, but I have a pretty decent ear for languages—that early exposure to French in Dakar, plus my multilingual expletive fluency, is finally paying off. Better still, I take my lunch breaks down at the water's edge of Monterey Bay, listening to language tapes in one of the most beautiful and inspiring places on the planet.

After just three weeks of hardship posting in Monterey, and with the tempo of Russian language training rapidly increasing at NASA, I'm pulled back to Houston along with several of the DLI Russian language instructors. They put me and several other astronauts and flight controllers into a makeshift immersive language program. Isolated in plain sight, the classrooms are behind the NASA Johnson Space Center. The atmosphere is disconnected and depressing, particularly in comparison to the scenery of the California coastline.

We are instructed to simply forget about the goings-on in the Astronaut Office a couple of miles away, to disconnect from email, staff meetings, and training, and to single-mindedly focus on our intensive language training. Sessions with our native-speaking instructors, conversations *po russki* with our peers, computer drills, and written exercises are well intentioned, but the fact that our exciting prior lives are just down the street makes the immersion less than effective. What it does for me, at least, is to begin to build my enthusiasm for the transition to a satellite existence in Star City, Russia.

Being forward deployed away from the hub of all astronaut activity, particularly in the early days of the US-Russian partnership, involves months away from the bustle of shuttle flights, close friendships, flight crew assignment announcements, T-38 flying, mission training, and the many unique activities that I personally identified as being part of the astronaut corps. I am heading out to exile, to the backside of the space program, and for all I know it's going to be as cold and forlorn as Fyodor Dostoyevsky's Siberia.

The Gagarin Cosmonaut Training Center in Star City, Russia, is a fading star of the former Soviet Union, a jumble of nondescript, rapidly aging buildings located in a beautiful birch forest about twenty-five miles northeast of Moscow. The cosmonaut training center is named for Yuri Alexeyevich Gagarin, the first human being to travel into space, and also to complete a full lap of the planet. In

April of 1961, Gagarin orbited the Earth in his *Vostok 1* spacecraft, safely ejecting from his craft just prior to landing.

The Russians won this first volley of the space race, with American astronaut Alan Shepard flying into suborbital space on a Mercury spacecraft the following month. The Russians also beat us in sending a woman into space, as just two years later, cosmonaut Valentina Tereshkova followed suit on *Vostok 6*. Sadly, it took us twenty years to catch up on that one; NASA didn't send a woman into space until Sally Ride went up on the Space Shuttle in 1983.[13]

I am thrilled to be going into training at the birthplace of space travel, so Gail and I pack up our belongings for storage and fly to Moscow for a promised two-year stint, leading up to my four-month mission aboard the *Mir* station. We move into a Soviet-era three-story apartment building called the Profilactorium, or the Prophy for short, which we nervously joke is a place for safe living. It had initially been constructed to house American crewmembers during the Apollo-Soyuz Test Project in the early 1970s, which culminated in the docking of an Apollo capsule with a Soyuz spacecraft in 1975.

Although we never have any direct evidence of our conversations being listened to, the Cold War origins of the place and the testing-the-waters nature of this new US-Russian space collaboration, called the Phase 1 program and leading toward a joint international space station (Phase 2), leads us all to believe the place is riddled with electronic-listening and observational technology.

Gail and I have a two-room apartment on the first floor, including a bedroom and a sitting room with a TV, along with access to a shared kitchen down the hallway. There are a few Western television programs dubbed into Russian, and on occasion I come home to see Gail watching TV, volume cranked all the way up to try to hear the English in the background. I'm not sure she even likes *The Rockford Files* all that much, but hearing some of our home language is comforting to us both at times.

Gail finds a job working part time as a nurse in an American clinic for traveling expatriates in Moscow, and the rest of the time she stays busy taking Russian language lessons and making weekly shopping expeditions to Moscow to a Western-style market called Seventh Continent, with access to decent produce and frozen foods, many imported from Western Europe. She also sets up several weekend trips for us away from the training center. Very few people speak

English, and while our governments have historically been at odds, the Russian people are incredibly welcoming.

Star City is housed on a formerly clandestine Soviet Air Force base and doesn't appear on any recent maps of the region, despite wide knowledge of its existence by foreign spacefaring nations. The somewhat grim-looking buildings of the training area are separated from the residential area by a very porous barbed-wire fence and ostensibly armed guards, but the warm good nature of our hosts makes us feel right at home. It is a family-friendly environment, with kids playing by the small lake out in front of the Prophy, and young families walking through the woods in search of wild strawberries.

To see General Yuri Glaskov, famed yet affable cosmonaut and Twice Hero of the Soviet Union, walking around the parklike grounds with his tiny dog defuses any tension or apprehension we might have felt in such an environment. Moreover, my background in war-torn areas has helped prepare me to make the best of any situation, so I settle in and go to work.

There is an unspoken, underlying tension in our evolving joint Russian-American flight program. Even I feel it, with delicate negotiations ongoing in terms of sharing information on things as fundamental as training manuals (called *Konspects*), the actual training content we receive, program finances, and other issues that are heavily infused with politics. The Russians are analytical and slow to make decisions, ask lots of questions, and carefully control their budget and intentions. They rarely let on what they are thinking until they are strategically ready to tell us.

The only other American I have much contact with is another Hog from my Group 14 astronaut class named Jerry Linenger. I will serve as his backup on the fourth long-duration American mission to *Mir* and then graduate to prime crewmember on the fifth. Two other astronauts, John Blaha and Shannon Lucid, are there at the same time, but they're living and training in another part of Star City, taking advanced classes for more imminent flights.

Jerry, also a med school graduate, had just completed his first Space Shuttle mission, STS-64, a couple of months before mine. He is in Russia solo without his wife, Katherine, and so we spend just about every day in training together. As a bachelor-in-absentia of sorts, he also eats many evening meals with Gail and me; thankfully, he never leaves us with leftovers and speeds up the cleanup process.

Beyond technical studies of the Soyuz life-support system and so on, part of our formal training is physical conditioning. Our Russian fitness coach, Anatoly, shortened to just Tolya, is determined to demonstrate his coaching brilliance by dramatically improving our current level of physical fitness. Three times a week we have swim sessions, interval sprints on a cinder track, and weight training in a well-appointed gym.[14] Jerry and I do pull-ups, sit-ups, bench presses, timed runs, and confidence-building dives from a three-meter-high platform. One of the highlights of the program is tennis, and sometimes the lighthearted competition between Jerry and me heats up to the point where we play insult tennis. It helps to keep us from going stir-crazy.

"I HATE . . . ," I shout with a powerful forehand, "your GUTS!"

"I can't WAIT . . . ," he replies with a lob, way over my head, "to leave you BEHIND!"

When we go to the track with Tolya, he marks the track for our first 100-meter sprint as a baseline, or "before Tolya" measure. I'm a little startled when Anatoly draws our finish line by dragging his foot across the cinder track at what I roughly judge to be a full 120 meters. A few weeks later, the line changes to more like 100 meters. I finally begin to see what he is doing when, ten weeks later, he draws a new finish line at 80-ish meters. With Anatoly's special custom measurements, I run the fastest 100 meters I've ever run, probably close to an Olympic gold medal pace. I'm certain Anatoly gets a nice bonus for our amazing improvement under his coaching.

Language training is a much bigger challenge. Jerry and I spend hours every day with the ultimate Russian drill sergeant, the kind-hearted Zinaida Nikolaevna. An older woman, and a classic babushka (or grandmother) in appearance with a warm soul and soft smile, she refuses to allow us to speak even a single syllable of English over our daily midmorning tea and cookies in the cosmonaut break room. Luckily, she also speaks French, and if there is ever uncertainty, I can communicate with her in a pinch, but typically we make a focused effort for mutual understanding in Russian, self-translating by context and with our ever-expanding vocabulary. She is a stickler for pronunciation and has a great ear for error. Social interaction is especially important to her, and will be for us on orbit, including an understanding of Russian culture and food. But even more important is learning the technical language of spaceflight.

All of our instruction and written materials, including system controls aboard the Soyuz, are in Russian. We also have to learn *Mir* space station systems—life support, electrical power, communications, guidance and control, onboard computer systems, and so on—in order to do our eventual simulator training and flights. There is no out. I have to become nearly fluent in speaking and reading Russian, because the two other crewmates I'll have aboard *Mir* will be speaking Russian with perhaps only a hint of pidgin English. The Soyuz is a very different launch vehicle from our winged Space Shuttle, even though the Russian and American space programs evolved at the same time, so we need to learn new launch, docking, and landing procedures, along with new spacewalk protocols and even different, higher-pressure spacesuits.

In the days before ubiquitous wireless Internet, Skype, and broadband, there isn't much opportunity for us to communicate with friends and family back home. As a result, the feeling of isolation and not belonging to the mainstream NASA flight crew office is real and grows stronger the longer we are there. Trying to figure out when we'll get a flight back to Houston for the home leave we were promised is especially frustrating for Jerry. Gail and I explore Moscow, St. Petersburg, Kiev, and other nearby cities by train on weekends when I have a little time, making good use of my evolving language skills.

I become acquainted with one of our instructors, Sasha, a Russian Air Force officer who is responsible for teaching us the operational details of the communications system on the Soyuz spacecraft. Like his peers, he has a very disciplined, regimented way of teaching, with schematic posters and the emphatic use of a pointer to make sure we understand. After I get to know him a bit, he sells me his Russian Ural motorcycle, complete with a sidecar, that he's been wanting to get rid of, for a mere $1,000. This is probably a fortune for him, and an incredible buy for me. I use it to ride around and explore the local countryside, and I know it will be a big hit once I get back home to Houston. Although just a few years old, it is a knockoff of a German World War II BMW motorcycle, straight out of *Hogan's Heroes.*

Four months into my training, it's time for plaster butt casting. A time-honored cosmonaut tradition, this is how the Soyuz capsule is customized for each crewmember who might need to come home in it, landing on very hard dirt in the steppes of Kazakhstan. Although the plan is for me to launch and land on the Space Shuttle, I could potentially need to use the Russian capsule in an emergency situation, and the seat needs to be molded precisely to my body to absorb the impact of what might amount to a controlled crash landing.

Russian engineers take great pains to create a custom seat for each cosmonaut, made to the exact specifications of a particular human body, from the head to the hips and thighs. Accomplishing this feat requires a detailed plaster cast of the cosmonaut's body. Thus, I find myself clad in a pair of form-fitting, paper-thin long johns underwear, very small for my torso and general anatomy, resulting in what can be best described as an atomic wedgie. As I self-consciously walk down a back hallway to the lab, very awkwardly trying to maintain a degree of modesty with my hands strategically positioned over my front and my back, I pass dozens of life-sized, anatomically correct white plaster casts of cosmobutts. Is this the necessary path to greatness? I'll soon find out. A few minutes later I am lying in an enormous steel vat as several dozen male and female engineers in white lab coats tend to the gallons of plaster of Paris encasing my nether regions. It is cold, wet, and sticky, with strangers poking, prodding, and rapidly jabbering about their progress, although my ears are mostly covered by a cap and my Russian lip reading is not up to par. When the process is finally complete, I feel like they owe me a dinner or flowers or something.

Two weeks later, after my plaster butt cast emerges and is analyzed, a seat is built to my exact specifications. I am called back in for a fit check, and a team of engineers straps me in for testing while I'm wearing a Russian Sokol launch and entry suit. Buttoned up in the suit, I can't hear all that is said, but I do see lots of frowns and heads shaking in animated discussion, and my suspicions are confirmed a couple of weeks later. I am given bad news—engineers have determined my six-foot, three-inch frame is too large for a Soyuz emergency-escape-capsule seat.

There is no appeal process. I am flunked out of a long-duration mission to *Mir*, and all of my fitness efforts, technical training, and language skill are going to be for naught. Gail is not too disappointed with the news—she is ready to head back to the States and return to her job at Texas Children's Hospital and to American life. We've pressed on through this assignment together, but it's not been easy.

But in the end, there are two positive outcomes. I will have the coolest motorcycle in the neighborhood. Even better, I have a new call sign. Yeah! No more Doogie. From now on, I'll be "Too Tall Parazynski," or just "Too Tall," for short.

CHAPTER TWELVE

Young Skywalker

For once you have tasted flight you will walk the
Earth with your eyes turned skywards, for there you
have been and there you will long to return.

—*Leonardo da Vinci*

TEXAS CHILDREN'S HOSPITAL, NICU, 1997

Although I'm back in the states with my cosmonaut career *nyet*, there is still hope for a visit to the *Mir* space station. I'll need a seat on the Space Shuttle, however, in order to accommodate my too-tallness. So back to work at NASA I go, hoping for another shot.

Meanwhile, Gail and I get ready for another new mission—becoming parents. Gail is pregnant with our first child, a son, and I follow this development with a rookie father's pride and euphoria, as well as a physician's fascination at the miracle of biology and physiology unfolding in my own home.

Once upon a time, as a medical student I'd seriously considered specializing in obstetrics and gynecology. I'd delivered at least twenty babies at the Santa Clara Valley Medical Center with a terrific supervising resident who exuded a passion for her work. I loved being part of the miracle of birth, even though babies always seemed to arrive in the middle of the night.

The incredible crescendo of teamwork and activity culminates in so many firsts—a baby's first breath of life, her first cry, and the first tender embrace with her exhausted mom. I'll never forget one particular mother who had already given birth to nine children, had only recently discovered she was pregnant again, and who went into heavy labor very quickly. I ended up delivering her tenth baby right there in the hallway. Luckily, all was well.

Any pregnancy involving a couple like us—an MD and an RN—is, of course, closely scrutinized and tracked by two people who know too much to just let nature take its course. But everything goes perfectly during those nine months of Gail's pregnancy. The ultrasounds and other tests are favorable, and we think about names, prepare the nursery, and look forward to becoming parents.

Eventually, however, a potential problem arises. Close to the due date, it's clear our baby is head up when he should be head down. A breech birth poses a real problem for delivery as the umbilical cord can wrap around the baby's neck, among other possible complications. Gail makes an appointment at the hospital for a procedure to attempt to reorient the baby, but he decides not to cooperate. Perhaps his resistance is a hint of his powerful personality.

Finally, Gail's obstetrician schedules her for a C-section, and on the evening before Luke's first day she craves, and eats, an epic omelet breakfast at Denny's. The next morning I'm there in the delivery room, breathless, back behind the curtain with the anesthesiologist. I peer over the curtain as they open up the uterus, and all of a sudden, there he is, energetic and ET-like! I want to climb over the curtain and grab him up and hold him tight. But my doctor's mind puts the brakes on my impulse and I wait. Luckily, our baby cleans up well, shedding his alien appearance, and Gail and I joyfully welcome our first child, Luke Andrew Parazynski, into the world on January 8, 1997.

Luke shares a birthday with Elvis Presley, so I tell everyone it's the second coming of the King. But more truthfully, he gets his name from Luke Skywalker. I wanted a name with character, and with a last name like Parazynski, his first name needs to be both short and memorable. Better a fierce Jedi warrior than a tapped-out rock 'n' roller.

At eight pounds, eleven ounces, Luke resembles a squirmy, miniature, bald sumo wrestler with piercing, wonderful eyes. I have a beautiful son! My heart is racing out of my chest with excitement, and I'm overcome with huge, unadulterated love. Luke is the most wonderful little thing I've ever seen in my life, and I can't believe I am finally getting to meet him.

My elation is short lived, though. Luke's color is a little dusky when he should be getting pinker, and after an examination, our pediatricians determine he is actually two weeks early, put him on oxygen, and send him off to the nursery.

Two weeks early isn't really that early, and to my eyes Luke looks like he is big and strong enough to bench-press the other babies in the surrounding incubators. But while his color improves due to the extra oxygen, Luke huffs and puffs and struggles to breathe. Within about ten hours, it becomes clear that Luke needs a few more days in the oven and his early arrival is enough to warrant the label of hyaline membrane disease, also known as infant respiratory distress syndrome.

Sometimes hyaline membrane disease happens because premature babies lack enough surfactant, a substance in the lungs that helps keep the alveoli, or air sacs, open and functioning. Without enough surfactant, Luke's lungs aren't transporting enough oxygen in exchange for carbon dioxide. With time, most babies do well, but as an excited, and now a very worried brand-new dad, and with Gail still recovering from her surgery, I find myself in almost as much distress as Luke. I stay by his side and hold him whenever I can, but every time I look at his nostrils flaring and his blue-tinged lips, I feel like I can't breathe, either. He will need to have surfactant delivered to his lungs via a breathing tube and spend a few days in a neonatal intensive care unit up in Houston.

As soon as Gail is able, we both begin working the phones to call in all of our favors with medical colleagues. Gail arranges for him to be transferred to neonatal intensive care at Texas Children's Hospital, where she works, in downtown Houston. Luke will make the forty-minute ride by ambulance, accompanied by a skilled and devoted pediatric intensive care transport team known as the Kangaroo Crew. Gail has to stay behind for a couple of days to recuperate so I am on my own. Distressed and very worried, I drive to downtown Houston like a maniac and even beat the ambulance by fifteen whole minutes. As the plan to move Luke comes together, I call both sets of parents, who make immediate plans to fly to Houston to lend physical and moral support.

As soon as Luke arrives and gets checked into the ICU, I begin a three-day vigil, alternating between confidence that my son is receiving the best care and will be fine, and sheer terror. Besides worrying about his immediate survival, I begin to worry about the future. If he does get better, will this have a long-standing impact on his life? Will weak lungs or a damaged heart handicap him? I feel desperate, saying prayers and sometimes dissolving into tears. But there is nothing much I can do to affect the outcome. Going into any sort of hyperfocus or flow state won't fix this problem. My visualization techniques aren't going to work here. Instead, I'm forced to wait, watch, and trust the experts.

I'm there every time the ICU team comes by, and they address me as a father, but also as a physician, going through the data and sharing the treatment plan. I press them for answers. "I'm not hearing the next layer of this. Why is he running a fever?" I demand. "What is the real prognosis? What do we do if things start to spiral down?"

I know there are no easy answers or magic bullets; Luke's lungs need time to develop. Sometimes, when I can't keep my eyes open any longer, I go to the small waiting room the hospital had very kindly converted into a bunk room for me (because of Gail's position at the hospital) and steal a quick nap. But I don't want to be away from my son for any longer than absolutely necessary.

I bring a small CD player and speakers to play Mozart for Luke in his ICU bassinet, and I wonder if he is listening above the rhythmic sound of the respirator and the beeps of the monitors. The "Mozart Effect,"[15] playing classical music for a child while still in the womb, and soon after birth, to elevate IQ, may or may not make a difference in cognitive development. But I want to stack the cards in his favor in any way that I can.

His tiny blue eyes are so full of life, engaging mine. *You are such a miracle,* I think as I look at him with the deepest love I've ever known. *How did you come from two tiny cells?* This beautiful, complex human being has arrived, defenseless and completely dependent on Gail and me and the team of pediatricians, nurses, and technicians supporting his breathing. I have so many hopes and dreams for him. While part of me knows it's unrealistic, I don't want him to ever have to want for anything or suffer pain or heartbreak. I want him to have a good, full life, and I hope to take him with me to travel around the world, like my parents did, and to experience life to the fullest. Fearing for his life and future in those first days is agonizing, with so many variables well beyond my control.

After a week in the hospital, the longest seven days of my life, Luke's lungs mature enough for release and we take him home. He grows fast and becomes my best friend and playmate. I'll never forget taking him to the astronaut gym when he's just a few months old. He loves to play with the basketball, even at a very early age, and he is so engaging with everyone he meets. I remember seeing astronaut-in-training Jim Pawelczyk there one Saturday; "Luke smiles with his whole body!" he says.

My goal as Luke's dad is to try to share as many wonderful experiences and opportunities with him as I can, and to try to give him a full set of keys to find whatever path through life he might dream of.

The year is intense: it started with joy that quickly descended into despair, but knowing Luke is thriving and being a proud dad launches me back into a season of unbridled optimism and opportunity. At NASA I'm assigned to my next mission, and it is going to be epic. I will be part of a shuttle crew docking with *Mir* on STS-86, scheduled to launch in September. I'll get to use my Russian after all.

And not only do I have my own chunky little Skywalker greeting me each day as I walk in the door, but I am going to be a skywalker, too! I go into flight-specific training for my first spacewalk, what NASA calls an Extravehicular Activity (EVA). I am beyond excited, since I've been studying the art of EVA since my first days and first Astronaut Office job at NASA. Riding a shuttle into space is one thing; being given the opportunity to leave the spacecraft and venture outside in what is essentially a personal spaceship, an Extravehicular Mobility Unit (or EMU) most of us would simply call a spacesuit, will be the ultimate human experience.

With the ISS program ramping up, walking in space will soon become an important part of most missions. Robots can't do all the necessary work of module installation, activation, and repair. Human adaptability and creative problem-solving will be crucial for complicated missions to update the Hubble Space Telescope and later build the ISS. Spacewalkers will now be called upon to do increasingly complex tasks in support of ISS assembly and maintenance, and I hope to help develop some of the tools, procedures, and contingency plans for the EVA work ahead.

As a doctor, I am fascinated by the EVA suits, which must nurture and sustain spacewalkers in an environment completely hostile to the human body, and without any margin for error. In the freezing, oxygenless vacuum of space, one of the biggest dangers is a leak in the spacesuit. Micrometeoroids, some the size of a grain of sand on the beach, could tear the suit and cause almost instant death, your body exploding within. To protect the human occupant, the outer layers include materials like Mylar insulation, along with a pressure bladder, a fireproof layer, and Kevlar, also used to make bulletproof vests.

Another serious danger is decompression sickness, or the bends, something I was very familiar with from my scuba diving background. If the pressure inside the spacesuit isn't managed properly, going outside into the vacuum of space could cause nitrogen gas bubbles to expand inside an astronaut's blood vessels, causing severe pain, cramping, and even paralysis or death. Higher suit pressure decreases the risk of decompression sickness, but lower suit pressure increases the astronaut's flexibility and dexterity. Like a deep-sea scuba diver doing decompression stops to prevent the bends, astronauts must purge nitrogen from their bloodstream before going outside, accomplished by breathing 100 percent oxygen. The oxygen and other critical systems of the suit are housed in the Primary Life Support System, which resembles a large backpack.

Body temperature control is another issue. In the shade, space can be as cold as 157 degrees Celsius below zero (minus 250 degrees Fahrenheit), and in the sunlight it can be as hot as 121 degrees Celsius (250 degrees Fahrenheit). To combat these extremes, the Primary Life Support System circulates water through hundreds of feet of flexible tubing, manufactured into a formfitting, stretchable undergarment.

An additional grave danger is accidental detachment, floating away into space. EVA suits have two safeguards. One is the use of a tether linking you to the shuttle itself. The other is a mini jetpack, called the Simplified Aid for EVA Rescue, with just enough power to propel a loose astronaut back to the shuttle.

All of this wearable equipment is incredibly complex and unwieldy and requires help to get into and plenty of practice to utilize properly. That's where the pool comes in. The EVA instructors train crewmembers for microgravity underwater, simulating the weightlessness of space through the neutral buoyancy of the pool. I begin my EVA training in a huge pool called the Weightless Environment Training Facility in Houston. The pool is seventy-five feet long, fifty feet wide, and twenty-five feet deep, and contains a full-size mock-up of the shuttle payload bay for spacewalkers to practice in.

I'll be flying with an American crew commanded by Jim Wetherbee, aka "WXB" (phonetically: *wex-bee*), a highly experienced Navy fighter test pilot and veteran Space Shuttle Commander who had flown the first rendezvous and close approach to *Mir* on his last flight, STS-63. This time WXB and crew will actually be docking with the station, and I'll be walking in space with legendary Russian cosmonaut Vladimir Titov.

Vladimir "Volodya" Georgievich Titov is a veteran Soyuz Commander and also the first human to spend 365 consecutive days off the planet. He is also famous for having survived several life-threatening experiences, including the closest call on launch ever, a seventeen-g launch abort. A large fire had erupted at the base of his *Soyuz T-10* rocket just one minute before launch, and the automatic abort sequence failed due to burned wires. Two launch controllers manually aborted the mission via radio and Titov and his crewmate were propelled by the launch escape system to land safely a few miles away from the launch vehicle, which had already exploded.

Mike "Bloomer" Bloomfield, a good-natured Air Force pilot and academy football player, would be the right-seater on the flight deck. Charismatic Frenchman Jean-Loup Chrétien, a Brigadier General and fighter test pilot who'd previously flown twice with the Soviet space program, would be a fellow Mission Specialist. As a new dad and a first-time spacewalker, I have a lot of work to do to measure up to the challenges ahead. Not to mention brushing up on my Russian. *Поехали!*[16]

Since the very first terrifying beep of *Спутник-1* or *Sputnik-1* in 1957, Russia and the United States had contested a technological and ideological race in space. Although we won the ultimate prize of landing a crew on the moon, one area where the Russians dominated was in designing and successfully operating the first space station, *Salyut 1*, in 1971. While the United States briefly tested the waters by sending three crews to the *Skylab* space station in the mid-1970s, the Soviets continued to invest and learn from successive *Salyut* stations and eventually constructed *Mir*.

Mir is the first continuously inhabited long-term research station, remaining in orbit from 1986 until a fiery reentry into the South Pacific in 2001. Crews conduct experiments aboard this microgravity research lab running the gamut from plant biology and human physiology to material science, astrophysics, and meteorology, along with operating innovative life support systems with the goal of a permanent occupation of space.

One of the main objectives of my upcoming shuttle mission will be to retrieve NASA astronaut Mike Foale after 145 days on *Mir*. Strangely enough, if I had been just an inch or so shorter, it would have been me up there instead of Mike. But I am delighted to be slated for a rendezvous with *Mir* and to welcome him back onto American soil, aka the Space Shuttle *Atlantis*.

A complication we'll be facing on the upcoming mission is due to a wayward *Progress* resupply ship, which depressurized the station's *Spektr* module during an ill-fated test of a new rendezvous and docking method during his stay. Foale and his cosmonaut crew saved the day, preventing the loss of the entire station, so I am sure he'll be relieved to be coming home after such an exhausting mission.

Another odd coincidence is that a second American cosmonaut replacement will be on my upcoming shuttle mission. Her name is Wendy Lawrence, a fellow Hog in my astronaut class with a master's degree from MIT and a background flying Navy helicopters. Wendy most recently served as Director of Operations in Star City, Russia, until she was tapped to step in as a replacement for the next long-duration flight.

Wendy's diminutive stature puts her at the opposite end of the anthropometric spectrum from me. As fate would have it, following the *Progress* collision with the *Mir* station, a number of repair EVAs will be required. Wendy is an incredibly capable astronaut in all respects, but unfortunately the Russian Orlan spacesuit is ginormous on her petite frame; she can even wriggle her arm out of the pressurized Orlan suit arm and scratch her nose! Weeks before she is due to launch on STS-86 to the *Mir* as Mike Foale's replacement, she, too, is pulled from the long-duration increment. Maybe you can guess her nickname—"Too Short." Collectively we refer to ourselves as "The Russian Rejects."

Next in queue is a bewildered physician-astronaut named Dave Wolf, who mistakenly thought he wouldn't be flying for many months. He enthusiastically jumps into an accelerated training flow, with certain shortcuts necessary to join our shuttle crew for launch. We have to Photoshop him into our crew portrait, and a small tab is tacked onto the bottom of our mission patch that simply says *Wolf.* For some strange reason he doesn't care too much for his new call sign—"Too Average."

CHAPTER THIRTEEN

Mir MacGyvering

Maybe it's about time I expanded the
realm of possibilities around here.

—*Richard Dean Anderson as MacGyver*

SPACE STATION* MIR, *1997

As the Too Crew trains for our upcoming mission, I'm thrilled when I realize that these two former adversaries, the US and Russian space programs, are now working together at unprecedented levels of cooperation to manage some significant crises on *Mir*. Even before the *Progress* resupply collision, there had been a major near miss that could've proven fatal to Jerry Linenger and his five crewmates. As Sasha Lazutkin initiated an oxygen-generating cartridge in the *Kvant* module, contaminants likely resulted in an uncontained fire aboard the spacecraft. A frightening jet of flames blocked three crewmembers' pathway to their Soyuz lifeboat, and the closed space station environment filled with blinding, asphyxiating smoke. Thankfully the torch didn't melt through the paper-thin aluminum shell of the module. All six crewmembers survived thanks to a limited number of emergency oxygen masks, their thorough training, and a healthy dose of luck.

It wouldn't be too much of a stretch to say that *Mir* was snakebit thereafter, with rolling brownouts of power and a variety of gremlins seemingly infesting their life support systems. We will be taking up a replacement Vozdukh carbon dioxide–scrubbing system with us, not to mention a replacement attitude-control computer.

A potential docking problem has also emerged: the station begins to experience significant problems maintaining the correct orientation during tests on the three consecutive Sundays before we are set to launch. It dawns on me that we are going up to attempt to rendezvous and dock with a space station that is past warranty. But to be fair, *Mir* has already exceeded its design life, and the Russians' recovery from several near misses has taken space MacGyvering to a whole new level. The Russians don't have a Space Shuttle to deliver resupply kits up to *Mir*, so the cosmonauts are adept at taking apart old, defunct equipment and salvaging parts and wiring for necessary repairs.

I will be serving as the rendezvous navigator during the approach and docking maneuvers, floating just to Jim's right, and looking up through the overhead windows toward our destination. Bloomer, our Pilot, will be working the shuttle's flight control software from the forward cockpit. It is my job to integrate the various sensors we have for range and for our relative motion toward the station, along with monitoring the precision of our alignment between *Mir* and the shuttle's docking system, and feed this information to the Commander flying the approach.

When we are still far away from the station we will use a radar system and lasers, but within one hundred feet to docking we will rely heavily on video cameras looking through our docking system hatch up toward a special target, enabling me to determine if we are co-aligned. Because of the computer and attitude-control problems they'd been experiencing on the station, we have even trained to dock with a space station that is rotating, and one that might not be pointing in the precise direction we've been told to expect. We train in a domed virtual reality simulator with a surprisingly realistic rendering of *Mir* orbiting the Earth, complete with a spinning planet below and the dynamic lighting we can expect on the real day. Our flight control team, in coordination with Russian engineers and specialists, believes we can still dock safely with *Mir* using our contingency plans and additional training. If necessary, we will manually reorient the shuttle and match the erroneous rotational rates of *Mir*. "Their systems are so good, I predict we'll never have to do manual fly-out" (or reorientation of the shuttle to match the *Mir* station), Jim assures us before flight.

We launch aboard *Atlantis* from the Kennedy Space Center in Florida at 10:34 in the evening on September 25, 1997. Since it's my second launch, I'm not quite as tense, but I'm even more excited. More than anything, I am looking forward to floating out on my first spacewalk, which will also be the very first joint US-Russian EVA from the Space Shuttle.

The evening of launch is pretty special, with an energetic lightning show tap-dancing off the coast. Everyone I know and love is about five miles away looking at me, our shuttle bathed in high-intensity xenon lights, but obviously not seeing me. As Mission Specialist 2, the shuttle's Flight Engineer, I am the very last crewmember to board the ship. I have the 195-foot level of the launch tower mostly to myself as my crewmates are getting strapped in by the closeout crew. My beautiful baby boy is over there, along with all of my family and friends. What are they thinking at this point? I wish they could see my beaming face right now to calm their nerves.

Launch is successful and uneventful, with only 8.5 minutes for the 4.5-million-pound shuttle system to accelerate from zero to 17,500 miles per hour, securing us in orbit. I feel right back at home, and we all quickly set out to convert our rocket ship into an orbiting laboratory and resupply ship. If all goes well, we'll be docking with *Mir* on our third flight day.

As we approach *Mir*, it transitions from a bright star on the horizon to an enormous spider overhead. WXB and I keep our eyes locked on our target. We have plenty of data from our onboard instruments, but at about one hundred feet away we do an early visual assessment to make sure the Russian space station is in the proper alignment. But it's not. WXB and I both sense something substantially amiss. We are still too far away for us to see the target cross on the *Mir* hatch on our small CCTV monitor; you have to be more like thirty feet away to do a precise visual assessment. But even at a hundred feet, it is easy to see that the whole space station is cocked to one side. WXB even postulates that the target had somehow been bent from the summertime collision. "Look at that," he says, tapping Bloomer on the arm. He makes a call to Mission Control

Houston, reporting the misalignment, and lets them know we'll probably be doing a manual fly-out. We don't have much time for discussion as we are still closing in on docking.

Being two degrees off in any one of the rotational degrees of freedom—pitch, yaw, or roll—constitutes a real problem. What I am seeing on my CCTV monitors suggests that we are off that much in all three axes. *Mir* was not supposed to ever be this far off, so our instructors had never programmed such an outlandish error into our virtual reality training. Based on what I can see on the monitor, and using different alignment cues, including a guide wire and a cross, our reality is wildly "off nominal."

I quickly establish that we are indeed off in multiple axes. Can this be real? I know that if we proceed as planned, we'll bounce off *Mir* and cause some serious damage. Aviators often joke about moments with serious "pucker factor," meaning the adrenaline response of an *oh, crap!* moment that causes your cheeks to tighten uncontrollably. This is one of those big moments, although to a casual observer all would appear to remain calm in the cockpit.

With the shuttle still thirty feet away, WXB fires jets to stop *Atlantis* and hold us in place while we talk to Houston on audio downlink as they visually assess the situation on the ground. Immediately, I calculate and then recalculate the fly-out to make sure we orient the shuttle to the proper angles for docking. "Let's fly it out," orders WXB.

In our cramped cockpit and with our tiny TV monitors, I am the only one with a clear view of the situation, although WXB and Bloomer are doing their best to back me up by looking over my shoulders. With full knowledge that screwing it up will be a huge deal, and substantially on my head, I call out the final angular corrections to Bloomer, who types them into our flight computer. Once the maneuver takes effect, I hold my breath as the target centers up and WXB flies us the rest of the way in.

Then, success. We make it, and I can't believe it was such a huge fly-out. But I'm also excited because I've been looking out the window at a former Soviet space station, and in a little less than an hour I'll be floating inside it. How crazy is that?!

Later, the misalignment is determined to be an understandable human error. The cosmonauts had locked onto the wrong star in their daily update of the navigation system, roughly six degrees off from the intended target star. The misalignment was thankfully unrelated to the collision damage from before. As for the docking itself, success was a result of our great training, excellent teamwork, WXB's calm leadership, and a wonderful demonstration of NASA's philosophy of backup and redundancy. Planning for multiple failures means a better chance of ultimate survival and success.

Floating through the hatch and flying into *Mir* for the first time is extraordinary, especially seeing our friends Mike, Commander Anatoly Solovyov, and Flight Engineer Pavel Vinogradov move so gracefully in their orbital home. The docking module is crammed full of old, inoperative payloads and mesh bags full of gear and trash, tethered, clinking, and floating off the walls, ready for a trip home on *Atlantis* in a few days. The next module, *Kristall*, is so stuffed I almost have to suck in my gut to squeeze through the dark central passageway. There is a musty, humid odor to the place, reminding me of my late great-grandmother's home in upstate New York. I am so glad to be here right now, but I'm also glad I'll be leaving in five days.

Greeting the Russians and seeing Mike in the flesh again is exciting, but my thoughts turn very quickly to preparing for my first spacewalk in a couple of days. Most importantly, we will also be running a major U-Haul operation during our docked days, exchanging Dave Wolf for Mike Foale on the station, along with all of their scientific and personal gear, not to mention lots of other logistics for the station crew, including food, the carbon dioxide scrubber, and the attitude-control computer, ten thousand pounds in all.

Vladimir and I will have our hands full during a planned five-hour spacewalk. We'll be retrieving four experiments from the outside of *Mir* that had been exposed to the vacuum of space two years prior, capturing minute traces of orbital debris on special collector plates and aerogels. We'll also be attaching a cap onto the exterior of the docking module that might one day allow *Mir* spacewalkers to seal off the leak in the hull of the *Spektr* module, thought to be underneath the attachment point of one of its solar arrays.

And—what I am most excited about—I'll be testing out our new emergency jetpack! I'm going to be the first to ever power up the operational "space parachute" and fire some thrusters.[17] It was designed to be worn by every future NASA spacewalker as a lifesaver, to propel them back to their spacecraft should they ever become detached. Our safety tether reels were never supposed to fail, so we shouldn't ever really have to worry about such things, but it was an important insurance policy I hoped I wouldn't need to make a claim on. Spacewalkers had been known to occasionally float away from their handrails on past missions, although thankfully so far they'd been able to reel themselves back in.

Like a quarterback on the Saturday before Super Bowl, I don't sleep much the night before, my mind busy going over and over the next day's procedures. Volodya and I get up early, and after being assisted into our EVA suits, this time in outer space, I feel mentally and physically ready for one of the biggest days of my life. I ask the shuttle crew to keep the payload bay lights off so I can see the stars as I float out the hatch, just like when you turn off the back porch light so you can walk outside and try to spot the Milky Way.

Turning the hand crank to release the hatch mechanism, I pull the hatch in toward myself and then hinge it down beneath me. Pressing open the white thermal cover that stood between me and the enormity of the universe, I pop my head and torso out into space. I focus first on hooking up to my safety tether reel and getting Vladimir hooked onto his, doing my best to try to ignore the otherworldly environment I am experiencing for the very first time. Once we are secured and can really go outside, it hits me: I can see trillions and trillions of stars in a fine blanket overhead. And then I see Anatoly, world record holder for the most time spent outside on EVAs, smiling down at me like a benevolent outer space deity from a tiny porthole in the Base Block of *Mir*.

But as soon as I begin to relax and savor the experience, another pucker factor moment materializes. Out of the corner of my eye I see something odd. Vladimir isn't even out of the hatch yet, so what is moving to my left? When I pivot in that direction, not an easy feat in the bulky suit and helmet, I see far too much braided steel cable floating around me.

The safety tether is a fifty-five-foot steel braid cable housed in a casing with a spring retraction mechanism, designed to prevent slack cable from floating around and snagging onto us or the sensitive spacecraft we're crawling on. The reel is our lifeline, designed to keep us from floating away. The retraction system seems to be frozen for some unknown reason. I look down in a brief moment of panic as the metal cable snakes around me, slithering around in zero gravity as if alive. What if it wraps around my arms or legs, or traps Volodya?

I reach down and give it a gentle tug, but the reel ignores the gesture, refusing to pull it back in. I cycle the lock-unlock mechanism several times. I try to push the cable back in, tap it on the side, and try every combination and permutation I can think of to coax it back to life. I realize that my spacewalk might possibly be about to end before it even begins. I'm dying of nerves; are we going to have to call this whole thing off?

Volodya waits patiently as I finally resort to a variation of the Russian safety-tether method, using both of my long waist tethers almost like ice axes, as if I'm climbing a waterfall of ice. I put one tether on a handrail, then move the second tether to the next handrail beyond. Mission Control Houston approves, and we are thankfully going to be allowed back to work. But first we bundle up the wayward tether reel—again, not an easy task with the big, stiff-with-pressure EVA gloves—then continue to the *Mir* station using a hand-over-hand tether protocol. As I pull myself along and establish a comforting rhythm, I finally begin to relax and realize I am going to get everything on our to-do list done, even if it doesn't all go as originally scripted.

It's tense-going those first minutes of that "walk" (or actually crawl) in space, with my heart rate initially up as high as 112 beats per minute. Once my anxiety subsides a bit with the knowledge that Houston isn't going to have me "abort EVA," a terrible-sounding procedure name for prematurely ending a spacewalk, elation floods through me. As I propel myself hand over hand along the yellow handrails of the shuttle and transition up the shuttle's docking system onto the *Mir*, my heart eventually settles as low as 42, and I find my stride. I am now a real spacewalker.

The test of our jet backpack, known as SAFER, or the Simplified Aid for EVA Rescue (actually a rare nested acronym), requires me to toggle the power switch on, and the checkout proceeds more or less as we trained, with various messages visible on the small liquid crystal display. I eventually hear clicking transmitted through my suit as the twenty-four jets are programmed to fire in sequence, but I feel no motion whatsoever. Houston calls up to me: "*Atlantis*, Houston, for EVA. Scott: Did you feel the jets?" I so want to say that I had, and I fear I lack the sensitivity to record them, but thankfully I report: "Negative, no appreciable movement, but I did hear clicks." After the mission, it is determined there wasn't enough current available from the battery to fire what is called a pyrotechnic valve. Everything else worked just fine, but no gas ever made it to the jet thrusters. Man that would've been embarrassing if I'd reported the opposite!

After five hours and one minute, we are back inside with all of our EVA tasks successfully accomplished. We've attached the *Spektr* solar-array cap to the docking module with a pair of Russian tether hooks. We've retrieved four suitcase-sized environmental experiments from the outside of *Mir*, designed to characterize the environment surrounding the station. And we've evaluated some common spacewalk tools to be used with both Russian- and American-made spacesuits, and even established a critical failure in my jet backpack. The SAFER testing took place with me safely in a foot restraint, so I was in no danger of floating away, but I'm also glad I didn't require a space parachute on this particular day, since my safety tether had decided to crap out on me. I feel elated at being a small part of some very important firsts, even with some unexpected challenges.

During the mission, the Space Shuttle *Atlantis* circles the planet 169 times and travels more than 4.3 million miles. And during those 259 hours in space, like a handful of Shuttle-*Mir* crews before us, we demonstrate that space exploration is no longer a competition between superpowers, but a demonstration of peaceful and very productive cooperation. Our international crew merges resources and expertise to accomplish a very complex mission, boding well for the future of space collaboration, including the planned construction of the *International Space Station*—and maybe even joint missions to Mars. It's the best adventure I've had so far. Except for meeting Luke, that is. Now we are both Skywalkers.

CHAPTER FOURTEEN

Physician to the Stars

You know, old folks can have dreams, too.

—*John Glenn*

NEW ORLEANS, 1969

I'm almost eight years old and glued to a black-and-white tube TV on July 16, 1969, with Mom, Dad, and 530 million other people. We're about to watch Neil Armstrong, Michael Collins, and Buzz Aldrin rocket out of Cape Kennedy and into space on Apollo 11. Halfway through the eight-day mission, Armstrong steps onto the moon with those unforgettable words: "That's one small step for [a] man, one giant leap for mankind."

During that epic week, the space program is front and center, and our lives revolve around the unprecedented events unfolding in our living room. I soak it all in. One astronaut in particular has already made a huge impression on me: John Glenn, the first American astronaut to orbit the Earth. Photos of his confident smile as he climbs into the tiny hatch of the Mercury capsule in his shiny silver spacesuit are burnt into my neural circuits.

A highly decorated Marine fighter pilot from Ohio who flew a combined 149 combat missions in both World War II and the Korean War, John was also known for personally shooting down three Russian MiGs in the last few days of the Korean War. He made even more history in 1959 when he set the world record for transcontinental flight with supersonic speed from California to New York in three hours and twenty-three minutes. Forget about Superman. This guy was the real deal.

On February 20, 1962, John entered the ranks of the immortals when he piloted *Friendship 7*, the name he gave his Mercury-Atlas 6 spacecraft. Walter Cronkite passionately narrated the launch for CBS News and about fifty seconds into the launch, excitedly called out, "Looks like a good flight . . . Go, baby!"

As those incredible Mercury and later Gemini and Apollo missions played and replayed on news programs and documentaries, I was riveted to the screen, memorizing the images, sounds, and dialogue. A condensed version of the four-minute launch conversation played in my head over and over like a tape on rewind. I visualize fire . . . steam . . . vibration. Then the rocket lifts off the launch pad alongside the tower while I hold my breath and lean forward.

CAPCOM: 3 . . . 2 . . . 1 . . . 0[18]
GLENN: Roger. The clock is operating. We're under way.
CAPCOM: Hear [you] loud and clear.
GLENN: Roger. We're programing in roll okay . . . Little bumpy along about here . . . Have some vibration . . . coming up here now . . . Feels good . . . smoothing out real fine. Cabin pressure coming down . . . flight very smooth now . . . All systems are go.

Once in orbit, Glenn utters the line that sparks a million kids' interest in space, including me: "Roger. Zero-g and I feel fine."

I idolize the humble coolness of John Glenn. He rode a rocket into outer space all by himself, pulling seven g's in a dangerous machine, doing something no one had ever done before, and with no guarantee of coming home. His voice sounded almost enthusiastically effortless, with a little aw-shucks mixed in.

Glenn ended up orbiting our home planet three times at a speed of approximately 17,500 miles an hour. A wayward heat shield called into question whether he could safely deorbit, and his planned seven-orbit mission was cut short to just four hours and fifty-six minutes.

He safely splashed down in the Atlantic Ocean near Grand Turk Island in the Bahamas. Two years after his Mercury flight, Glenn resigned from NASA and joined the business world, later running for and eventually being elected to the United States Senate. John Glenn was a national hero and celebrity without peer, and even if he had not resigned from the space program, it was widely believed that the space program would not have risked his life by allowing him to fly again. No one wanted to lose the first American orbital astronaut. This same fate reportedly befell his Soviet golden boy counterpart, Yuri Alexeyevich Gagarin, who had only one opportunity to fly a pioneering orbital mission before his untimely death in an aircraft training accident in 1968.

Fast-forward thirty-six years, eight months, and nine days after his historic flight and John Glenn is going back. At the age of seventy-seven. And I'm about to be assigned to serve as his personal physician in space.

Chief Astronaut Ken "Taco" Cockrell singles me out at our Monday morning staff meeting, asking me to stop by his office immediately afterward. I had a great outcome three years ago when the Chief asked me to stop by after the weekly all-hands meeting, but this time it's way too early to even dream about getting reassigned to fly. Maybe he's going to ask me to move over to Russia to serve as Director of Operations, or worse yet, to wear a tie in Building 1 as a Management Astronaut. The latter will probably mean limited training and a longer wait until the next flight, but I'm prepared to do either one—maybe I'm due some desk time since I feel like I've had an almost charmed flight career so far.

But out of the blue, Taco asks me to join the mission we've all been whispering about, slated for October 29, 1998, on Space Shuttle *Discovery*. No spacewalks are planned, which is a disappointment for me after my first taste of EVA, but having a living legend like John aboard more than compensates. Instead, STS-95 will be dedicated to carrying out eighty-three different science experiments, including deploying and later retrieving a three-thousand-pound satellite called Spartan to study the Sun's corona, or atmosphere, and testing a new cooling system to prepare for the next Hubble Space Telescope servicing mission.

I can't believe it, as it has only been a year since my last flight. After coming back from the docking flight to *Mir*, I was resigned to going to the back of the queue and waiting a few long years for my next flight. But since I'm a physician-astronaut, I got lucky and I happen to have the unique skill set needed for this mission.

It feels too good to be true, like solving the physical mysteries of nature with Albert Einstein, summiting a Himalayan peak with Sir Edmund Hillary, or playing basketball with Michael Jordan. For an astronaut, this is about as exciting as it gets. There is no one else like John Glenn. He is deeply respected among the Mercury, Gemini, Apollo, *Skylab*, and Space Shuttle astronauts as well as in the world at large. He has now been elected to his senate seat four times and was even a serious contender for the Democratic Party's presidential nomination in 1984.

Not everyone is as excited about launching a senior citizen into space as Senator Glenn is. Even though he's in tremendous health for his age, no one is quite sure how the rigors of spaceflight—and returning home—will affect him. He has to lobby hard to make it happen, but he's a Marine and naturally tenacious. While some voices in the government and in the media accuse NASA of pulling a publicity stunt, John comes in with a compelling case that his participation will further the understanding of age-related issues, one of his passions as an elected official. Experiments are planned for assessment of his overall physical health in space, including the adaptation to space of an aging body, along with his balance, muscle strength (will his muscles atrophy at a faster rate?), cardiovascular endurance, immune function, and sleep patterns. Essentially, John will be a human guinea pig for geriatric studies in space.

When John flew the first time, as the lone crewmember he served as Commander, Pilot, and his own physician. Back then no one knew what orbital spaceflight would do to the human body and the Russians certainly weren't sharing any information. So *Friendship 7* had a very small medical kit, including morphine for pain, mephentermine sulfate (a cardiac stimulant) for shock symptoms, benzylamine hydrochloride for motion sickness, and a stimulant called racemic amphetamine sulfate (now sometimes used to treat ADHD) for focus.

Discovery's medical kit will be far more substantial since we have more room and crewmembers aboard our spacecraft, and we'll be spending several days, versus just hours, up in space. Add an enormous complement of medical experimentation and a senior astronaut into the mix, and some additional medical tools and supplies beyond the typical Space Shuttle medical kit will be flying with us.

Although John passes his medical-screening tests with flying colors for his age, we will have a defibrillator and a more complete set of Advanced Cardiac Life Support medications on board, just in case.[19] I feel the weight of the world that comes with being labeled "John Glenn's personal physician in space," the title I am often given when delivering speeches prior to the mission. I also realize if something bad happens to John during our mission, I might as well take a spacewalk without a spacesuit. Hey guys, excuse me while I step outside for a second to clean the windows and check the fluids. No need to wait.

STS-95 will be conducting other studies as well, including a complex experiment from Japan featuring two live toadfish with electrodes surgically implanted into their large, semicircular ear canals. The toadfish's inner ears allow them to judge which way is up and down, but how will things work up in space, without an appreciable gravity vector? Dr. Chiaki Mukai, a Japanese cardiovascular-surgeon-turned-Payload-Specialist-Astronaut with a radiant personality and boundless energy, will be in charge of the toadfish, which look like big-faced catfish sporting huge whiskers. Chiaki affectionately nicknames them Payload Specialists #3 and 4. She will monitor the adaptation of our "astrofish" to the challenges of launch and weightlessness to help us better understand the problem of space motion sickness.

John walks into our new crew office for the first time, our full crew in attendance. Even though he will be our crewmate, we are all a bit starstruck and confused as to how to properly address him. Sensing this, he immediately says, "Please just call me John, *or* I'll answer to Payload Specialist #2. If any of you call me Senator Glenn, I'll ignore you!"

He jumps right into participating as a full member of our crew, putting us and our training team completely at ease. I can't help but tease John that I was only seven months old when he first flew into space, which induces a playful grimace on his face. I also tease him that I have more spacewalking time than he'd spent in space. To his credit, he takes it all in good humor.

Chiaki, who flew on a prior life-sciences shuttle mission known as STS-65 four years earlier, is Payload Specialist #1, and the toadfish are Payload Specialists #3 and 4, so John notes that he's just ahead of the fish in the rankings. It's a bit of a demotion, but it doesn't seem to bother him much. Steve "Stevie Ray" Robinson, a veteran Mission Specialist and a brilliant jack-of-all-trades aeronautical engineer from UC Davis and Stanford, will oversee the dozens of different scientific payloads on the mission as our Payload Commander, robot arm operator, and Mission Specialist 1. He'll make sure we are properly cross-trained to get all our work done "upstairs."

I will serve as Mission Specialist 2, or Flight Engineer, along with operating lots of experiments, some flying of the robotic arm, and performing my medical duties. Rookie Pedro Duque of the European Space Agency will also be a Mission Specialist on the flight. Almost immediately he becomes known to us as "Juan Glenn," in reference to soon becoming the first Spaniard in space. I'll be flying with Curt Brown again (from STS-66), who will be in the Commander's seat this time. Air Force Colonel Steve "Pinto" Lindsey, a master at finding the perfect one-liner for any situation, is our talented Pilot. "I'd like to thank all the little people I stepped on to get where I am today" is one of his favorite lines whenever about to step to the podium to give a speech. I'm still not sure of the true origin of his *Animal House*–inspired call sign, but he definitely has the entire movie committed to memory.

John throws himself into training and takes on every experiment and task he is assigned, even those involving bloodletting. As a subject in ten different life sciences experiments to quantify how his adaptation to space and return to Earth's one-g might differ from younger astronauts, he has to deal with his lifelong fear of needles (something we have in common). Our preflight medical data collection requires me to take countless tubes of his blood, earning me the new call sign "Count Parazynskula." Seizing the opportunity to tease him a bit, I make a mental note to bring along a set of plastic vampire fangs to make the in-orbit bloodletting a little more fun, at least for me.

Even though John's participation in our shuttle mission might be controversial to some, it turns out to be a huge shot in the arm for NASA. The publicity is overwhelmingly good, and so is the science.

Launch morning, October 29, 1998, is an absolute circus outside with perhaps the largest gathering of spectators since Apollo 11 in and around the Kennedy Space Center. All are joyously celebrating John's return to space. Half of the US Congress is in attendance, too, along with President Bill Clinton and his wife, Hillary. But for us in Astronaut Crew Quarters, it's just as we practiced three weeks earlier during our Terminal Countdown Demonstration Test, or TCDT, the final dress rehearsal for launch. The only difference is, we're going to play a big practical joke on the *hermanos* Glenn.

We'd poked at John that he was actually a space rookie like Pedro, since he hadn't been able to get up out of his seat and truly float during his first flight all those years ago. We veteran flyers therefore have specially prepared laminated green boarding passes tucked away in the zippered pockets of our orange Launch and Entry Suits (LES). Upon arrival to the pad, we're greeted by a SWAT team officer as a Black Hawk helicopter circles overhead. We're sternly told to present our STS-95 boarding passes as we exit our ride, a converted motor home simply known as the Astrovan. I still laugh, thinking about the frenetic energy John and Juan put into trying to find their tickets to space!

The launch itself is both exhilarating and thankfully uneventful, with one brief exception when the Range Safety Officer announces, "The radar is saturated," implying that there are unknown aircraft in the vicinity of the launch pad. Tensions are very high with Iraq at the moment, so I wonder for an instant whether Saddam has somehow managed to get some of his jets trained on us. But it turns out to be a couple of Cessna pilots taking the most insane joyride of their lives, an incursion into restricted airspace with a loaded Space Shuttle on the pad. I can't even imagine getting chased down by a Black Hawk helicopter gunship and forced into an emergency landing.

Once safely established in space, it is a very special moment to see John float up to the flight deck to see his home planet from space for the first time in nearly thirty-seven years. I try to snap a quick photo to document the moment, and I think I may even see a tear well in his eye.

Meanwhile, at the exact same moment back at KSC, another form of tears is in my twenty-two-month-old son Luke's eyes. Little Luke has been held captive in the Launch Director's office in the Launch Control Center, along with the other family members, while awaiting a visit from the President. Much like me at his age, he just wants to get out and roam the corridors; sitting still in an office is plain torture for him.

Finally, the Clintons arrive for a meet-and-greet with photos. But when it is time for Luke and Gail's photo with President Clinton, the stressed-out photographer announces he is out of film. Gail does her best to lasso Luke in her arms for the lengthy wait while film is located and the camera reloaded. But immediately after the photo is clicked, Luke turns and slugs the leader of the free world in the arm. Regaining his footing, Luke then kicks the First Lady in the shin and runs out the door, with most people in the room laughing hysterically. Luke even comes home with a couple of Secret Service stickers.

Although John is one of the original group of seven astronauts, his historic flight had been just a few hours long and he had never experienced eating and sleeping in space. On the shuttle, he agreeably participates in a sleep experiment that requires him to sleep two nights in complicated headgear studded with electrodes to monitor his brain waves. He and Chiaki, who also participates in the sleep study, wear microphones along with special black tank tops wired to track other vital signs. It takes me, Stevie Ray, and Pinto an hour or so to help put their scalp electrodes and other gear on before bed. They then float into coffin-sized sleep stations and zip themselves into their sleeping bags so they won't float away. They cheerfully wear the gear for the good of science and reportedly get reasonably restful sleep. Their Halloween-worthy appearance is probably more disruptive on my rest than their awkward sleep gear is for them.

One of the best parts of having an international astronaut (or two) on your crew is that they're able to bring one or two special dishes with them on board our shuttle flights. Pedro brings some delicious and pungent Spanish manchego cheese, and had aimed to bring some tasty *jamon* (raw dried ham), but the latter failed microbiology testing. Chiaki's contribution to our galley is a Japanese curried coconut rice that beautifully permeates the entire ship.

Each crewmember's family gets to pick a song for us to wake up to. Mine is "What a Wonderful World" by Louis Armstrong. But even better, I wake one morning to the soothing sound of John's good friend Andy Williams singing "Moon River," the song that won an Academy Award in 1962, the year John first flew into space. I'm also privileged to witness a special greeting by the people of Perth and Rockingham in Australia, who leave their lights on while we pass overhead in the shuttle, just like they did during John's *Friendship 7* flight.

We complete dozens of experiments in a pressurized laboratory module called *Spacehab* back in the payload bay, which is connected to the middeck of the shuttle by a long tunnel. Interspersed among scientific discoveries in plant biology and metal crystallization, we have time to set up a "transport accelerant" between the two compartments. We fasten a taut bungee cord between two handrails and by pressing your feet into the catapult, you can launch yourself like an F-18 Hornet leaving a carrier deck. As the mission wears on we get more and more confident with our thrust vector control, and one crewmember nearly ends up getting stitches. Stevie Ray floats into the middeck as if nothing happened, completely unaware that he has a glob of dark, shimmery blood on his forehead, and that the "third eye" is growing. Chiaki and I look at each other, first with concern, and then with excitement. We're going to be the first docs to actually do surgery in space! Naturally we tease Steve to no end, but he is a great sport. Poor bedside manner and teasing aside, he really only needs a butterfly bandage to close his small laceration.

The sleep study results show John is sleeping about six and a half hours a night, pretty normal for a shuttle mission, although it takes him longer to fall into REM sleep than a younger person, which means he developed some cumulative fatigue during the journey. Also, even though he is incredibly strong and fit for seventy-seven, upon landing he is a little wobbly, quite nauseated, and shuffles around until his body and inner ear get readjusted to Earth's one-gravity.

After we return home, as a crew we make one more orbit of the planet at much lower altitude, visiting our respective space agencies and doing media and school events across the United States, Europe, and Japan. On our very last night together as a crew, right before we go our separate ways, we're riding a hotel elevator up to our respective rooms in Kyoto, Japan, when John gets that twinkle in his eye we've all come to know so well. He turns to Curt, our mission Commander.

"You know, Curt, you're the second best Commander I've ever had."

Quite a compliment, since John had been his own Commander on his solo spaceflight.

After nine days, nineteen hours, fifty-four minutes, and 3.6 million miles traveled, *Discovery* lands at Kennedy Space Center in Florida just after noon on November 7, 1998. All the Payload Specialists (including the toadfish) make it back safely and in good health on my watch, and I am privileged to be a part of Payload Specialist #2 racking up an additional 150-plus orbits to his spaceflight resume.

When I grow up, I want to be like John. He's never stopped dreaming.

CHAPTER FIFTEEN

Strength and Honor

The only thing expected about spacewalking is the unexpected.

—*Told to me by physician-astronaut Story Musgrave, the only astronaut to have flown on all five Space Shuttles*

INTERNATIONAL SPACE STATION, 2001

The secrets of flight crew assignment and reassignment are closely guarded by those in the corner office. My attitude is always to keep my head down and keep charging, do my work to the very best of my creative abilities, and trust good things will eventually happen. I'd be an abject failure at office politics, so I try my best to steer well clear of it all.

I'm told my name has been penciled in for a future space station assembly mission to develop the spacewalking procedures for a flight that will one day install the centerpiece truss of the complex, known by the catchy name S0. Then, out of the blue, my buddy Robert "Beamer" Curbeam is pulled onto an earlier mission to install the US Laboratory module, called *Destiny*. He's been training as a spacewalker for STS-100 alongside my classmate, Canadian Chris Hadfield, and all of a sudden there's an empty seat in need of an occupant. Thankfully I'm the lucky one to get the nod from Charlie Precourt, the boss man at the time. I don't have to spend much time coming up with a response: Let me check my schedule. Yes, sir. I think I can fit that in.

Chris and Beamer, along with EVA and robotic flight controllers, flight directors, and engineers, have been developing the mission plan for several years by the time I come on board. I'm late to the party, but there's still plenty of time for me to catch up and contribute. Space Shuttle *Endeavour* is the scheduled vehicle for STS-100, the mission to the *International Space Station* to deliver and install a nearly billion-dollar robotic arm called Canadarm2. There will be at least two spacewalks involved, and I am over-the-moon ecstatic.

Chris Hadfield was accepted by the Canadian Space Agency from a pool of over five thousand applicants and subsequently joined our 1992 Hog class. I don't know Chris all that well as we begin working together on STS-100. He exudes tremendous confidence, and yet as I really get to know and understand him, I discover a very humble but exceptionally capable guy. Chris is a Royal Canadian Air Force fighter pilot who'd been the top graduate of our US Air Force Test Pilot School at Edwards Air Force Base and had flown intercept missions for NORAD. He was the first McDonnell Douglas CF-18 pilot to intercept a Soviet Tupolev Tu-95 long-range bomber in the Canadian Arctic. He's also a guitarist and talented singer for Max Q, the all-astronaut band. As the guy Canada chose for many of its space firsts, Chris would become the first Canadian astronaut to fly both the shuttle's and space station's robotic arms (although he wasn't scheduled to do so), the first to do a spacewalk, and the first to command the ISS (a few years later). And despite all his disgusting accomplishments, he is a really nice, funny guy who can take a ribbing.

As we train for the upcoming mission, including Chris's first spacewalk, he proves to be a good sport whenever we quote "Great White North" McKenzie Brothers lines to him. Bob and Doug McKenzie are two fictional Canadian brothers played by Rick Moranis and Dave Thomas. The dense, beer-guzzling bros first emerged onto the pop culture radar on the comedy show *SCTV*, wearing puffy down jackets and ending most sentences with a heavily accented "eh?" or calling someone a hoser. During training in our big Neutral Buoyancy Laboratory pool, I make frequent references to our EVA "toques," aka helmets, and our crew references the Canadian national anthem as simply "The Hockey Song."

Our STS-100 Pilot is Jeff "Bones" Ashby, a Navy Captain with over a thousand carrier landings and an equally innumerable stream of witty retorts. Our Flight Engineer John Phillips, Mission Specialist 2, can't be seen in public without a Hawaiian shirt. He had been the number two graduate in his US Naval Academy class, later becoming an A-7 pilot and then a PhD geophysicist. Italian Umberto Guidoni and Russian Yuri Lonchakov round out the fun-loving crew.

Isn't it amazing that politicians, engineers, scientists, technicians, and astronauts from all over the world have come together to build the ISS? Many of the people who designed the hardware and experiments in the far corners of the globe probably never even get to meet one another. Moreover, many parts of the ISS never physically touch until they are assembled together in space, and they have to fit and work flawlessly. I am very lucky to fly with people from all over the world, including a record-setting four nations on STS-100 (United States, Canada, Italy, and Russia).

Our STS-100 Commander is Kent "Rommel" Rominger, a Navy test pilot with 685 carrier landings on his resume. An old friend, he was also in the same astronaut class as Chris and me. Not only had he proudly gifted me with my Doogie Howser call sign, but his mantra is, "If you're not having fun, you're not doing it right." On the job he is always the consummate professional and a truly inspirational leader, although he's well known to be a wild man on snow skis, water skis, dirt bikes, and anything else that moves fast.

The eleven-day mission will be jam-packed with important tasks, the most crucial of which is the installation of the "Big Arm" onto the space station. Canadarm2 is slated to become a workhorse for installing modules and trusses, capturing free-flying payloads, and serving as a cherry picker platform for spacewalkers building and repairing the station. We will also be installing a new UHF radio antenna for space-to-space communications during shuttle rendezvous and ISS spacewalks.

Soon after we've all been assigned to the flight, we need to settle on roles and responsibilities. I know I'll be spacewalking and actively involved in the rendezvous and docking with the station, but I am also a very experienced shuttle flight engineer. On my way out the door one afternoon, Rommel asks me to stay behind for a quick chat. He's always straightforward, so I know I won't have to guess what he's thinking.

"Hey, Scott, here's my plan. But you're probably not going to like it."

What an opener. I brace myself.

"You're very experienced, but I want to share the wealth and give the rookies some of the primary responsibilities, so I'd like to give you a special assignment."

Wait, isn't the pilot supposed to be responsible for taking care of the space potty?

"I'm going to put you on middeck. Both ways, launch and landing."

The shuttle has three levels. On top is the flight deck, where the shuttle commander and the pilot sit up front with great forward cockpit views and the primary flight controls. Two mission specialists sit in a second row behind, close to the action. The second level, down a short ladder, is the middeck, with up to three seats for more mission specialists and no windows. The middeck also contains the galley, our vacuum-operated space toilet, dozens of storage lockers, and a side hatch where we would be crawling into the shuttle prior to launch. The airlock is on middeck as well and includes another hatch that opens to the payload bay. The bottom level is below the floor of the middeck and serves as utility space, with air and water tanks, along with the carbon dioxide scrubber system.

Rommel, Bones, Chris, and I have all flown before. But the others are new to space, and Rommel wants to give our rookies some valuable experience by rotating them in seats up on the flight deck.

I quickly decide to make the best of it. "I'm perfectly fine with that." I certainly thrive on being in the heart of the action and would love another window seat with flight-critical duties, but the crew needs me elsewhere.

Rommel looks relieved.

But before he can relax too much, I jump in with a request. The assignment could be viewed as a bad deal, but instead I vow internally to make my middeck the best-run middeck in Space Shuttle history. "Since I'm on the middeck both ways, can I be in charge of post-insertion and deorbit prep, coming and going? I'm going to be the best Middeck Commander you've ever had."

"Sure, Doogie," Rommel says with a big smile. I'm pretty sure no one has ever appointed themselves Middeck Commander, before or since.

One training technique I've added to my arsenal in the days just before launch is taking a T-38 jet trainer from the Shuttle Landing Facility at the Kennedy Space Center out over the Atlantic to pull some g's. The science isn't conclusive, but it sure is fun to do a launch pad flyby and then commence a series of sustained, seventy-degree banked turns, resulting in three g's of loading. It seems to attune my body to the physical exertion I'll soon feel on launch. This is somewhat tame in comparison to the aerobatic flights we sometimes do in the Gulf of Mexico just beyond Galveston, back home in Texas. If you don't prepare for a six-g pull by bearing down, clenching the muscles in your legs and abdomen, you can easily gray out and even lose consciousness.

I'm as ready as can be when *Endeavour* launches at 2:40 p.m. on April 19, 2001. The crew is a bunch of fun guys, slightly bawdy and over-the-top enthusiastic on the pad. A middeck launch is different—basically a face full of lockers and no window seat. I feel a degree of helplessness at T minus nine minutes without being able to see everything that's going on up top. It's like being on a commercial airline flight in an aisle passenger seat, instead of in the cockpit.

We're loaded to the gills with expensive and complex hardware, including Canadarm2, folded in half and carried on a pallet we call the Lab Cradle Assembly. The new robotic arm is a generation beyond the original Space Shuttle Canadarm, which flew to and from orbit on each and every shuttle mission that required robotic support. The new arm will stay permanently in space. In addition, it can move end over end like an inchworm to reach much more of the *International Space Station* than the old arm, whose reach was limited to its fifty-foot physical length.

The new arm loosely mimics a human arm, with a three-jointed shoulder, an elbow, and a three-jointed wrist. Unlike its human counterpart, Canadarm2 is able to change base locations, like a kid in a playground swinging along from one hanging metal ring to another. All seven joints can rotate 540 degrees, a much larger range of motion than a human arm. Canadarm2 also has force moment sensors to provide a form of force feedback, an advanced automatic vision feature to assist in capturing equipment, and a basic collision avoidance system. And it is powerful, capable of handling a payload of just over 250,000 pounds, as compared to 65,000 pounds for its predecessor. It will be invaluable for completion and maintenance of the space station. Canadarm2 is the centerpiece of the Canadian Space Agency's contribution to ISS and a source of enormous national pride. Chris will be designated the lead spacewalker, or EV-1, for both the mission and for his country.

On the fourth flight day of the mission, Chris and I float out the hatch for a seven-and-a-half-hour spacewalk. As Chris begins to hook our safety tethers up just outside the hatch, I quote a favorite STS-100 crew movie, *Gladiator*, that we'd watched in crew quarters the morning of our launch.

"Strength and honor, Chris." I think it's a pretty catchy phrase to start our EVA, although perhaps less spontaneous than that of first-time spacewalker Bill McArthur, on STS-92, a few missions prior. He'd simply blurted out: "Oh, sweet Jesus."

"Strength and honor, Scott," replies Chris.

The UHF antenna bolts on and pivots up into place, just as we'd trained in the pool back in Houston. Now it is time to power up, unbolt, unfold, and assemble the Big Arm, with Chris positioned in a foot restraint on the shuttle's robotic arm, and me zipping all around the *Spacelab* cradle, what we termed free-floating.

Chris and I work together to remove eight one-meter-long "superbolts" holding the arm onto the cradle and then stow them in what we call a quiver. A scare happens as I pivot the booms roughly thirty-five degrees to allow us clearance to bolt the arm together. The first time I try, applying lots of force, absolutely nothing happens. The second time, I try with more force and feeling, to no avail. I take a deep breath and finally give it my best Olympic clean-and-jerk weight-lifting effort, and the booms grudgingly begin to move.

Chris then unfurls the Big Arm from his cherry picker position on *Endeavour*'s robotic arm, and we set about installing and tightening eight fasteners, working opposite one another as if tightening the lugs on automobile wheels. It is physically demanding, exacting work, and each of us is sweating a bit.

About thirty minutes into this heavy effort, Chris begins to have a problem with one of his eyes. Fighter pilots never like to admit a physical problem for fear of being called off the mission, so characteristically, he doesn't say much at first. But something is creating burning pain in his left eye, causing the eye to clamp shut so he can't see out of it.

At first he continues working, using his functioning right eye. But his left eye quickly begins to fill with tears. Because of the absence of gravity in space, the tears don't flow down your face. The surface tension of the moisture just holds the tears together in a kind of gelatinous ball over your eye. (Ever see the movie *Flubber*?) After a few minutes, the ball of tears grows big enough to flow over the bridge of his nose and into his right eye, causing it to also burn and clamp shut. Now Chris is essentially blind, both eyes burning. It's no small thing, being suddenly blinded outside the Space Shuttle in the vacuum of space. It is turning into a bit of a situation.

Chris starts to describe what's happening. I clamber up on the edge of the cradle and get all up in his grill, visor to visor, trying to determine the source of the problem. I see big globules of tears, and Chris is grimacing as he blinks repeatedly, trying to clear his eyes. I run through the possibilities—it could be just salty sweat, soap from his anti-fog on his visor, or perhaps a response to a more serious failure of the lithium hydroxide canister in his spacesuit, used to scrub carbon dioxide out of the breathing gas. Mission Control Houston instructs him to open up his helmet purge valve to see if that will help.

There is nothing else to do at this point, with no way for Chris to retract his hand inside the suit and touch his face to rub his eyes. There is no way to wash them out, either. It's up to Chris's tear ducts. The alternative is for me to perform an Incapacitated Crew Rescue, and we don't have much time.

Back on the ground, I'd helped develop a method to bring in an ill or injured spacewalker in the pool, involving first attaching my waist tether to the incapacitated party in a sort of daisy chain. I would then drag and float him or her along the outside, before unceremoniously stuffing him (in this case) into the airlock and shutting the hatch. But I didn't want to do that if we didn't need to. As a testament to Chris's calm demeanor, we decide to wait it out and see what might transpire. Maybe, just maybe, his eyes will flush out whatever the irritant is, and soon.

In what seems an eternity, but is probably only ten minutes or so, Chris's eyes generate enough tears to begin to remove whatever irritant is there. The burning sensation begins to resolve, and when it is clear that Chris will be able to proceed and finish the work, I heave a sigh of relief (although not loud enough to be heard over the comm channels; I want to play it as cool as Chris). Later, we find out the episode was caused by too much residual anti-fog solution, basically Joy dishwashing soap used to prevent condensation on the inside of our visors. If you don't judiciously apply and then aggressively wipe out the excess soap, it can interact with your sweat, and droplets can migrate into your eyes, with painful consequences. It is exactly like the very painful experience of getting soap in your eyes in the shower, except there's no way to immediately flush the soap out.

While all of this is going on with Chris, however, I am developing a situation of my own. I don't want to whine about it in real time over the comm loops, but I am having some sort of problem with my spacesuit's boots, causing intense pain across the bridge of both feet. The boots are made up of multiple layers, including special insulation to protect against the extraordinary temperature extremes in orbit, along with Kevlar, central to bulletproof vests' bounce, used to protect against micrometeoroid orbital debris (or space junk). As we would find out later, the protective outer layer of the boots had been cinched down a bit too tightly, forcing the stiff pressure-bladder lining of the suit to bunch up directly onto the tops of my feet, creating ridges. The suit is pressurized to 4.3 pounds per square inch, which means stiff as a board. The pressure is pushing those ridges of material down onto my feet like a hacksaw blade, and I have to endure it for seven long hours. I keep trying to wriggle my feet around to alleviate the pressure, but it only temporarily helps. My right foot is worse than my left, but I do my best to tune out the searing pain. (When we finally finish the work and get back inside, I find my right foot blistered, the skin broken down by the unrelenting pressure. Who knew it would just take a little extra soap and stitching to handicap two highly trained spacewalkers?)

But the spacewalk isn't over yet. Chris and I are wrapping up the first EVA of the mission, almost seven hours into the job, and putting away tools in the payload bay of *Endeavour* when we get an unexpected call from our Capsule Communicator (CAPCOM),[20] Canadian astronaut Steve MacLean. Would we mind staying out an extra fifteen minutes or so? No explanation, and no special tasking, just "stay out?"

Is this a trick question? You never ask a spacewalker whether he or she wants to stay out longer, since there's only one (obvious) answer to that question.

What we don't quite realize is we are about to fly over Canada, and Steve has some nice words to say first. There is a beautiful dusting of snow over parts of Canada, including the very prominent Manicouagan impact crater, and just 1,400 kilometers to the southwest is Chris's hometown of Sarnia, Ontario. Steve reflects on the success of the transfer of the Big Arm to the ISS, along with Chris's performance of the first Canadian spacewalk. He even declares that I am now an honorary Canadian citizen, just before piping up to us the beautiful Canadian national anthem.

We are all happy, punchy, and relieved. I can see my crewmates inside celebrating, high-fiving and laughing, saying something about "The Hockey Song." It has been a great day, and I am grinning from ear to ear, but I'm also doing everything I can to not laugh while the anthem is playing. My spacesuit's communication system is "hot mic," meaning everything I say and every noise I make, including heavy breathing or laughing, will be broadcast through my microphone to Mission Control Houston.

I'd make it unscathed if it wasn't for Bones. Seizing the moment, he jots three simple words on his robotics checklist and then floats over to the aft flight deck window to show me his little sign:

Beer me, Hoser!

Projectile tears of laughter shoot like fire hydrants from my eyes, temporarily blinding me. I'm not certain I've ever had a better laugh in my entire life. My guess is that my honorary citizenship is immediately rescinded, since I've never received an honorary Canadian passport.

But international incidents and burning eyes and feet aside, there is one more spacewalk to do. Chris and I have to do some delicate rewiring of the robotic arm to allow it to walk off its pallet and become a permanent resident of the station. I'm also looking forward to a long, sweeping ride on the end of the shuttle's robotic arm, with me carrying a large, spare electronics box from our payload bay over to the side of *Destiny*, the US Laboratory module. In the pool and in the Virtual Reality Lab, Bones and I had trained the heck out of the maneuver, and I'm expecting a thirty- to forty-minute one-way trip with a God's-eye view. On the actual day of the spacewalk, however, Rommel is manning our IMAX camera as Bones drives the arm. In the spirit of getting a great action shot, Rommel eggs Bones to really speed up the motion. With me loaded up with a massive box and Bones wagging me around on the tip of the arm, I feel like I might get spit out of my foot restraint and into deep space, beautifully captured for the *Space Station 3D* IMAX movie. I'm cheated out of my view, but it's a hell of a ride.

After the successful completion of those two spacewalks and other tasks inside, it's time to unpack our Hawaiian shirts. We want to have a special parting meal with our space station crewmates, Yuri Usachev, Susan Helms, and Jim

Voss, who haven't been to a party or enjoyed houseguests for over two and a half months. Taking John's fashion lead, we have put together the universe's first official space luau, complete with Don Ho music, a meal of pork and pineapple, and a toy hula dancer doll I had sequestered away as a gift for the station crew. There may or may not have been live hula dancing. You'll have to ask Bones about that.

CHAPTER SIXTEEN

Fire and Rain

The potential possibilities of any child are the most intriguing and stimulating in all creation.

—*Ray L. Wilbur, third President of Stanford University*

EDWARDS AIRFORCE BASE, CALIFORNIA, 2001

With heavy clouds and rain in Florida, we fire *Endeavour*'s orbital maneuvering engines on the tail of the ship to shave off just about 500 feet per second from the 25,400 required to stay in orbit. Earth's gravitational tug now exceeds our centripetal momentum, and we are literally falling out of the sky a half a world away from Edwards Air Force Base in California.

Graceful and weightless at first, we very slowly begin to sense the force of gravity on our bodies and notice it visibly in the cockpit around us. We will soon need to exchange most of our kinetic energy for heat, slamming through the thickening atmosphere and creating a fireball of superheated gases around our craft, generating a pulsatile orange light show for the lucky dudes on the flight deck. I can hear them oohing and ahhing over the amazing views, and I point out how much I hate them from the coach seats down in the middeck.

We're choking down water and salt tablets to rehydrate our bodies for the impending challenge of Earth's 1-gravity and briefly feel about 1.6 at its heaviest during the deorbit process. Blood is being pulled toward our toes, and we're feeling the weight of our bodies and our seventy-pound spacesuits for the first time in nearly twelve days. I figure this is what a one-hundred-year-old man probably feels like on a regular basis, hunched over and straining. I rotate the dial of my g-suit on my right leg a couple of clicks, resulting in a firm squeeze to my legs and abdomen, helping my heart focus blood to my brain, where it's needed most.

It isn't until we finally slow to the speed of sound—and then go subsonic—that the senses truly go into high gear. The ship rattles like a train at full throttle that's about to go off the tracks, and I hope it all holds together. After a few seconds of rock and roll, the vibrations abate and Rommel smoothly takes over control of our massive glider from the autopilot system, using precise guidance information rendered on a Heads-Up Display (HUD). This allows him to fly a very prescribed glide path and ground track to get us to touchdown at just the right airspeed, about 195 knots, much faster than any commercial or even military aircraft land with. "Wheels stop, Houston" is calmly reported home to Mission Control, despite the exhilaration of recent days and the added challenge of dealing with body weight once again.

We are now a family of four. In between my last two shuttle flights, STS-95 and STS-100, a beautiful baby girl named Jenna joined our world. Luke, now two and a half, is so excited to meet his blonde, bright- and blue-eyed sister, a bundle of energy (I'm not sure who she got that from). I, too, fall in love with her from the first instant our eyes meet.

Just like with Luke, baby Jenna arrives by C-section, and she is healthy from the get-go. Within her first year, she hits and exceeds most developmental milestones, learning how to walk fairly early and beginning to speak. As I watch her play and navigate the world, she seems very mechanically adept, superfocused and attentive to every detail, and precocious. I have astronomical hopes and dreams for her, and begin to visualize her as a brilliant, overachieving superstar. There will be no glass ceilings for my daughter.

But by fifteen months, Jenna starts to fall off the developmental curve. We notice she is easily agitated and incredibly noise sensitive, prone to intense, inconsolable tantrums. She doesn't like to be comforted, or even touched. When she is two years old, after my return from STS-100, Jenna is behind in language development, doesn't seem very interested in people (including us), and lives in an almost constant state of agitation. She cries to the point of becoming drenched in sweat, and it becomes clear that her anguish is far beyond a normal toddler's moods and behavior. We can't take her out anywhere without provoking more anxiety, and she needs care 24/7, with a nanny at home when we are at work.

At first we attribute her constant state of upset to multiple ear infections and colic, hoping she'll grow out of it. A well-meaning family friend observes, "I think there might be something wrong here," but I brush the words aside, unable to process that she is spot-on. We take Jenna in for a comprehensive ear workup, hoping the pain and inflammation of recurrent ear infections might be the root cause. Maybe an antibiotic, some steroids, or even a surgery will solve the problem and get us back on track as parents and as a couple. The strain is great as we search for answers. But it isn't to be. At just over two years of age, our daughter is diagnosed with autism spectrum disorder, a mysterious developmental disorder I've only read about in medical school but have never seen clinically.

Much of the little I knew about autism comes from seeing the movie *Rain Man* a decade earlier. I read every scientific and pseudoscientific paper I can find on the web, zeroing in on anything where I can find some hope. Certain experts suggest extreme measures such as chelation therapy (removing heavy metal ions from the bloodstream), immune globulin and secretin (hormone) injections, and even stem cell infusions that supposedly result in complete cures. Other therapists offer different unconventional treatments, charging desperate parents large amounts of money for unproven nutritional supplements, craniosacral massage, and auditory integration therapy (specially filtered music to help address oversensitive hearing).

What science does clearly show is that early intervention with an approach called Applied Behavioral Analysis (ABA), a systematic approach to targeting desired behaviors, can be extremely effective. Texas Children's Hospital, where Gail works, is just setting up an intensive ABA program called Bridges in Houston. We are fortunate to get Jenna enrolled in the very first class, and we hope that with early intervention, perhaps Jenna won't have much more than a mild developmental delay.

But it is very slow going. I am scared and don't really know the right strategies for interacting with my baby girl. Should I try to reason with and redirect her, discipline her, or let her temper flares run their course? The ways I'd been able to console Luke when he was younger fail miserably. For the first time in my life, I don't have a clear vision for what to do or what the final destination will look like. I can't study or train or wing my way out of this one. I have no previsualization techniques for this particular summit. I am out of my league, but thankfully therapists at Bridges and others who will follow, like Dr. Gerald Harris and his team, patiently and relentlessly train both Jenna and her parents for the long road ahead.

I yearn to understand how she is processing the world around her, and how I can best interact with her to help her begin to navigate what to her is a frightening and overstimulating world. A number of program staffers become very invested in Jenna—I would go as far as to say they deeply love her—and I am so grateful. Witnessing Jenna's anxiety is torture, and yet these dedicated professionals are completely committed to helping her cope, communicate, and learn.

Jenna absolutely adores Luke, trying to emulate him and his friends as best she can. She loves being around him and his friends and she especially loves to go swimming with him, where they play and dunk each other. She thrives in the water, so it's sometimes a tumultuous scene pulling her out of the pool, her fingers and toes completely pruned.

At home, Jenna plays with dozens of tiny little dolls, endlessly arranging and rearranging them into massive lineups. She also begins to collect Luke's Lego pieces and Star Wars action figures and line them up on her dresser. If anything is knocked out of place, she throws a chaotic, sweaty temper tantrum. We try hard to respect her rituals to keep her on an even keel and avoid meltdowns, while at the same time struggling to maintain some family routines.

When Gail and I realize Jenna's developmental journey is not going to be a brief one, we decide to pack up and move from Clear Lake up to Houston. We need to be closer to the programs that can help her long term. Gail sometimes works the night shift to be available for Jenna's appointments and is extraordinary in her networking and researching of options. She is relentless in finding the very best therapy for our daughter. But Jenna's diagnosis and the ongoing struggles put a heavy strain on our marriage.

For a time, I mourn the loss of my traditional hopes and dreams for Jenna, realizing she might not ever achieve a fully independent life, have a career, get married, or have children. It's so much harder to deal with the pain your children experience than to manage your own ailment. I become consumed with grief, ultimately going through the equivalent of Kübler-Ross's five stages of managing death in rapid succession: denial, anger, bargaining, depression, and eventually, acceptance.

I come to realize that autism isn't a death sentence at all, and we are resilient fighters. I've grown to adore Jenna's beautiful idiosyncrasies and ignore the stares we often get when we're singing and dancing to music in the car on the way to school. I push Jenna through the aisles at Costco one morning, while she nestles in the shopping cart, hugging a stuffed pink hippopotamus she grabbed as I tried to negotiate oncoming cart traffic. We happen upon a very nice family of three who appear to be of Chinese origin. In perfect accent and intonation, Jenna says to them: *"Ni Hao!"* The family seems to perceive her developmental challenges and responds with love. Watching the Nick Jr. show *Ni Hao, Kai-lan* taught Jenna the expression, but making that social connection at such a young age is so amazing that tears well in my eyes.

When Jenna is about three years old, and Luke five, I am assigned to my fifth Space Shuttle flight: STS-118 on the Space Shuttle *Columbia*. Our Commander is Navy Captain Scott Kelly, who will later go on to fly a nearly yearlong mission to the *International Space Station* while his brother, Mark, also an astronaut, serves as a medical control on the ground. Our assigned Pilot is a Marine Colonel by the name of Charlie "Scorch" Hobaugh, a boisterous and fun-loving guy who always has just one more question in any class or simulator session.

I will serve as Mission Specialist 1 and the lead spacewalker, with Canadian Mission Specialist and physician Dave Williams joining me for three or four ISS assembly EVAs on the flight. Our other Mission Specialists are Navy Captain Lisa Nowak, who will be the Flight Engineer, and my good friend Barbara "Babs" Morgan. Babs had been Christa McAuliffe's backup on the ill-fated *Challenger* mission in 1986; she will be living out Christa's legacy by conducting lessons in space, among many other tasks assigned to her as a full Mission Specialist.

The crew begins to train together for what promises to be a very exciting mission, including delivering and assembling a truss segment of the space station, along with an external stowage platform and a replacement Control Moment Gyroscope used for attitude control of spacecraft. We'll also be carrying a *Spacehab* module similar to the one I'd flown with on STS-95, a pressurized aluminum habitat carrying a variety of cargo, supplies, and science for the ISS. The upcoming mission will be *Columbia*'s twenty-ninth flight, and the spacecraft's first visit to the *International Space Station*. I am beyond excited to embark on my fifth shuttle mission, and I begin to train hard, as usual, as the post-diagnosis routines at home begin to normalize.

Meanwhile, I've been asked to serve a different, more personal mission as the family escort for my buddy Rick Husband. Rick and his crew will be launching on an earlier *Columbia* mission, STS-107, scheduled for January of 2003. Rick is a country boy from Amarillo, Texas, but something draws us together even though we come from very different backgrounds. He is always upbeat, technically outstanding, and a great leader. There is something so impactful about him.

Rick is also a man of incredible faith, but never preachy. He's a man of easy grace with a positive view of the world and of people. If I have to log some extra T-38 flight hours, I search him out to see if he has the time to fly with me. A "gas and go" to his family home base in Amarillo, ideally with a slice of pie and a cup of coffee at the English Field House restaurant right on the flight line, is our favorite destination. At any sort of astronaut gathering, I usually gravitate toward Rick, and he often drawls out, "You can't swing a dead cat in here without hitting an astronaut."

Serving as a family escort is both a great honor and huge responsibility. You commit to looking after your colleagues' families as you'd like yours treated under the stress of launch. And if the unthinkable were ever to happen, you would be supporting them through unimaginable loss. I'd supported Rick, Rommel (Kent Rominger), Ellen Ochoa, and their crew on shuttle mission STS-96 a couple of years back, and Rick returned the favor for me on the Canadarm2 STS-100 mission.

The night before we launched on STS-100, Rick had visited the astronaut beach house for a barbecue. A truly gifted singer, he and fellow astronaut Dan Burbank serenaded us after dinner. One lyric really stuck out that evening—James Taylor's haunting song "Fire and Rain," about the loss of James's friend

Suzanne, suggesting an airplane accident. The line about "sweet dreams and flying machines in pieces on the ground" shook me quite a bit, knowing the risk I would be willingly launching into the next morning.

When Rick is assigned to command STS-107, he asks not only me but also three others to serve as crew family escorts. Because of the added security and fanfare around the launch of Israel's first astronaut, Ilan Ramon, we need more family support to manage the chaos of launch day.

Rick's crew includes Pilot Willie McCool, a lanky runner and gifted pilot who had been a cross-country star and team captain at the US Naval Academy and is passionately in love with his beautiful wife, Lani; Mike Anderson, an Air Force pilot, husband, and father of two great girls who is a thorough, thoughtful, and gracious instructor to me in our NASA T-38s; Kalpana "KC" Chawla, an Indian-born aerospace engineer with a perpetual smile and a love of all things aviation; Laurel Clark, a Navy Flight Surgeon and a wonderful, doting mom to her son, Iain, and who lives in our neighborhood with her husband, Jon; Dave Brown, an exceptional overachiever who is not only a Flight Surgeon but also a naval aviator—making him a rare breed indeed—as well as a former competitive gymnast and even a circus performer; and Ilan Ramon, an Israeli fighter pilot, descendant of Holocaust survivors, and a national hero who'd taken part in Operation Opera, striking the Iraqi nuclear reactor Osiraq in 1981. He, too, is a great family man who gushes with life and would become Israel's first astronaut.

The entire crew along with their significant others have a night-before-launch barbecue at the beach house on January 15, 2003. These "kiss and cry" gatherings are always emotional, the very last face-to-face time for couples to say their goodbyes. The crew is about to take on an enormous risk by launching into space, and the awkward elephant in the room embodies the possibility that they might not ever see each other again. Crewmembers have to make sure their financial affairs and wills are in order, and I always write contingency "I love you" letters to be given to all my family members in the event of a fatal accident. These evenings are bittersweet, as we all have to deal with the uncertainty of what could happen the next day, and over the course of the mission.

Writing a farewell letter you hope will never be read is probably the hardest thing to do when getting ready to leave the planet, typically in the rushed week before flying to KSC for launch. In the event of a "contingency," a NASA euphemism for a flight that doesn't make it home, our family escorts will hand deliver our letters to our immediate families. Shopping for a blank Hallmark card, I have to figure out which cover is appropriate for saying both "I love you" and "I am so, so sorry for not making it home." Then the really hard part is expressing in a couple of paragraphs how much I love my family and how proud I am of them. I want them to know that somehow I'll be there as a guardian angel to support them in whatever way that I can. I can barely breathe thinking about my kids growing up without their dad, but with trembling hand, I always begin: *Dear Luke and Jenna, You are the greatest gifts of my life, and I am so sorry I won't be there to share more of it with you . . .*

As the evening of the STS-107 kiss and cry comes to a close, the mood becomes more serious. I am struck by Willie and Lani McCool's strong bond, palpable even in the way they lock eyes. They are so in love you can't be in the same room and not know how crazy they are about each other. I feel a pang of regret because my marriage isn't like that anymore, and maybe never was. Things are becoming more strained and I'm wondering what the future holds. Gail and I have started living separate lives, dividing and conquering family responsibilities and trying to keep it together for the kids.

Tears begin to flow as Rick draws the culturally diverse group of astronauts, their families, and us family escorts together into a circle of prayer. He quotes a Bible verse, Joshua 1:9, from memory:

> Have I not commanded you? Be strong and courageous. Do not be terrified. Do not be discouraged for the Lord your God will be with you wherever you go.

None of us know what the future holds in these moments, but his calm, strong voice resonates through the room and brings us all a measure of peace.

Columbia launches successfully the next day, January 16, 2003, at 10:39 a.m. from Kennedy Space Center Launch Complex Pad 39A. I stand on the roof of the Launch Control Center with the immediate families of the crew, including Rick's wife, Evelyn, and their kids, Laura and Matthew, and we are elated when they make it safely into orbit. We can hear the excitement in the crew's voices for the orbital days ahead. The sixteen-day mission will be devoted to microgravity research, with dozens of experiments designed by scientists and students from around the world. The experiments range from testing specialized cancer therapies and evaluating a new technology for recycling water on the space station to ozone investigations, and every second of the flight will be busy.

I fly home from Florida to Texas and get back to work. But like everyone else at JSC, I keep close tabs on the ongoing mission, periodically checking in on the families. I take some of them into Mission Control for brief family conferences about halfway through the flight. In Houston, we joke about the NASA television channel doubling as a screen saver, since it often shows an almost-static video feed of the flight control room, engineers sitting and staring at consoles. In reality, it's pretty amazing that anyone can watch and stay up on the latest developments on NASA missions, including periodic feeds from space and from other NASA centers. I keep tuned to the channel, and on the surface, the mission progresses flawlessly, the crew ably completing more experiments than any prior stand-alone shuttle flight in history.

But under the surface at NASA, a riptide begins to develop and gather strength. Some flight controllers and engineers voice concern about a piece of foam insulation that broke off from *Columbia*'s external tank about eighty-two seconds after launch, appearing to strike the left wing of the orbiter. However, pieces of insulation have been observed falling off four previous successful shuttle flights in a phenomenon called foam shedding. When *Columbia* shed this suitcase-sized piece of foam, it was noticed two hours later from video recordings taken during liftoff. The next day, higher-resolution film confirmed that the foam debris struck the left wing, but the exact location of the strike was not clear, and the viewing angle didn't show any obvious damage. Mission managers deliberate and eventually conclude the foam that had come off was "in family" with prior launches, and they choose not to pursue trying to get the crew or other space assets to take a look and make sure the shuttle is okay.

The night before Rick and his *Columbia* crew are scheduled to land, I go to bed looking forward to seeing the crew and families when they land at Ellington Field the next day, high on life from a perfect mission and reunited with their loved ones. I'm not planning to be at the landing site in Florida. There will be much less fanfare as compared with launch, and NASA honestly considers the majority of spaceflight risk to be tagged to the launch. Landings happen like clockwork and had been accomplished over one hundred times without major incidents. So I asked to remain in Houston to work, and also to deal with pressing personal matters. After a prolonged tense and unhappy period, I feel like my marriage to Gail is just about over. We've gone through counseling and it hasn't helped. I've scheduled a meeting with a divorce attorney for the following afternoon to gather some advice, and I am deeply preoccupied.

At 8:15 (Central) in the morning, February 1, 2003, just after I awake to my alarm clock, I get a call from my friend and upcoming mission Commander, Scott Kelly.

"We've just lost *Columbia*. Turn on the TV."

"What? What do you mean?" My groggy brain isn't making sense of the words I'm hearing. For an instant I think he means NASA has moved our mission to another shuttle, no big deal.

"Just turn on the TV."

CHAPTER SEVENTEEN

Remorse and Resurrection

To leave behind Earth and air and gravity is an ancient dream of humanity. For these seven, it was a dream fulfilled.

—*President George W. Bush*

HOUSTON, TEXAS, 2003

Barefoot and in boxers, I run downstairs and punch the remote until I hit CNN. Across the bottom, the banner headline screams, "Breaking News: No communication with shuttle since 9AM ET." I stop breathing for a second, hoping it's some kind of communications issue. But within a minute or two, while listening to my friend and CAPCOM Charlie Hobaugh make continued solemn attempts to communicate with Rick and his shuttle crew, I know. My gut and my heart tell me the truth. I can't believe it, but I know it. *Columbia* is lost, and seven beautiful people are no more.

Still no official word yet, and news anchors fill the empty space with mindless chatter while waiting for some confirmation on what is going on. Video begins to come in, showing disordered streaks of light when there should have just been one bright, hot Space Shuttle high over the skies of Texas. There is a live feed of the control room, the various flight controllers seemingly frozen at their consoles, staring like zombies at their monitors. Then, as if on cue, several stand up and converge to talk. Their faces are blank, tight, and controlled.

If *Columbia* and its crew have perished, I know what is going on at Mission Control—the same procedures that had been carried out when *Challenger* exploded seventeen years before. Flight Director LeRoy Cain would already have received reports from the long-range radars at Merritt Island Tracking Station, which should have locked onto the incoming shuttle at 9:04 a.m. and followed its final approach. But if *Columbia* isn't on the radar, Cain knows *Columbia* is no longer in the sky.

By 9:12 a.m., Cain had issued instructions to the controllers: "Lock the doors," meaning, there really was no hope for *Columbia*. Flight controllers were not allowed to leave the building and everyone present was to begin preserving data and writing up their logbook notes for use in the subsequent investigation. No phone calls or data, in or out.

On the screen I see one controller stand up and briefly bring his hands up to his face, in clear distress. But that is the only emotion on display. They are trained for disaster. So am I.

My mind is reeling, my heart on fire. *Columbia* is gone. Rick, Willie, Dave, KC, Mike, Laurel, and Ilan, gone. I picture their families, there at the landing site, waiting in the grandstands for a shuttle that will never come. The countdown clock ticking down to zero and then hauntingly counting up, with no sonic booms and no sign of the shuttle.

The families. I need to get to them, now!

I know they'll be coming back to Houston as soon as they can be pulled from the landing site and put onto planes. I need to scramble. The news anchors are now showing multiple vantage points of footage of what had once been *Columbia* streaking across an otherwise blue sky. Reports of hydraulic issues are mentioned. "There's no doubt we've had a bad day," says a reporter at the landing site as the video clips play over and over. The shuttle is breaking up on television screens before the eyes of the world.

I skip my shower, throw on clothes, and take one last glance at the TV. Under the Breaking News banner, I read the words, "NASA HAS DECLARED

AN EMERGENCY." I hear NASA Public Affairs Officer Kyle Herring's voice. He is still talking to the news anchor, answering questions this time about the crew and the possibility of their survival.

"If something was going wrong at this point, what are the options for the crew getting out if they need to?" asks CNN's Miles O'Brien.

"Well, I'm afraid, Miles, that there is not really an option at this altitude." Kyle's voice is quiet, matter-of-fact.

I shudder, knowing the shuttle would have been traveling about twelve thousand miles per hour at an altitude of two hundred thousand feet at the point the vehicle appears to have disintegrated.

Kyle continues. "The bailout procedures that are in place for a shuttle, either during or after an engine problem on launch or on reentry, are bailout procedures that would take place or be in effect below about twenty thousand to thirty thousand feet or so . . . So much, much lower than what you're seeing here."

Luke and Jenna are home with me since it's Saturday morning, but Gail is already at work. I call her at the hospital and tell her what has happened and how I need to get down to the space center as fast as humanly possible. Now the responsibility of being there for the families as they arrive back in Houston is all I can think about. I hadn't been at the landing site, crushed under the heavy struggles of my personal life, but now I feel extraordinary remorse for not having been there for the families.

Gail rushes home and I meet her at the curb. "They had babies," she says, beginning to sob and giving me a quick embrace. It is every astronaut's and every astronaut's family's nightmare. Our marriage problems seem to recede in the face of this tragedy. Gail and I are still a team for now, albeit a struggling one.

As I drive to NASA, I picture Evelyn, Rick's gracious wife, and his kids, Laura, twelve, and Matthew, seven. They would have been sitting with the other astronaut families and the three family escorts in attendance on bleachers at the viewing site, about midway down the runway. Hundreds of others were sitting nearby, the public along with VIPs, NASA managers, and reporters. No one expected any problems. The sixteen-day mission had gone off brilliantly. I imagined all the families, expectant, smiling, and ready to jump into the arms of their returning astronauts. The kids, bored with waiting, would have been running around and playing.

Coincidentally, I know Rommel, my Commander on STS-100 and now Chief of the Astronaut Office, is there at the landing site, too. This morning he would have been flying the Shuttle Training Aircraft, a NASA jet modified to handle like a Space Shuttle, making practice approaches to assess visibility, winds, and turbulence on the shuttle approach. But whatever information he had gathered that morning would never be needed.

I head south to Ellington Field, where the families will soon be landing. I'm about to do a job I hoped I'd never have to do, but astronauts take care of their own. I was also a designated CACO for Rick, a US Navy term for Casualty Assistant Calls Officer, with the responsibility to help the next of kin. Along with Steve Lindsey, a very close friend of Rick and Evelyn's (and a crewmate of mine on STS-95), we will be ready and available for the next several months to do whatever Evelyn and the kids need us to do. I will be there for them and treat the family as I would have liked my own family to be treated if something like this had befallen me. Somewhere in the back of my head I hear again those haunting words to the James Taylor song Rick sang almost two years ago. I know that song will forever be linked to this day, this moment.

As I drive, I wonder what happened to *Columbia*. Was it something related to the foam strike on liftoff? Or some other mechanical failure? Could it have been human error? I doubt so, with Rick in charge and a very well-trained crew. Or maybe it was something else? I know a full-scale investigation will be launched, and I decide I will be a part of it, as deeply involved as possible.

I also briefly wonder about the future of the space program, and whether there will ever be another Space Shuttle launch. Somewhere on the drive, I have a sudden, sharp realization. My upcoming mission was scheduled for *Columbia*. This could easily have been flip-flopped, with Rick driving to meet Gail, Luke, and Jenna after my demise.

On top of everything else, I feel another horrible wave of guilt that I wasn't there with the crew's families at the landing site when the disaster was unfolding. There were three other astronaut family escorts in attendance. It was considered enough coverage, but I wish I had gone. I feel awful. But now I have the chance to make it up to Evelyn, Rick, and the rest of the crew and their families.

Almost the entire astronaut corps is there at Ellington, some of them preparing to get into jets and fly into *Columbia*'s flight path over Texas to begin recovery efforts. As I walk down the corridor at the hangar, I see huge maps being prepared to track debris recovery, my colleagues' faces grim but resolute.

Soon, two Gulfstream jets arrive with the families. Usually when a crew arrives home from a mission there is a big celebration at Ellington with flags, speeches, and euphoria, but not this time. The jets pull up in front of our main hangar, and we have their cars lined up and ready to roll. Evelyn and the kids come down the steps, and I give them hugs. What do you say to someone whose life has just changed forever? And in such a public way? I feel inadequate to even address them.

Evelyn and her family need lots of time and privacy to begin to deal with losing Rick, and so Steve and I spend most of those early weeks there at the Husband residence, including late nights and weekends. We help secure the Husband home from media attention, answer the door, and deal with countless well-intentioned deliveries. I drive them around, go shopping for them, take them to events, and spend time with the kids. Matthew wants to drive go-karts, so I take the kids and try to have fun. When all of them have had enough attention and need some privacy from whatever event is happening or person is visiting, we have a code phrase. If they mention "Aunt Edna," I know it's time to whisk the family away and get them home as soon as possible.

The next few weeks are a blur of funerals, memorial services, and dedications. President George W. Bush's comforting words are some of the most powerful of his presidency, honoring the crew's work and sacrifice:

> My fellow Americans, this day has brought terrible news and great sadness to our country. At 9:00 a.m. this morning, Mission Control in Houston lost contact with our Space Shuttle *Columbia*. A short time later, debris was seen falling from the skies above Texas. The *Columbia* is lost; there are no survivors. . . . The same Creator who names the stars also knows the names of the seven souls we mourn today. The crew of the shuttle *Columbia* did not return safely to Earth; yet we can pray that all are safely home.

Meanwhile, many other astronauts, engineers, first responders, and the general public comb the fields and roads of northern Texas for pieces of the spacecraft, along with human remains. Thousands of fragments are ultimately recovered, and the investigation begins. Initially, everyone at NASA is overwhelmed with grief. How could this have happened on our watch? There is much soul-searching, a sense of shared responsibility, and plenty of dark emotion, including guilt. *I'm never going to do this again,* I think. I have kids, and I don't want my family to go through this. I'm going to hang up my spacesuit. I've had four shots in the barrel without any major problems. I've had a great career in space already, and I don't want to tempt fate again.

But then two to three weeks after the accident, though we are still in national mourning, the recovery effort begins to shift to finding and fixing the problem. The folks in Mission Operations, Engineering, and the crew office come together like one big family in crisis, honoring our own by doing our best to find out what happened. If we can understand the root cause, then we can try to develop strategies and tools to prevent a reoccurrence in the future. I begin to poke around, asking questions. I meet with colleagues and try to figure out how we could use spacewalks to repair damage from possible foam strikes. Later, it becomes very clear that the chunk of foam that had come loose on launch had indeed caused damage to a panel on *Columbia*'s left wing. The hole created allowed hot reentry gases to penetrate, melting the aluminum structure of the wing and leading to disintegration of the Space Shuttle.

As a veteran spacewalker, I want to see if my colleagues and I can potentially work on the shuttle's inaccessible and delicate outer thermal-protection system up in space. Can we develop repair materials and toolkits for the job and then teach other astronauts to perform contingency repairs? That is, if we are given the chance to fly the Space Shuttle ever again. For now, all missions are on hold, including mine.

People in Mission Operations, Engineering, and our Astronaut Office begin to propose big ideas, and the next year or two becomes one of the most creative times in my life. I help our team develop and test different materials, tools, and procedures to do work that has never been conceived of before, even in the wildest of imaginations. We also dig back into spaceflight history, including the first Space Shuttle mission, which even then had planned to carry a tile repair kit the size of a suitcase. The idea had been that a spacewalker would use an as-yet-to-be-built jetpack to fly out and repair tiles on the belly of the ship. It was an early primitive concept, never used, and would have been very difficult to carry out.

One big barrier to the development of a repair procedure is that the underside of the Space Shuttle, covered with delicate heat-resistant tiles, had never been designed to be visited by spacewalkers. Handholds and safety features are not built in. In addition, tile repairs would have to be precise and exacting, which would be difficult with the existing equipment and tools while wearing a full pressure suit. If you make a mistake and underfill or overfill a hole or divot in the tile with a repair material, you could potentially cause turbulence as the shuttle returned through the atmosphere, resulting in overheating and actually making the problem much worse.

One of the most far-out ideas I contribute to is a concept to use high-tech sticky pads, something like the stickiness of those picture-hanging strips that don't damage your walls, to anchor a spacewalker to the belly of the shuttle long enough to make repairs. We develop a specialized "lander" that would be flown to the damage site using our SAFER jet backpack I'd tested on STS-86. We evaluate this and many other possible repair procedures in the Neutral Buoyancy Laboratory (a much larger training pool that had long since replaced the one I'd first trained in), in parabolic flight, and in our Virtual Reality Lab. It feels good to be working on the problem together as a team, although there are heated discussions as we bat ideas back and forth. We all want to contribute to the effort and to make the best decisions. Emotions run high at times, but ultimately we're all proud of the work we are doing.

During this time, the EVA Branch Chief, my former STS-66 crewmate Joe Tanner, gives me some of the best advice I've ever gotten; in his folksy way, and I'm paraphrasing here, he kindly suggests I need to "shut up more," giving the newer folks around the table more of a chance to contribute to the brainstorming. My seniority and spacewalking experience, coupled with my confidence and energy, had given me something of a reputation as a Jedi Master. It was slightly embarrassing, and I didn't want that to intimidate some of the others into not voicing their opinions. To this day I'm still not anywhere near perfect, but I try to keep this lesson in mind as I work with groups of people. Listen and learn first, then add value, whenever possible.

While we're working on nuts-and-bolts solutions, the *Columbia* Accident Investigation Board is at work to determine the root cause of the tragedy. There were procedural failures as well as a failure of the NASA corporate culture, including an unwillingness to consider dissenting opinions, contributing to the loss. The findings point at something pilots call get-there-itis, or what mountaineers call summit fever. It's the drive to achieve a big milestone, in this case the urgency to complete the American part of the *International Space Station*. This artificial ticking clock turns out to be undue scheduling pressure. We'd had failures of the external tank foam before, with large chunks of foam coming off in similar fashion, although in all previous cases the shuttle had returned safely. This resulted in a complacency and a lack of intellectual curiosity about the potential damage this foam problem could impart.

That complacency, combined with an unrealistic or unsafe schedule pressure, prompted decision makers to cut corners and not use the proper rigor necessary to maintain a high level of safety. Smart people had in fact stood up and asked to have *Columbia* inspected on orbit, perhaps by EVA. *Columbia* didn't have a robotic arm installed, but the crew could have done some form of inspection spacewalk to take a look at the wing. Or national security satellite assets could have possibly swung their cameras over to see if anything was amiss. All of us at NASA felt like we had let the crew down, whether or not we were directly or indirectly involved.

We also felt we needed to focus more on crew survival. There had been a shuttle on the ground nearing readiness for launch. The shuttle might have been prepared quickly enough, launched, and steered toward a rendezvous with *Columbia*. The *Columbia* crew would've needed to know very soon after launch that their ship had sustained catastrophic damage and to have powered down all but the most essential life support systems, but a rescue was not out of the question. A small rescue crew might have been able to transfer the *Columbia* crew using EVA, and it's quite possible, although I will never really know for certain, that I might have been assigned to the rescue team. It would have been a cosmic Hail Mary play fraught with challenges and maybe another major accident, but the fact is we didn't try it, and we'll never know if it would have worked.

Ultimately, the shuttle program is shut down for about two and a half years. But the shuttle is cleared to fly again, beginning with mission STS-114. We still need to finish the space station. And after some personal soul-searching, I will fly again, too.

It takes some time but a dawning conviction rises inside of me. I owe it to Rick and the rest of the *Columbia* crew to carry on. They loved the space program and would have wanted it to continue. I'll do all I can to help the NASA team deliver a repair capability, and I'll ride the rocket's red glare one last time.

CHAPTER EIGHTEEN

Hail *Columbia*

After a storm comes a calm.

—*Matthew Henry*

COLUMBIA POINT, COLORADO, 2003

The idea for Columbia Point is hatched around a table in Evelyn Husband's kitchen. A few days after the accident, we're sitting there together with her parents, a wonderful couple named Dan and Jean Neely.

The Neelys had raised Evelyn in the rugged oil and gas town of Amarillo in the Texas Panhandle. Salt-of-the-earth people with a strong faith, they tell me about Rick and Evelyn's courtship at Texas Tech and the gift of their two terrific grandkids. We start to discuss plans for Rick's upcoming memorial service in Amarillo, which will be followed by a hike with close friends and family to Palo Duro Canyon, a mini Grand Canyon of sorts. Like a bolt of lightning it hits me; there needs to be a Columbia Point.

A few years back I'd visited the Colorado summit of a 14,081-foot peak called Challenger Point, dedicated in honor of the Space Shuttle crew who had perished in 1986. I'd wager I was the first astronaut to ever stand up there, and I was moved to the point of building seven small rock cairns on the summit, one for each of the fallen crew. As I start to describe this experience to Dan and Jean, they lean in with greater and greater intent, and within minutes, we three agree on the need for *Columbia*'s peak. In June of 2003, just a few months after we lost *Columbia* and after lots of footwork and applications, the United States Geological Survey approves the renaming of a neighboring 13,980-foot peak in Colorado. Columbia Point is born.

I travel to Washington, DC, where Secretary of the Interior Gale Norton makes the formal announcement:

> Seven brave astronauts perished during her final mission. . . . Those who explore space in the days ahead may gaze back at Earth—and know that Columbia Point is there to commend a noble mission. The point looks up to the heavens and it allows us, once again, to thank our heroes who soared far beyond the mountain, traveled past the sky—and live on in our memories forever.

Columbia Point is a prominent sub-peak of Kit Carson Mountain, part of the beautiful Crestone Group in the Sangre de Cristo Range of the Colorado Rockies. As was done with its twin memorial peak, Challenger Point, we will install a memorial plaque on the summit and—adding a considerable layer of difficulty—I want to invite the families of the fallen *Columbia* astronauts to make the trip. The logistics of plaque installation at almost fourteen thousand feet are not trivial, let alone getting that many people to high altitude. The journey will require a heinous four-wheel-drive journey to a distant trailhead at the South Colony Lakes, followed by a long hike to the summit. Even though I'm a lifelong optimist, I am surprised when our wish comes true and we quickly receive NASA approval. The *Columbia* crew families and several fellow astronauts sign on. I also draft a handful of my best and most skilled climbing buddies, along with many locals who agree to help.

Several members of the team carry out preliminary scouting of the route and summit with me, and we pre-drill our chosen summit rock to match the plaque currently in production. I also reach out to friends at the National Outdoor Leadership School,[21] or NOLS, who had taken the STS-107 crew on a very memorable team-building and leadership trip to the Wind River Range of Wyoming before their mission. NOLS is instrumental in outfitting the Columbia Point trip, along with providing their unmatched mountain expertise.

Despite so many memorial events to attend, as well as dealing with the tragic and public loss of a loved one, the families are still very positive about joining in on the experience. My hope is there will be some healing for everyone involved. I throw myself into the planning, hoping the expedition to Columbia Point might be one bright spot for spouses and kids in a very dark time.

The trip will take about five days, as the almost fourteen-thousand-foot altitude will be a challenge and require some acclimatization. Not everyone has been camping before, nor is everyone in the best physical shape at the time. And most are not all that used to wearing a backpack and eating food cooked over a campfire, either.

Every family joins the mini-expedition, including six spouses (two men, four women) and nine children. There are kids as young as five years old, so my team and I work hard to attend to the details and make it as easy and pleasurable as we can for the families. We establish a base camp, with tents set up and food ready. There is no bathroom or shower, but the kids don't seem to mind, and because this is a private trip, with no media or outsiders allowed, they can be themselves and act rowdy when they feel like it.

On the day of the dedication, a group of four climbers sets out in the predawn hours to reach the top, mix the Quikrete concrete, and have it bolted in place by the time our fifty-person procession achieves the summit. August days in the Rockies can be unpredictable, however, and I see dark storm clouds moving into the area much earlier in the day than usual. With safety paramount and the peak in view, I decide to halt the families on the ridgeline below the mountain at about thirteen thousand feet above sea level, still no mean feat for lowlanders. We hold our dedication ceremony on the saddle of Humboldt Peak as the summit team finishes their work above.

In the immediate aftermath of the accident, being thrust into full-time family support, I don't really have time to process the loss of my friends. There are certainly many tearful moments with the families and more heartfelt memorial services than I can count, but there isn't ever time for me to grieve with all that is going on. That all changed on Columbia Point, with the family members and all the astronaut family escorts in attendance. As I stammered out the true meaning of this special place, now and into the future, the tears finally flowed freely. Getting hugs from the family, I felt them consoling me, which was the last thing I'd wanted, but the first thing I really needed.

The bronze laptop-sized plaque is emblazoned with the STS-107 mission logo and these powerful words from our President:

IN MEMORY OF THE CREW OF SHUTTLE *COLUMBIA*
SEVEN WHO DIED ACCEPTING THE RISK,
EXPANDING HUMANKIND'S HORIZONS
FEBRUARY 1, 2003

"MANKIND IS LED INTO THE DARKNESS BEYOND
OUR WORLD BY THE INSPIRATION OF DISCOVERY
AND THE LONGING TO UNDERSTAND. OUR
JOURNEY INTO SPACE WILL GO ON."

Then, from over the horizon comes a roaring sound underneath a low cloud deck. Before I can catch my breath, a group of four F-16 jets streaks directly toward us, white contrails behind. We watch, heads tilted back, as the Air National Guard team zooms in a Finger Four Formation overhead. I look over at my climbing buddy and fellow astronaut John Herrington, in direct radio contact with the jets. After they cross over us, the lead jet pulls straight up and, in an instant, roars up and away through the clouds. This Missing Man Formation is the traditional aerial salute to honor a fallen pilot. Or in this case, the seven lost *Columbia* flyers. There is not a dry eye for miles.

Before we leave the peak, the family members pose for a group picture in a loose attempt to re-create a photo the *Columbia* crew had taken on their NOLS expedition. Then it's time to head down the mountain, with the kids pretty exhausted. Eight-year-old Iain Clark, who lost his mom, Dr. Laurel Clark, runs out of steam. I grab him up, throw him on my back, and carry him down the mountain as I walk next to his father, Dr. Jon Clark. Jon is a very important part of the ongoing investigation, with a special interest in crew safety and survival. During the investigation and return to flight, crew safety has become a priority.

Iain told his dad he is going to become a scientist and invent a time machine to go back and warn his mom and the crew.[22] The astronauts had to leave their families behind, but they also left something of themselves behind in their families, especially the young ones.

About a month after the accident I picked up my mail in the Astronaut Office mail room, only to find a stunningly thoughtful and haunting gift: the crew had all signed a stamped cover with their mission logo before the launch, and they'd had them postmarked at the date of their launch and also the day of their intended landing. They'd actually given me and their other family escorts a gift from beyond the grave. I'm certain that no other crew had ever arranged such a profound gift.

Back home, all flight assignments are up in the air. I know my former assignment on Scott Kelly's crew for STS-118 will likely be changed. As I work and wait, another storm comes into our lives. Hurricane Katrina is a different kind of storm from the *Columbia* tragedy, but her fury threatens to devastate the lives of hundreds of thousands of people.

Katrina brews up over the Bahamas in August of 2005. The National Weather Service warns she will be a monster, predicting that much of the Gulf Coast area could be uninhabitable for weeks. In Houston we're used to wild, wet weather, but this one seems different. As Katrina surges into New Orleans, it plays havoc with the aging system of levees and seawalls the Army Corps of Engineers had built to keep the city, six feet below sea level on average, and in some places as much as nineteen feet below sea level, from flooding.

The day before Katrina arrives, the mayor of New Orleans issues the city's first mandatory evacuation order. Many people heed the order, with 80 percent of the population leaving, but many of the poor and aging simply don't have the means to leave the city. Thousands go to shelters, and thousands more decide to stay at home, sheltering in place. So when the levees burst and the city floods, they really have nowhere to go. The Superdome in New Orleans is packed with people and strapped for resources, and tens of thousands more desperately need help.

The people of Houston respond, and I decide to be a part of it. The Houston Astrodome takes in twenty-five thousand people after canceling all events through the end of the year. I ask for two weeks of annual leave and volunteer to help at the Astrodome. I walk in on a sea of humanity, thousands of exhausted, traumatized people arriving in a steady stream, day after day. Many people have spent considerable time in contaminated waters and are suffering from rashes and skin infections. Others with medical conditions such as high blood pressure and diabetes have been without medication for two or three days; I send a number of them off to local emergency rooms for stabilization. We set up a little medical clinic, cordon it off, and see lots of elderly folks who need medicine, young kids with asthma, and people of all kinds with injuries and illnesses needing attention.

Whenever there is a lull in our clinic, I zigzag through the rows of cots under the giant dome of the stadium. There are so many people here, many still wearing the tattered clothing they've escaped with. I am overwhelmed by the survivors, as well as the volunteers. People come from miles around to give clothes, food, toys, books, and games to the evacuees.

In line at the clinic, a guy flirts with one of our volunteer nurses. She is a beautiful young Jamaican woman with a lilting accent, and he is a strapping and confident thirtysomething with a pair of tears tattooed beneath his right eye. She rolls her eyes, smiles, and hands the simple chart to me. It's fairly clear he'll get nowhere with the nurse, but he has a bad case of bronchitis and I can help.

It is pretty extraordinary, our meeting, just shooting the breeze and hearing a little bit of his story. I realize our paths would probably never have crossed if not for the tragedy of Katrina, but I am glad I can be there to help in some small way. I stop for a minute, surprised, as emotion sweeps over me. I suddenly feel a part of a much larger effort, sharing what I can with people who have lost their homes and neighborhoods in such a traumatic way and are now facing a very uncertain future without a safety net.

I've always felt like something of an outsider in Houston. Since I didn't grow up a Houstonian, I don't much feel like a local in the sprawling city hemmed in by rings of suburbs. I'd grown up in so many different places that I don't really have a place I call a hometown. I am a global nomad, not having full ownership or roots in any of the places I had lived. Behavioral scientists have coined a term for individuals like me who spend a significant part of our developmental years outside our parents' passport culture: "third culture kids." We are a blend of cultures, but I've learned that many of us sometimes feel rootless and restless because we're so used to letting go of relationships as we move from place to place.

Third culture kids have advantages, too: understanding how to navigate in different cultures and traditions, and knowing there is more than one way to look at a situation or solve a problem. We know how to integrate elements from all our experiences, we're creative, and we weave together our own networks of other third culture kids, passionate adventurers, and avid explorers.

Maybe that's why I so love climbing mountains and frozen waterfalls with my friends, forging strong, almost familial bonds with others that follow me from place to place. And it's also why I love what I'm now experiencing in Houston, as my adopted city opens its arms to busloads of people who need a helping hand. For the first time, I feel a deep rootedness to Houston as the city, my city, rises to the occasion and answers the call to help. I'm proud of my city and her huge heart, and I finally feel like I belong.

CHAPTER NINETEEN

Scott vs. the Volcano

Don't send me flowers when I'm dead.
If you like me, send them while I'm alive.

—*Brian Clough*

LICANCABUR, CHILE, 2004

Out of the blue, one day I get an unexpected call from Greg Kovacs. "Hey, how about going to climb a big mountain in the name of science?" Greg is a perpetually wisecracking MD/PhD inventor and a Professor of bioengineering at Stanford. Your typical slacker.

"Is this some kinda trick question? Don't you already know my response?!" I say. I don't need to hear anything else. He has me at "Hey."

"Sorry, my bad," says Greg. "How would you like to travel to the Andes to climb Licancabur and possibly dive in the world's highest lake?"

Licancabur is a pretty special place, a 19,409-foot volcano in the Andes on the border between Bolivia and Chile. The conical mountain conceals a small, seventy-meter-long, emerald-green body of water just below its summit. A few butterflies began to stir in my gut. "Tell me more, and please don't try to talk me out of it."

"Dr. Nathalie Cabrol from the SETI Institute [Search for Extraterrestrial Intelligence] is leading the expedition. We're taking a team of NASA scientists, and we'd really like you to come along as an astronaut field scientist."

I remember an old explorer's legend about the Incas throwing a gold statue into the lake as an offering to the gods. Not that we'll find actual gold, more like scientific gold, but now my mind is racing with excitement and questions. "Put me in, Coach!"

Greg cackles. He clearly knew my answer well before he'd asked and explains that the team of astrobiologists would be studying extremophile[23] life forms in the lake, in a similar environment to those that likely existed on Mars 3.5 billion years ago. My role would be to support the team as an experienced mountaineer, and one of two team docs (not to mention the token astronaut, since NASA was looking into greater use of Martian and lunar analog environments for use in future astronaut training).

My mind reels at the possibility of diving where very few have ever ventured before, and in the name of science. The freshwater lake contains a planktonic fauna thriving on the slight heat generated by the mild geothermal (read: volcanic) activity inside Licancabur itself. The expedition aims to determine how the diverse, microscopic organisms that live in the lake have adapted to the low availability of oxygen at such a low atmospheric pressure, coupled with exceptionally cold temperatures and unfiltered, damaging ultraviolet rays. The UV irradiance is roughly seven times greater than at sea level.

A few months before departure, I fly out to NASA Ames Research Center in California, my old stomping grounds, for an expedition team kickoff meeting. I listen intently to the science team's report on the survey of the caldera lake they'd performed the previous year. Porters had hefted an inflatable raft to nearly twenty thousand feet above sea level and then, already exhausted, had to pump it up with the wispy high-altitude air, half as dense as compared with sea level. Scientists then paddled said inflatable raft across the lake and took individual depth measurements along the way, requiring a diver in the water with a plumb bob and Greg in the raft taking notes and recording GPS positions.

Photos of the raft on the windswept lake make it look like a frigid cold, miserable tribulation, but the pictures also give me an idea. Why not use human-tended robotics to do the job? I ask for—and receive—an allotment of $500 to come up with another way to measure the lake floor, an important task to help us understand whether the lake is growing or receding over time.

First, I head to the hobby shop and buy a battery-operated, radio-controlled toy boat. Then, it's the sporting-goods store for a GPS-enabled fish finder. In my garage workshop at home, I add pontoons to the boat for stability in choppy water and prep a special bow for the depth sensor up front. If everything goes per plan, my roboboat will map the floor of the highest volcanic lake on Earth in substantially greater detail than has ever been possible before.

After more planning and a long three-day journey involving multiple plane flights and a jolting microbus ride into the hills, my adrenaline surges with my first look at Licancabur. The volcano rises out of the Atacama Desert and looks like the driest, most scorched place on the planet, making me feel like I'm about to backpack on Mars. The higher we climb, the colder and windier it gets. We acclimatize for a few days adjacent to Laguna Verde, with its stunning but arsenic-tainted green waters. As we ascend, I pull out my down jacket and balaclava hat, a stark contrast to the board shorts I'd worn the week before while sandboarding the dunes of the Valle de la Muerte (Death Valley) near San Pedro de Atacama.

We camp fitfully on lumpy terrain behind a rock barrier halfway up the stratovolcano, then set off for the summit with a team of local porters and lots of science gear to spend two or three days up top. My first glimpse of the crater lake dazzles me—clear, windswept emerald water with a shallow, rocky bottom. We launch the roboboat and gather phenomenal data, allowing us to start mapping with great precision the half of the crater lake that isn't covered in ice.

Greg, Nathalie, and I prep for diving by putting on dry suits with warm layers underneath to keep us comfortable in the just-at-freezing water. We will be snorkeling and free diving, holding our breath and not using a tank or rebreather. As I ease into the lake, I don't spot any Incan gold, but I do see brilliant mats of red cyanobacteria as I collect small samples of water and the hardy life forms inside. I wear a wet suit hood and thick gloves, but they leak a bit, and the icy cold water shocks, then numbs the uncovered portions of my face and lips.

At one point I bump into what I think is another diver (Greg and Nathalie are both diving with me, someplace), but it turns out to be a large layer of ice on the surface of the lake. I shudder and realize how lucky I am. I could've been blown and perhaps trapped underneath the mini ice cap by the wind and the current, or had my dry suit torn to shreds.

After three weeks at high altitude—hiking, diving, working the roboboat to map the lake bottom, collecting priceless data, and living in this harsh, Mars-like environment—I'm ready for home. We pack ourselves and our gear into a cramped van for a four-hour ride to Antofagasta, Chile. I draw the short end of the stick and have to ride in the tiny back seat, cramped and curled up like a roly-poly bug. Then I endure an abbreviated night of sleep in an airport inn before a twenty-four-hour travel day via Santiago and Miami.

Finally, I make it home, exhausted and ready to hang out with my smiling kids. I'm jet-lagged and windburned from the extremes in travel and altitude. But I'm home and I'm happy. I sit on the couch and watch a football game with Luke. It's always great to watch football with him, enjoying his knack for stats, and playing catch at halftime and in between games. He's perfected a better spiral than mine.

During the game, I get up to try to use the bathroom. I'm constipated from the hours of inactivity on the long return trip from Chile, and when I look in the mirror, I see what looks like a sunburned Stay Puft Marshmallow Man. I need to do something about my bloat or die trying. And I really do almost die trying. Straining on the toilet with all my might, my gastrointestinal system finally responds.

But I also feel a strange popping in my chest, almost like the popping in your ears when you take off or land in an airplane. Bizarre. Probably nothing. I head back to the couch to get an update on the game from Luke. Within minutes, however, something feels very wrong. I'm light-headed, in a cold sweat, and when I stand up, my right eye has gone half dark.

I call the NASA flight medicine clinic, which keeps close tabs on us, and talk to Pete, the flight surgeon on call. Once I tell him my symptoms and presumptive diagnosis, and that I've just been diving at extreme altitude, he vectors me to get to the hospital as soon as possible. Within minutes, Gail is driving me to the Methodist Hospital ER, and we both worry about a detached retina. A surfeit of medical knowledge—knowing what exactly can and might go wrong—is one disadvantage of being a medical family. As we drive, Gail calls anyone who's ever worked, or known anyone who's ever worked at Methodist. She is calling out the cavalry, and even though it is late on a Sunday night, she successfully pulls in attending physicians and specialists to check me over.

One call goes out to our good friend NASA optometrist Keith Manuel. With his urging, I see a retinal specialist that very evening, called in from home to see me in the ER. At first, the leading diagnosis is a detached retina from my straining on the toilet, even though the ophthalmologist can't see it with his special lenses and devices.

No, that's not at all embarrassing.

After four hours in the ER and lots of baseline tests, I am discharged home with instructions for visual field testing the next morning at Keith's eye clinic. I'm anxious, don't sleep much, and arrive early for my appointment the next day. I have to stare straight into a half globe for a seeming eternity, an eye patch over my left eye, clicking a button anytime I see a flashing light. After I repeat the test for the other eye, a computer will analyze my responses to determine any visual field deficits. Keith and Pete step out to review results. I wait, anxious and impatient.

When Keith steps back in, his eyes are turned down, uncomfortable.

Uh-oh.

Keith is always the guy with a good-humored twinkle in his eye, the one you can count on for a quick joke and big laugh. This is the first time in fifteen years that I've seen him look serious.

"What we have here is either a bleed, a clot, or a space-occupying lesion." He goes on to explain that I have visual field deficits in both eyes, not just my right eye, and something serious is happening deep inside my skull.

I have brain cancer. I know it. Or maybe a ruptured aneurysm. Or a stroke. Whatever it is, my life has just changed forever.

I wait. What more good news does he have for me?

"We need to get you scheduled for an MRI as soon as possible. I will make the call right now."

In a hurry? *Not good.*

I barely remember what else he says. I'm thinking the absolute worst, preparing for my imminent death and the somber scenario of my kids growing up without a father. I can't explain exactly why I'm going to worst-case scenario, but maybe it has something to do with the *Columbia* tragedy, still so raw in my mind and heart. Or the struggles in my marriage. Or maybe it is just the serious expression in Keith's eyes.

I say goodbye and walk out to the car. Gail is at work, so I am alone. Tears begin to well up in my eyes as I unlock the car and sit down inside. *What is the MRI going to show?*

I start the car and pull out of the parking lot, starting the twenty-five-mile drive home. I think about Licancabur. What had seemed like a great adventure, diving in the highest lake in the world, had lost some luster. After three weeks at significant altitude, my bloodstream had become sludge-like, denser, with more red blood cells to carry the limited oxygen at great heights. That, plus the extended time sitting in buses, airports, and airplanes, meant trouble. Strokes in high-altitude climbers are not that rare, probably as a result of blood clots forming in their bloodstreams.

I call Gail from the car, a tear starting to run down my face, and tell her I am facing a very uncertain future. Gail, ever practical, asks, "Should you be driving if you have something terrible going on in your brain?"

Probably not, but too late to change that.

That afternoon, I am admitted for my MRI and points unknown. Directed to sit in a large, padded chair, I begin to feel light-headed again, this time as I look at the IV rack next to me. I can already imagine the sting of the sliver of metal sliding into my arm and the gallons of blood they'll need from me. I'm a doctor, yes, but I hate needles unless I'm pointing them at someone else. I can't control it. So not only have I practically popped out my eye while on the toilet, but now I'm about to faint with a simple needle poke.

The nurse gets the needle into one of the huge pipes that run up and down my arms and starts to draw blood, not knowing she's at risk of having an astronaut collapse onto the floor in abject fear.

"What are you here for?"

My head clears and I focus on her words. I want to answer, but I'm about to lose it. "I'm not sure, but it's not good," I force out, my heart about to beat out of my chest. So much for stoicism. *What's up with me?*

Riding down the hospital corridor on a gurney, flat on my back and staring at the tiny holes in the ceiling tiles, I am at one with my patients in a way I've never experienced before. For the first time in my life I feel like I have absolutely no control over my future. I suddenly have a view of how patients must face life's uncertainties.

I also wish I could muster up some better composure. I always admired President Ronald Reagan under duress. After being shot by John Hinckley, he was wheeled into the trauma room and pulled himself together enough to grill his surgical team. "Please tell me you're Republicans."

But just like I survive the blood work, I survive the gurney ride and the MRI. I barely survive the diagnosis, though. The MRI shows a thrombotic left occipital hemisphere cerebrovascular accident.

I have just had a stroke.

Does that mean I'm going to be permanently crippled?

OR DIE?

The most likely cause is the passage of a small blood clot from the right side of my heart to my left, through a patent (or open) foramen ovale (PFO). The foramen ovale is a small, flap-like opening in the wall between the right and left upper chambers of the heart (atria). It normally closes during infancy. When the foramen ovale doesn't close, it's called a patent foramen ovale.[24] It's not a rare condition—one in four adults have them—but most people who have them don't know it. Thanks to Licancabur, I now know it.

My PFO situation is dangerous. Like an open door, it had allowed a clot from my altitude-induced sludge-like blood to pass through and travel, an unwelcome and uninvited visitor, up to the back of my brain. Lodged in the occipital cortex, the region of the brain where visual inputs are processed, the clot had caused the vision issues, compromising peripheral vision in both eyes.

With the test results now in, I have plenty more to worry about. First, is this fixable? Second, I am not happy knowing there will be plenty of blood draws and needle sticks in my near future. And now I have to be afraid of the bathroom. I don't want to pull an Elvis and die on the white porcelain throne. I am terrified of becoming the victim of a fatal stroke the next time I need to have a bowel movement.

After I stew over these things for a while, another horrific thought comes to me. Will I ever be able to fly again? Am I done being an astronaut? Even though I'd thought about hanging up my spacesuit after *Columbia*, I had made the decision to do one final mission to honor Rick and his crew. Will I be able to carry out that promise now with a blood clot on my brain, damage to my eyes, and a hole in my heart? My life is at stake, and so are my dreams. This just might be the end.

CHAPTER TWENTY

Iron Man Smackdown

Far better is it to dare mighty things, to win glorious triumphs, even though checkered by failure, than to take rank with those poor spirits who neither enjoy nor suffer much, because they live in a gray twilight that knows not victory nor defeat.

—*Theodore Roosevelt*

METHODIST HOSPITAL CATH LAB, 2006

The first Space Shuttle mission after the *Columbia* disaster, called Return to Flight, had already launched a few months back in July of 2005. But with my altitude-induced stroke and the receding blood clot in my brain, I know even though the shuttles are flying again, I am grounded. Maybe forever.

But first things first. Before it can be determined if I'll ever be able to fly into space again—and before I can sleep restfully at night without fear of another stroke—we need to do something about the hole in the heart wall connecting the right and left atria of my heart. The vast majority of people with a PFO remain asymptomatic, and often it can only be detected after death (in the event an autopsy is performed). Given my recent history, however, the open door in my heart needs to be shut permanently to avoid the chance of future strokes, and I am all for it.

Soon after my porous heart is diagnosed, I receive a care package from my good friend and Licancabur teammate Greg Kovacs. Inside is an envelope simply labeled *PFO Self-Repair Kit*. Not knowing where this is going, I'm already smiling as I open the envelope to find a single Band-Aid. Laughter is one of the best medicines of all, but I probably still need something a bit more definitive. Enter CardioSEAL.

The CardioSEAL patch is a specialized repair implant used to close leaky heart walls like mine. The device is made of nonferromagnetic metal so you don't trip the metal detector at the airport, and you can still have an MRI. In the past, fixing a PFO required open-heart surgery, a long and invasive procedure where a patient undergoes general anesthesia with the surgical team cutting into the chest, cracking open ribs, and then repairing the hole by suturing it closed. It required about a dozen professionals in the operating room and a week in the hospital, plus four to six months' recovery time afterward. Luckily, the technology has evolved, and PFO closure can now be accomplished with a heart catheterization, instead of open-heart surgery.

During surgery, a small device will be fed into a vein in my leg and advanced into the right side of my heart and through the PFO opening. The CardioSEAL patch, like a pair of closed umbrellas, has two small double arms attached to Dacron fabric with special springs. Each side is then slowly opened up and covers each side of the hole, like the slices of bread on a sandwich. This closes the hole and, in time, my own heart tissue will grow over the implant, and the device will become part of my beating heart.

On the day of my heart cath, the medical knowledge I've accumulated doesn't quite prepare me for one unexpected pre-op moment—the equivalent of a Speedo-worthy bikini wax. This hair-raising procedure is followed by local anesthesia in parts of the body no sane person ever wants to have impaled by needles.

The actual CardioSEAL procedure is monitored by fluoroscopy, or real-time X-ray imaging, along with an ultrasound camera inserted into my esophagus to view the back side of my heart. The whole procedure takes just a couple of hours, plus a few hours of recovery time, while I am laid flat with sandbags on my groin to make sure my femoral vein and artery don't spring a leak.

After coming to, I am relieved by the good report of my cardiologists, Doctors Clem Defelice, Al Raizner, and Ron Grifka. The seal is in great position, and there is no longer a shunt between the chambers of my heart. It has been a long six weeks of waiting since the stroke, all the while on anticoagulants (or blood thinners). I've also undergone a series of hyperbaric oxygen treatments, breathing pure oxygen at higher atmospheric pressures to help recover my peripheral vision, and this had been surprisingly effective. The wait has been agonizing because I've still been afraid I'd suffer another stroke with any kind of straining. And just to be safe, Gail and I have updated our wills.

Happily, with my heart repair complete, I explain to Luke that I now have a metal patch in my heart. "You're like Iron Man!" he says. I'd prefer *The Six Million Dollar Man*, but that shows my age.

With my heart mended, it's time to rehabilitate and work my way progressively back into a spacesuit. I haven't done much working out in the period of time leading up to the cardiac cath, so I have to get back into shape, starting with fast walks around the leafy Rice University campus, then elliptical cardio, weights, and swimming. Meanwhile, my eyes are almost back to normal as the clot absorbs into my body and my brain's visual cortex heals. I go through exhaustive testing during the next four months, and miraculously only the most sophisticated of test equipment can now discern a very small peripheral visual field deficit.

The night before my first dive back into the astronaut training pool, I can barely sleep. First will be scuba, then a few weeks later I'll be back in my second skin, the Extravehicular Mobility Unit (EMU, our spacewalking suit).

On another empowering day, I am finally allowed to fly in a T-38 again; punching through a cloud deck like a bullet is another major milestone toward spaceflight requalification. Everything feels raw, intense, and exciting, like I am a brand-new astronaut experiencing everything for the first time again. I'm so grateful to the doctors and nurses who have brought me back to good health, and Dr. Pete Bauer and several other NASA flight surgeons who are working to get me safely back onto flight status.

The desire to get back to space grows, and with my CardioSEAL and the resolution of the damage from my stroke, it just might be a possibility. But first,

I have to go before the NASA Medical Review Panel, made up of a large group of medical experts who will need to agree that I have fully recovered with no residual impact of stroke, and no increased risk of a recurrent stroke.

Jon Clark, the NASA Flight Surgeon and neurologist who lost his wife, Laurel, on *Columbia*, has been a huge support. Jon was one of the first NASA docs to come see me in the hospital back when the stroke had first been diagnosed, and it was his pressing that enabled me to participate in hyperbaric therapy, still somewhat of an experimental method to recover penumbral neural tissue—nerve cells adjacent to the ischemic stroke whose blood flow had been compromised but were possibly recoverable. Jon is a no-nonsense kind of guy, and when he had first begun to talk about the process of getting my flight status back in such a matter-of-fact way, I remember sitting up in rapt attention and thinking, *Did Jon just say, "when you fly again"?* It's tough to look serious in a loose-fitting pastel-blue hospital gown that immodestly flashes the world wherever I go, but this was no time for self-consciousness.

Other hospital visitors, like Rommel (who is now Chief of the Astronaut Office) and Scott Kelly, my Commander on STS-118, also spoke positively about the chance to fly again if I got a green light from the flight docs. I hadn't been in a mind-set to start thinking about STS-118 yet, but their encouragement meant a lot.

In what might be a breach of etiquette, I ask for permission to attend the Medical Review Panel when my complex case is evaluated for full spaceflight duties. As a physician who's monitored my own restoration of peripheral vision, including measuring my visual fields in the hyperbaric chamber with a crude device of my invention, I want to describe my observations and share my appreciation for the team who has brought me this far. I know I can't be in the room for the subsequent discussion or the vote, but I really appreciate the fact that the NASA flight surgeons have worked diligently to give me a fighting chance. During the meeting, I wait, anxious and hopeful while they deliberate. Finally, a couple of hours later I get a call with the incredible news. I have cleared medical, and once again, I am "Go for Launch."

As expected, NASA reshuffles missions due to the Space Shuttle tragedy and investigation, and I am shifted from STS-118 on the ill-fated *Columbia* to a later mission, STS-120, on Space Shuttle *Discovery*. My new Commander will be Colonel Pam Melroy, Air Force test pilot and veteran of Desert Shield and

Desert Storm. Pam is a veteran Pilot-Astronaut and will become only the second woman to ever command a Space Shuttle. She had been an essential part of the *Columbia* Reconstruction Team, although I didn't know her well in those days. Other team members are Shuttle Pilot and Marine Colonel George Zamka, spacewalker and Army Colonel Doug "Wheels" Wheelock, Stephanie Wilson, our Lead Robotics Driver and shuttle Flight Engineer, and Dan Tani,[25] who will stay behind and live aboard the *International Space Station* for another several months. Also joining the team will be Paolo Nespoli, an Italian representing the European Space Agency.

Rounding out the crew on orbit is Peggy Whitson, Commander of the *International Space Station* and the first female to serve in this capacity. Clay Anderson, an exceptionally proud Nebraska native, will trade places with Dan and come home on the shuttle with us after five months on orbit. Finally, Russian cosmonaut Yuri Malenchenko is an essential part of the ISS flight crew. And the real work on the ground will be led by NASA Flight Director Derek Hassmann and his brilliant team of flight controllers.

Although this will be my fifth mission, I am as excited as a restless rookie on a rarified rocket. Maybe even more so, because I want to honor Rick and the rest of the *Columbia* crew. Maybe it's because of my unexpected health crisis, and the distinct possibility that I might never have been able to fly again. Or maybe it's because I know this will be my last flight into space. At last year's Astronaut Office Christmas lunch featuring skits by the latest class of astronauts, the youngsters half jokingly made it clear they want guys like me and astronaut relic-legend Jerry Ross gone: "Don't let the door hit you in the ass on the way out!"

The crew moves into a common office, and we start a new training flow together. STS-120 will require several challenging spacewalks, which I will lead. We are slated to deliver and install *Harmony*, a new module on the *International Space Station*. This module will open up the capability for future international laboratories—already nearing completion in Europe and Japan—to be added to the station. Canadarm2, the robotic arm Chris Hadfield and I had helped install on STS-100, will get a good workout on this trip, as we'll also be relocating part of the solar array that powers the station. This tricky tasking means many hours in the astronaut training pool, one of my favorite places in the world.

To build camaraderie and develop team problem-solving skills, our crew and our Lead Flight Director, Derek Hassmann, leave for a National Outdoor

Leadership School (NOLS) sea-kayaking trip to Alaska. I think it sounds like a great adventure vacation, but others on the crew are much less comfortable in the wilds. The reality is the conditions could very well be punishing, leaving us cold, hungry, and grumpy a good percentage of the time. The planned route takes us through Prince William Sound past tidewater glaciers, the water a balmy 45 degrees Fahrenheit with small blue icebergs bobbing in the water and black bears foraging on the misty coastlines.

Getting dumped off on a remote Alaskan beach with all our gear and kayaks is exciting at first. We stand in a circle as our two NOLS instructors brief us on the upcoming ten-day exercise. But it's hard for me to concentrate on what they are saying with sunny skies, dense evergreens, and deep-blue water all around. Unbeknownst to us, this is pretty much the last time we'll see the sun, and the last time we'll feel warm and dry until a skiff picks us up at the end of the expedition.

The journey is designed for us to take turns navigating and leading, and a win-win day means we beach the kayaks at a predetermined spot and make camp just off the beach, then cook dinner and thaw out around a warm campfire well before sunset while we debrief the day's events and have a few laughs.

A bad day means whoever was leading screwed up in one way or another, whether during breaking camp, route finding, landing on the beach, setting camp, and/or making dinner. And the worst day belongs to me, on day seven, in the mother of all screwups. When it is my turn to lead, I'm not too worried. With my wilderness experience and being an Eagle Scout, I feel like I have it in the bag. Read a map, paddle, and pick a place to camp. Easy.

Wrong.

The day starts with rain, unrelenting rain. But the rain in Alaska is not like the rain in Houston. It's more like having ice water poured down your back while you float on ice water. Air temperatures hover around 40 degrees Fahrenheit, and on this day, we'd already paddled for over twenty miles. Our first potential campsite isn't going to work because there is no beach, just ledges, and it would be extremely tough to get out of our kayaks. Plus, the seaweed line is too high. The tides in the Sound are plus or minus twelve feet, which means you are guaranteed to go through a high tide cycle during your night's sleep. With the change, at high tide your beach might be underwater, and the kayaks could even float away. Which would be really bad.

Places that look like a good campsite on a chart might end up out-of-bounds because you can't tell what the tides are going to do. As the day wears on, I feel like everyone is looking at me with that cold, hungry, *what now?* sort of look. I'm pretty hangry myself and just want the day to end.

At the second possible stop, a thrashed salmon tosses in the surf, obviously torn apart by a bear looking for an appetizer. Judging by its fresh sashimi appearance, the furry gourmet has probably passed through the area within the last couple of hours. No one wants to end up the main course at the Alaskan bear buffet so we need to leave, and in a hurry. I hear, or maybe just sense, the collective grumbles intensifying. We confer about which way to go and which cove we are at on the nautical chart, and I find I am at the point where I simply don't care to discuss and analyze any further. What I do feel like I know for certain is that we will have to cross the mouth of a river on our right, passing by an island within our plain view, and we will then find a favorable beach on the other side. I don't want to plot it out on the map, and I just want to get the hell going. My frustration might be leaking through a tiny bit.

Finally, we find a suitable spot and pull up, unfold our chilled, soaked bodies, climb out of the kayaks, and go about setting up camp. Wheels, an Army veteran who's spent most of his life with various pyrotechnics, eventually builds a rip-roaring bonfire in the pouring rain, taking full advantage of our alcohol-based hand sanitizer as fuel. I slam down my dinner and want nothing more than to remove myself to my tent. The day has been exhausting, with everyone miserable, and nothing had come easy.

But first we need to talk about the day's events, a nightly discussion led by Pam and the instructors. It seems like an hours-long discussion when it is probably only fifteen or twenty minutes, but as we go around the circle with people describing their unhappiness with the day's events, I sink lower and lower in shame until I feel like I am one with the freezing cold sand. Pam and one of the NOLS instructors lay into me pretty heavily, pointing out that I hadn't sought out consensus and that I failed to apologize when it became clear my waypoint was off, when others had made the right call.

It is an unrelenting, brutal talking-to, with all eyes on me. I walk away feeling rotten, and I run to bed soon after my public crucifixion, stewing in my sleeping bag. The purpose of the daily debrief is to put the leader under scrutiny and point out what errors and mistakes were made, no matter how small, and what can be done to avoid those in the future. But it feels more like a smackdown, like one of the worst moments of my life, especially since I've never really been smacked down before. As the most experienced astronaut on the crew with a lot of responsibility on my shoulders, I feel like I've let my new crewmates down.

I couldn't control the rain or the temperature, and I sure as hell didn't have a crystal ball to know which campsites would work and which ones wouldn't. It is the worst day of the trip. I keep going over the day in my mind, examining and reexamining my decisions, then replaying the crew debrief. It was my responsibility, and ultimately I feel ashamed that I have screwed up and let everyone down. My signature cheer and goodwill have been scoured away by the cold Alaskan drizzle.

Three days later, after yet another epic paddle to another new campsite, Pam walks over for a heart-to-heart. I am not too happy to see her. She seems to feel a little discouraged, too. She is an intense leader, and I know she is making an effort to stand back and let her crewmembers take turns in the leader rotation so she can stay in observational mode. But NASA is a competitive environment, and by not taking a strong position, even on a little adventure trek like this, it allows our crew to give in to their irritation and become overly critical, leading to a tense atmosphere.

It becomes an important moment as we discuss the team dynamic. She is feeling the burden of leadership, and she is cold and exhausted, too, but I can tell that she cares about me and she cares about the crew. I still feel like something of a failure, and I'm guessing I will for a while, but something significant happens that day. I'd felt the collective hammer, but in the end Wheels had built us a fire, and Pam has given me the beginnings of a hand up.

More important, the NOLS trip shows I am not really an invincible Iron Man, just one part of a crew of very capable, smart, and experienced individuals who all have their own ideas and opinions and ways of doing things. I've learned something more about the concept of servant leadership, making decisions when it is my turn and also accepting the blame when the outcome isn't as successful as I hope. NOLS shows us that, as a crew, we are going to have to learn to work together in difficult circumstances to solve problems and to fix whatever needs to be fixed without smacking each other down, or taking ourselves too seriously. Because we have a space station to help build.

CHAPTER TWENTY-ONE

Rambonauts

Spectacular achievements are always
preceded by unspectacular preparation.

—*Roger Staubach*

HOUSTON, TEXAS, 2007

When our crew gets back from Alaska, I still feel a little tender from my smackdown. But within a couple of weeks, as I continue to stew internally, I begin to gain some perspective. My inability to quickly and effectively find an appropriate campsite wasn't the core problem. In my rush, it was my failure to listen, to communicate, and to draw on the power of the team.

NASA can be a strangely competitive place, and my way of working in challenging situations has always been to keep my head down and keep charging as hard as I can. I don't like to focus on how I'm stacking up against everyone else. I simply want to always be the very best I can be. I compete against myself, but in competitive environments I'm learning I'm not always as in touch with the group dynamic as some others seem to be.

I feel I've done a pretty good job at NASA and have certainly been rewarded. And sometimes it's simply because I've had the right skills at the right time. Even so, I am aware of some possible jealousy along the way. With four flights under my belt, and now on the schedule for a fifth, with a record-tying four spacewalks in a single shuttle mission, I sense a target on my forehead, especially with the new astronauts.

Head down, keep charging.

Except, that approach is perhaps not always the best method when you're a part of a high-performance team preparing for a high-stakes challenge such as STS-120. As a team member, I need to learn to be able to absorb criticism and my fair share of blame while maintaining a frank, honest system of communication. Everything Pam said about me and to me is absolutely correct. I need to elevate my level of communication, teamwork, mentorship, and servant leadership on this mission, and Pam is the iron fist in a velvet glove that got my attention. I got the message.

The NOLS trip hadn't been all pain and suffering, however. It was becoming clear that our crew has a strong appreciation for fun, and a penchant for having a good laugh. A sign of our growing camaraderie is a set of new call signs for our upcoming mission. Since Pam's aviation call sign had been "Pambo" and George Zamka had long been known as "Zambo," we adopt Rambo-style monikers to match. "Wheels" becomes "Flambo" as a tribute to his fire-building skills, roboticist Stephanie is labeled "Robeau," Dan Tani of Japanese heritage is now "Boichi" (pronounced *Bo-ichi*). Paolo emerges as "the Italian Stallion," and I transform into "Longbow," in deference to my height and long limbs. I like my new mythical-sounding nickname. It's even better than Too Tall, and I am not about to jeopardize it by suggesting I like it. Our Lead Flight Director, Derek Hassmann, is sometimes known as "Bo Derek" but, out of respect, rarely to his face.

The Rambonauts immediately start training runs in the pool. The pool's full-scale mock-up of the *International Space Station* is constantly updated to match the current configuration of the space station, down to every labeled handrail, electrical and fluid connector, nut, and bolt. The hours and hours of practice on the tasks and maneuvers we'll be carrying out in space will give us muscle memory and the mental programming we need to excel at our jobs in space, and to be aware and in the moment enough to deal with the inevitable problems that will arise.

Although EVA training is fun, it's not always easy. We have to work with complex mechanical interfaces and bulky tools, performing very challenging tasks in a very unforgiving environment. Working with our pressurized gloves is tiring, almost like trying to do brain surgery while wearing a baseball mitt. Something like grasping our Pistol Grip Tool (PGT in NASA-speak), which is really a sophisticated, electronic DeWALT-like power tool, requires considerable strength and concentration—gripping the handle in your pressurized gloves is like continually squeezing a tennis ball. You have to hang onto the PGT firmly and resist the forces pushing back through your gloved hand; otherwise, you risk spinning off the station like a top teetering at the edge of a table. Carrying out tasks in the pool can be even harder than in space, as you have the water's drag resisting your movements. But with time, the spacewalking suit becomes more or less a second skin. It feels like an extension of my body, and I don't really think about those inconveniences, or the subtle limitations in my mobility.

I feel totally at home in the water, even exuberant, and every session in the pool is like playtime for me. I always have a great time with the divers, suit techs, and medics who make our training safe and memorable. Moreover, it's fun getting to work with Wheels. This will be his first flight and first spacewalk, and he's beyond excited, soaking in everything and asking endless questions.

EVA instructors Dina Contella and Allison Bolinger, who will serve as EVA flight controllers when we're in space, form a trifecta along with spacesuit expert Sarah Kazukiewicz to train us for the mission. Dina is a spark plug of energy and creative problem-solving, and we'd forged a tight friendship, almost a Vulcan mind meld, through the *Columbia* recovery and this mission. We dub these three the "D-EVAs," with Dina serving as the senior D-EVA, and they enjoy ribbing us mercilessly. They begin to compare me and Wheels to the old Looney Tunes characters Spike the Bulldog and Chester the Terrier. In the cartoons, Spike is a tough, gruff veteran of the streets and Chester the hyper, enthusiastic follower who wants to learn how to be more like Spike. In our world, Chester morphs into Tike, which obviously rhymes better, and Wheels and I earn two new names: Tike and Spike.

During one particular Spike and Tike training session in the pool, we're running through our contingency EVA training, to anticipate the many things that could possibly go wrong on our mission. One contingency task requires us to get into an underwater foot restraint without any nearby handrails, a so-called one-tether ingress, much more difficult than usual. The D-EVAs are merciless, laughing and goading Tike.

"Let Spike do it first; watch him and do it exactly like he does. He's got those long beefcake arms." We hear the now-familiar sounds of D-EVA laughter ricocheting down through the comm lines and into the pool.

"How come Scott gets all the cool names?" Wheels whines through his helmet mic. "And why do I get all the crummy names?"

"You want a new call sign, Tike?" Dina says, not missing a beat. "We're gonna call you Cupcake. How's that? Beefcake and Cupcake!"

This time the safety divers surrounding us in the pool break up, too, convulsing with laughter as they exhale hard through their regulators.

But we're happy to take it. The NOLS trip, along with the dozens of hours in the training pool and other simulator sessions, has created a strong bond between Wheels and me, and the rest of our crew and training team. I'm still working on lightening up on my head-down-charge-ahead ways and learning how to be a more intentional mentor. Every time we step out through the airlock into the vacuum of space, our lives are in each other's hands and we have to trust each other.

I approach EVAs with confidence, and I want to learn how to pass that on. I think my years of mountaineering and rock climbing have given me a strong, innate sense of comfort with the demands of a spacewalk, with parallels between the vertical world of mountaineering and the weightless world of EVA. In both, you're tethered at all times and moving hand over hand around complex structures. Both require similar strength and endurance, along with a strong sense of situational awareness for your rope mate and the conditions around you.

Of course, being as sharp and as enthusiastic as anyone I've ever seen, Wheels catches on quickly, and before long he's crawling around the underwater mockups like a veteran spacewalker. Dan Tani will also be doing a spacewalk with me, with Paolo Nespoli serving as our EVA quarterback inside. Peggy Whitson, the ISS Commander, and Russian cosmonaut Yuri Malenchenko will do other spacewalks after we depart. We train hard, and as our October 2007 launch date approaches, I grow confident we're as prepared as we can be.

Although this will be my second visit to the *International Space Station*, the massive structure has evolved considerably from when I first visited on STS-100. The largest and most complex structure ever built in space, ISS is several times bigger than the US *Skylab* or Russia's *Mir*. The *International Space Station* measures 357 feet end to end, almost the length of a football field. The seventy-five to ninety kilowatts of power for the ISS is supplied by an acre of solar panels, longer than a Boeing 777, with a wingspan of 240 feet. It takes eight miles of wire to connect the electrical power system and fifty-two computers to control the systems on the ISS, with 3.3 million lines of software code on the ground supporting 1.8 million lines of flight software code.

The ISS orbits the planet every ninety minutes and has been continuously occupied since November 2000. At the time of publication, more than two hundred people from fifteen countries have visited.[26]

The station has matured into a microgravity laboratory where an international crew of six astronauts and cosmonauts can live and work year-round while traveling at a speed of five miles per second relative to the Earth's surface directly below. When it flies overhead, it can easily be seen with the naked eye as the brightest man-made object in the predawn or twilight sky. The visible brilliance is due in part to the enormous gold-backed solar panels, measuring twenty-six thousand square feet, that power the station's systems.

Since my son Luke grew up in and around the space program, he's about as impressed with astronauts as he is with plumbers and accountants. But sometimes he humors me. I go outside with him one night before my final flight to watch the ISS fly overhead.[27]

"Whoa! You're going up there?!"

"Yup." I nod, welling up with a bit of pride. "I've been up there once already to help get it started, and now one final trip to finish my part of the job."

Part of me wishes I could take him there with me. Part of me, the protective dad, is glad I can't.

Our shuttle payload, the *Harmony* module, also known as Node 2, is twenty-four feet long and weighs 31,500 pounds. If all goes well, subsequent missions from Europe and Japan will attach their modules to *Harmony* to complete the ISS. Ultimately, the module was designed to later have the shuttle dock onto its front end. *Harmony* has a variety of very complex systems, which explains why it will take a couple of spacewalks to fully activate it.

We'll also be relocating a truss called the P6, launched early in the assembly sequence to provide power to the ISS as it grew. It will now be relocated to its permanent home on the end of the truss. The trusses on the space station are permanent latticework structures, much like steel girders, that serve as backbones for the solar arrays and other equipment. Each truss has a name and at the very far end the P6 supports a pair of solar arrays, the massive gold-orange wings that jut out to the sides of the space station, along with their support structure. It's an enormous piece of hardware, somewhere around 35,000 pounds.

The P6 truss part of the mission reminds me of watching the relocation of a huge Victorian house when I was just a kid. I remember a team of construction workers coming to disassemble the connection between the house and its foundation, and then disconnecting all the electrical connections, along with the phone wires, plumbing, and other utilities. Then with jacks and cranes and flatbed trucks, they were able to transport this huge home to some unseen location in the faraway distance.

Fast-forward thirty years and I'm going to be doing a similar job as a construction worker, but at extreme high altitude. To relocate the P6 truss that holds the solar arrays, along with the solar arrays themselves, we will be using all sorts of specialized tools and equipment, including a robotic crane. We'll also be relying on crisp teamwork with the ground, coordinating with Mission Control to perform an orderly power down of all the systems on board the P6. We'll be disconnecting the cooling loops, the ammonia fluid lines, and the power and data connectors, and then unbolting the connections. The robot arm operators inside the space station will have already grappled the P6 to lift it off its perch on top of the space station. Over the next couple of days, the P6 will be handed off to the shuttle arm and then back to the space station arm to get it into position for Wheels and me to help steer it into its final location, all while giving verbal commands to Robeau and Boichi, on the arm controls inside.

Once the P6 truss is in the correct location, we'll bolt the two structures together. The truss's tremendous size and weight will require very precise robotic flying and careful coordination with us spacewalkers on the scene. Then, once it's all bolted together, we'll reconnect everything, including electrical connectors and data lines. Finally, we plan to all sit back and observe the majestic deployment of the massive solar-array wings. The wings are waiting for us, folded away inside large boxes, like a venetian blind accordioned up and tucked inside its metal box at the top of a window.

Just the year before, on STS-116 with Space Shuttle *Discovery*, my buddy Bob "Beamer" Curbeam had to go out on an unplanned spacewalk to coax one stubborn solar panel into its box by jostling it with a small, L-shaped stick. Wheels and I anticipate we could possibly encounter some sort of similar jam, so we practice this maneuver in the training pool, poking a mock-up solar panel with a mini hockey stick to get it to deploy again. After plenty of practice and joking around with the D-EVAs, we are pretty confident we've refined our space-hockey skills.

The team is ready, I am ready, and now it's time to ride one last rocket into space.

CHAPTER TWENTY-TWO

In the Blink of an Eye

If you're offered a seat on a rocket ship,
don't ask what seat. Just get on.

—*Christa McAuliffe,* Challenger *astronaut*

INTERNATIONAL SPACE STATION, *2007*

Déjà vu all over again, and I'm strapped into a seat on Space Shuttle *Discovery*, face full of storage lockers, focused and ready. It's October 23, 2007, and I'm going back to space.

Down in coach on the middeck, I realize I'd forgotten how long these two prelaunch hours are as I lean back, waiting for the rocket's kick in the pants. I'm in a seventy-pound survival suit with fluid shifted by gravity to my head and upper body, along with plenty of pressure on my bladder. There's not much to distract me other than a few lame quips about the poor in-flight service and lack of pretzels between Boichi, Paolo, and me. I try to concentrate on the systems in front of me, but there really aren't any, so it's an interminably long wait. I think about how I'm not the man I used to be, the greenhorn astronaut on STS-66, or even the ebullient spacewalker on STS-100. Jenna's autism and a struggling marriage, the death of my friends on STS-107, and even my blundering performance at NOLS have all made me humbler, stronger, and also more appreciative of the many gifts in my life.

My mind briefly wanders to *Challenger* and *Columbia* and everything bad that could possibly go wrong, all the way through to landing. I'm attached to 4.5 million pounds of shuttle and rocket, fueled by volatile, explosive rocket propellants. The shuttle's solid rocket boosters and main engines provide 7.5 million pounds of thrust to accelerate the vehicle from 0 to 17,500 miles per hour in just over eight and a half minutes.[28] There's no turning back; once the solid rocket boosters are lit, there's no "Off" switch.

Ten seconds before launch, I feel the vibration from the Sound Suppression Water System. Water pours from a 300,000-gallon tank through pipes and nozzles into the launch trench to protect the shuttle and launch tower from damage by shock waves and rocket exhaust.

Six seconds before launch, the main engines ignite, and the shuttle starts to sway a bit. I can feel a powerful, stuttering vibration, like a nitro drag racer applying full throttle while trying to hold full brakes.

At T minus zero, the solid rocket boosters ignite with a dull clank way beneath us, and the acceleration pushes me back into my seat, my bladder protesting. As we thunder upward, I feel pressure, up to three g's, three times my body weight plus the weight of my suit. It feels like a sumo wrestler squatting down on my chest. I forcefully take a deep breath, hold it briefly, and then relax as the air eases its way out of my lungs.

Two minutes into the flight, the solid rocket boosters drop away with a shudder. On my prior trips I had always exhaled with relief as we left them, and the downfall of *Challenger*, behind. But in a post-*Columbia* world, I now know there will be risk until the very last moment, when *Discovery* touches down in Florida sixteen days from now.

Eight and a half minutes into launch, we're at orbital velocity, the main engines having defied gravity once again. It's quiet, the invisible sumo wrestler has vacated my chest, and I can breathe again. I'm in space!

There's so much to do and to remember on this mission I don't have time to sit and think. It's not in my nature anyway, but I know it's my last shuttle flight, and I will try to savor every moment. Maybe someday I'll get a chance to fly into space again or even go to Mars on some other spacecraft, but that's a real long shot. This is what I have right here, right now. And it's enough.

I unbuckle and float upstairs to one of the flight deck's overhead windows, a huge smile across my face. I feel like I'm back at home, and as I look outside, I'm stunned by the beauty of the European landscape gracefully streaming along beneath us. As Thomas Dolby might sing, it's "poetry in motion . . ." And even though I've seen our home planet from above four other times, there's no way for the scientist in me to exactly describe this vantage point. I don't think there's a person alive with the eloquence to do the experience justice. Deep space is beyond beautiful, a tapestry of trillions and trillions of stars against the blackest of black. But Earth's blues always command your fullest attention, a rare jewel against the infinite blackness. It's a global—actually a universal—perspective that I wish more people could share, seeing the enormity of our universe in a way that can never be captured on camera. I quickly daydream a trajectory from my shuttle vantage point down to the coral atoll I see beneath me; I conjure the turquoise waters within, and then zoom back up to my orbital perspective.

I turn away wistfully, not sure if I'll ever get to have this profound experience again. But at least I'm here now, and I turn my mind toward the work ahead on this mission, arguably the most complex in the ISS assembly sequence. There will be challenges as we move the P6 truss, launched into space way back in 2000, from the top of the station to its very tip. It isn't clear to any of us on *Discovery* that the bolts and the electrical and fluid connectors will play nice and line up as they are supposed to after so much time in space. The thought of the complex coordination it will take, between robotics, EVA, and Mission Control, quite honestly makes my palms sweat. For an astronaut, this is a high-stakes, high-adrenaline, high-pucker-factor mission.

As I squeeze out of my orange Launch and Entry Suit (LES), I'm excited about the sixteen days ahead serving with this most affable of crews. All astronaut crews become an extended family of sorts, with so much time together in simulations, flying, diving, and more mundane office chores. This crew is special, though. Cohesive and always fun and funny, we sometimes find it tough to get past the joke and focus on whatever it is we are supposed to be doing. Pambo really has her hands full leading this talented but sometimes distractible crew, and as the guy with the most flights under his belt, I am supposed to help her "herd the kitty cats." The truth is, even I have a tough time keeping a straight face and maintaining focus with the constant banter.

A typical question from Flambo: "Does this spacesuit make my butt look fat?"

"No, but your fat ass *does* make your butt look fat," is the standard STS-120 reply.

I think about the beautiful piece of machinery in our payload bay—*Harmony*, slated to be the space station's utility hub, containing four racks that provide electrical power and electronic data, and acting as a central connecting point for European and Japanese lab modules via its six Common Berthing Mechanisms (CBMs). In addition, *Harmony* will add roughly 2,700 cubic feet to the station's living volume, an increase of almost 20 percent, from 15,000 cubic feet to nearly 18,000 cubic feet. With the successful installation of *Harmony*, NASA will consider the space station "US Operating System Complete" (meaning that all the planned United States–built modules and components will be operational). I feel a pang as I remember the "Countdown to USOS Complete" computer screen savers we all had prior to the *Columbia* tragedy, with so much artificial pressure applied to get to this major milestone mission.[29]

Delivering *Harmony* and relocating P6 comprise an inordinate amount of work for one mission, and we have a very aggressive schedule set out for us. My personal red-white-and-blue three-ring crew notebook is stuffed full of detailed notes, memory joggers, and last-minute reminders.

Bring it on. This is what I was made for.

After a few minutes "recalibrating" to zero gravity, the entire crew jumps into action to convert our launch vehicle into an orbiting construction zone. Reconfiguring shuttle engines, life support systems, and computers keeps Pambo, Zambo, and Steph busy on the flight deck, with the rest of us swimming in a sea of orange LES "pumpkin" suits, suit fans, seats, laptops, and cables.

The first and last days of any shuttle mission are always the most chaotic, with an unending list of chores required in what seems to be the blink of an eye. Keeping everything straight as you're floating in zero gravity can be a daunting challenge, especially if you don't tether or Velcro whatever it is you're working on. If you "drop" something in the spacecraft, then the next time you'll likely see it is two days later in the intake of the cabin air cleaner, also known as the Lost and Found.

After I zip myself into my sleeping bag on my first night back in space, Velcroed to the ceiling of the middeck, it takes me a while to fall asleep. We'd gotten most everything done we'd planned, and then some, but it was a hectic, high-adrenaline day. Finally, I doze off. Sometimes I dream about space, and tonight is one of those nights.

I'm 250 miles above the Atlantic Ocean, and I can hear the comforting sound of my suit fan, reliably circulating oxygen and aiding in the process of humidity and temperature control. Although we're in the vacuum of space, contrary to popular belief it's anything but silent, and we're always thankful for this reassuring hum in our suits. I am completely in the zone. With the last turn of a bolt holding two enormous trusses together, the putter-sized torque wrench clicks to verify it is tight and will stay for good. It's just like Wheels and I practiced it in the pool. I quickly glance down at my DCM, the Display and Control Module on the front of my suit, to see a rock-solid carbon dioxide level with plenty of oxygen and battery power to spare.

"Guys, check it out! Italia at three o'clock low," says Paolo, the astronaut from Milan.

A few moments later, passing over the Bosporus Strait, I smile as I catch some occasional snippets of wailing Turkish music on my suit's UHF radio. *I don't think I'll be downloading any of that from iTunes when I get home! Time to wrap this walk up*. After well over eight hours buttoned up in my suit, my stomach clock goes off with a vengeance, and I am looking forward to my tortilla-wrapped, thermostabilized steak sandwich and rehydrated and reconstituted shrimp cocktail, with plenty of horseradish sauce to clear out the sinuses. Trust me, it tastes much better than it sounds or looks.

And then it happens. A ferocious burst of kinetic energy, possibly just a small washer or even a measly fleck of paint from an expended booster launched decades ago, strikes the left arm of my EMU. A brilliant flash of light, searing heat, and then an instant fiery combustion of my spacesuit's limited, but highly pressurized oxygen.

I'll never know what piece of debris, closing in at the equivalent of twenty-five times the speed of sound or more, penetrates my pressure suit. After a secondary explosion ignites within the oxygen tanks on my back, there's not much left.

A human being. Me. Gone in an instant.

I wake up, heart pounding. I imagine the culprit—space junk. Because of gravity and drag, the tiny piece of debris has made its inexorable way back toward home, gently but persistently sucked toward the center of the Earth by a force first observed by Galileo and then described in Newton's universal law of gravitation in 1687. Although the paint chip is smaller and lighter than a postage stamp, the kinetic energy associated with the wayward chip's speed around the planet makes it a killer, especially when coming into contact with my spacesuit's highly flammable, pressurized oxygen.

This nightmare is not something I ever dwell on for more than a few fleeting moments the night before a spacewalk. You can't focus on the what-ifs that aren't in your control. Instead, I previsualize all the details of what I'm actually going to do—done perfectly, because it's all in your head—and drown out the uncomfortable and unproductive thoughts that might lead to insecurities the next day, when it would really matter. It's not simple bravado that makes astronauts compartmentalize this way. You absolutely must "see" your way to success and develop confidence through training so you're prepared to manage the vast majority of the risks you might face out there. I accept certain risks by venturing out into space, but I wouldn't haphazardly accept them if I didn't see the enormous value to the human race.

Legendary astronaut Gus Grissom, Commander of the Apollo 1 mission, expressed it best. "If we die, we want people to accept it. We're in a risky business, and we hope that if anything happens to us it will not delay the program. The conquest of space is worth the risk."

The uncomfortable truth is that a cloud of space debris is circling our planet, far above us. Not all launches into space are successful, and even those that get their payloads to orbit often shed small amounts of debris, or space junk. Sometimes rockets and satellites fail, break apart, or otherwise deteriorate. Since the first orbital success with the Soviets' *Sputnik* satellite in 1957, there have been over 2,500 satellite launches to orbit or beyond. As a result, 21,000 man-made objects, including rocket stages, payload shrouds, and other flotsam, have been cataloged and tracked by the US Air Force radar-tracking network.[30] But these radar sensors can only detect pieces three to four inches and larger. The rest, the small stuff like bolts, metal washers, chips of paint, and even explosive detritus from failed blastoffs, numbers in the millions and millions.

Thankfully, so far no human in space has been instantly obliterated by space trash, also known as Micrometeoroid and Orbital Debris (MMOD). But this gruesome possibility has marched through my mind before each of my seven trips out of the airlock hatch. It's a serious game out there. Every shuttle mission has returned home with dings in the exterior tiles and windows as a result of collisions with debris traveling thousands of miles per hour, often in the opposite direction.

MMOD is just one of the hazards I'll be facing on this mission. But as I rub my eyes and get ready to float out and make myself a cup of strong Kona coffee, the smile comes back. Just another day in the office.

In space.

CHAPTER TWENTY-THREE

Sew What?!

I guess we all like to be recognized not for one piece of fireworks, but for the ledger of our daily work.

—*Neil Armstrong*

INTERNATIONAL SPACE STATION, *2007*

We set off to transfer the *Harmony* module and relocate the P6 truss during the first three spacewalks. Much to everyone's relief, and with a bit of surprise on my part, everything goes according to plan.

As usual, laughter accompanies the work. "It sure looks like you've got a nice purse there, Scott," Paolo says about the launch thermal covers I've just collected on the outside of the *Harmony* module.

"It's a *murse*! It's European!" is my immediate defense.

As I learned anew with *Columbia*, however, even in the midst of the jokes and camaraderie, it's never good to get too comfortable or to forget that everything has to be done perfectly. Space is beautiful but it can kill. There is no room for mistakes.

As Wheels and I triumphantly float inside the *Quest* airlock module at the end of our third spacewalk, the truss moved and bolted into place, we're elated and oblivious to the drama unfolding at the robotics workstation within the *Destiny* laboratory. Peggy Whitson and Pambo see something funky as the second solar panel, P6-4B, is extended via a series of commands on a laptop.

"In motion," Pambo reports, observing the deployment of the segmented solar sail. "Continue."

At first everything looks good, with Peggy and Pambo monitoring the operation through cameras on the outside. Then they detect an abnormal wave in the unfolding solar panel just as the Sun's angle causes a flare of light. The camera feed whites out. "Aborting," Pambo says sharply.

A few key clicks on the laptop and the motors halt with the solar array just 80 percent extended. The two Commanders look closely and see something like a dark smudge on the wing. It's the shape of a triangle, and it shouldn't be there. Something is very wrong, but the glare makes it nearly impossible to see clearly.

"Houston, Alpha, we think we've detected some damage. We're zoomed in on it on Camera twenty-four right now," reports Pambo.

"Good call on the abort . . . We think we see it," Mission Control responds.

No one has to say anything. Right now, there is nothing *to* say. Everyone in space and in Mission Control below immediately knows it's one of those *holy crap* moments you never want to have 249 miles above the Earth's surface at 17,500 miles an hour.

It's a struggle to get more information, but over the next day and a half, with telephoto lenses and after tweaking the rotation of the solar panels and the attitude of the ISS, it becomes pretty clear: two thirds of the way up the delicate, accordion-like solar array is a rip that occurred for some reason when the billion-dollar panel began to unfurl.

Despite a legion of extremely smart engineers thinking and planning well ahead of this mission, no one anticipated this particular problem, and at this moment, no one is sure what to do or how to fix it. The solar panel can't be left in this tattered condition because with a damaged and partially unfurled sail, the ISS will not have the power it needs to support future science modules from Japan and Europe. Moreover, the force of the shuttle undocking from the space station could rip the structure apart and potentially cause serious damage. Billions of international dollars and an incalculable amount of human effort and resources are at stake, with no easy or readily available solution.

There is no Home Depot around the corner to grab tools and supplies for a quick, on-the-spot, unanticipated repair. Moreover, it would be a potentially very dangerous repair for a spacewalker who hasn't trained for it. There is nothing to hold on to, as the solar array was never designed for spacewalker servicing. And the rip is essentially out of reach, farther away from the airlock than any station spacewalker has ever gone before.

If that's not enough, the solar panels are "hot," always generating current. You can't turn them off even in the dark, during orbital night in Earth's shadow. Thus the panels are always extremely dangerous to a spacewalker in a suit pumped full of 100 percent oxygen. Maybe my nightmare the other night was prescient, foreshadowing an epic bad day in the vacuum of space. It might not be MMOD that gets me; I just might fry instead of blow apart. That's not a productive or cheery thought, so I quickly shift gears and start mentally preparing myself for the possibility that our fourth planned spacewalk to test out shuttle tile repair techniques will be postponed to a future mission. EVA 4 would instead become an emergency repair spacewalk.

While my mind runs over the challenges of this kind of unplanned repair, the folks on the ground at Mission Control begin to analyze the problem. There are just seventy-two hours to come up with a miraculous fix or else face the possibility of having us go out and discard a one-billion-dollar national asset. Taxpayers will probably not be too happy with that option.

As tense as the atmosphere is, the jokes start to fly about MacGyver, the ingenious television show character who seemed to be able to make or fix anything as long as he had a few rubber bands and some duct tape. We know Mission Control's Team 4, the problem-solving contingency team, will be hard at work developing options to solve what seems an impossible problem, especially considering we don't even have the reach with our ISS robotic arm to access the damaged and dangerous panel.

Apollo 13 comes to mind, too, the ultimate NASA-overcoming-the-impossible story.[31] Now it's our turn in the barrel. First, in order to make the necessary repairs, we need to get someone out to the far reaches of the space station, farther than anyone has ever ventured. The NASA teams working the problem, who are now calling in extra help, advice, and analysis from hundreds of engineers and specialists in Houston and across the country, realize that even with the reach of the robotic arm and the inspection boom, the damaged area might be beyond the reach of a typical spacewalker. My height is going to be an asset here, unlike in Russia. While I'd love to be able to say it was brilliant planning to have my largesse on the flight, it was just plain lucky, as we will need the full extent of my reach to give us a shot at completing the job. Being Too Tall is finally going to pay off. I'm champing at the bit to try, marinating in a strange mixture of excitement and cold sweat.

To fly me over to the damaged solar panel, Mission Control figures out a way to cobble together the space station's robotic arm, Canadarm 2, plus *Discovery*'s inspection boom, and then further add a work-site extension for my foot restraint. Altogether, it is a jury-rigged ninety-foot-long platform. This is brilliant and crazy at the same time. *Won't it spring like a diving board?*

Wagging this ungainly robotic contraption with a spacewalker on the end of it around other solar arrays, the Space Shuttle, and sensitive instruments on the outside of the ISS will be no small feat, either. Lead Robotics Officer Sarmad Aziz and his team must figure out from scratch how to fly a safe trajectory to get me to and from the solar array, but time will be of the essence. I'll only have about seven and a half hours of "consumables," the term NASA uses for my suit's battery, oxygen supply, and carbon dioxide removal capability, and the repair job will likely be difficult and time consuming. My emergency backup oxygen (called the secondary oxygen pack) will only have enough extra oxygen for thirty minutes and, at best, I'll be forty-five minutes away from the safety of the airlock. Because the stakes are so high, Houston agrees to "waiver" the flight rules in this one case. No one is getting much sleep. The robotics team maps it all out and transmits Steph and Dan the plan, a complex, full-forty-five-minute maneuver in each direction.

Last, and most important, in just seventy-two hours, the army of engineers, flight controllers, and astronauts on the ground needs to improvise a set of tools to repair the solar array from supplies available to us on the shuttle and the space station. As the clock ticks down, we turn our new *Harmony* module into a metal shop as Peggy and Zambo use their shopping lists created by engineers on the ground to pull items from different parts of the space complex. They start gathering up seemingly random wires, bolts, nuts, aluminum stock, and tape to begin fabricating tools for me and Wheels to use. As the repair plan develops, it looks like I will be doing some suturing.

My only real experience in this area involves suturing *people* back together, which I've done thousands of times as an ER doctor. But that was easy—in those cases, I wasn't perched on a jury-rigged ninety-foot springboard traveling at over 17,500 miles an hour, at risk of either electrocution or spontaneous combustion, while wearing a thirteen-layer pressure suit.

There was, however, that one time in Dakar, Senegal. It was a clear, warm West African day on a beautiful beach called Sali when I experienced perhaps the most dreaded of all middle school fears—a public wardrobe malfunction. Of biblical proportions. Several of my Dakar Academy classmates and I were on a field trip to a pristine, sandy shoreline with modest waves, perfect for playing chicken.

I was jousting with friends, holding a pretty, bikini-clad girl named Eroica (yes, that was her real name) on my shoulders. It should be noted that the academy was run by Baptist missionaries, who held an hour of Bible study each day. As I look back, my avid adolescent interest in girls might not have been congruent with the mission of the school, although I hadn't quite figured out what to do with girls just yet. As I dodged and parried with Eroica, writhing and wet on my shoulders, the both of us trying to avoid getting dunked in the waist-deep ocean water, I heard something no one in that situation ever wants to hear.

Riiippppp.

As the sound of shredding denim rose above the roiling water and our grunts of exertion, I knew exactly what had happened. My cutoff denim shorts had chosen that particular moment to fail spectacularly, and very prominently, in the crotchular region.

In a split second I dumped an oblivious Eroica off my shoulders and hunkered down to do my best to cover my privates. Several of my schoolmates began to laugh and shout. I hunched over, scuttled up out of the water like a hermit crab, and launched myself into a thatched hut where the teachers sat.

"Does anyone have a sewing kit?"

With great tenderness, Ms. Susan produced one from her purse. "You just never know when you might need one of these," she said with a knowing smile and a wink.

After a few quick sewing pointers from the teachers, I retired to a neighboring hut and stripped off my shorts. Mind you, I'd never sewn as much as a button before and now I had to perform solo critical repairs on the only article of clothing I had to cover my nether regions for the rest of the day, including the long ride back home. With Eroica.

My bare buns perched on an icy cooler, I fumbled my way through it and ended up with wearable shorts. I was quite proud. Little did I know that half a lifetime later, I would have the potential to enter the big leagues of sewing by being asked to suture a billion-dollar solar array back to health—in space.

CHAPTER TWENTY-FOUR

That Day

The solar array repair . . . was somewhat of a perfect storm.

—*John V. Ray, NASA Chief EVA Training Officer*

INTERNATIONAL SPACE STATION, ***2007***

After three days of working around the clock and trying out solutions on scale models of the solar array, NASA's Team 4 has a cunning solution. The repair concept is inspired by simple, albeit giant, cuff links made of large metal tabs attached to a stretch of twelve-gauge wire, with everything thoroughly wrapped in nonconductive tape.

The idea is for me to carefully coax the metal tabs through openings in the solar panel on either side of the two tears in the panel, with the wire then taking the load and allowing the panel to be fully extended. It will be like fitting a cuff link through a buttonhole in the arm of a shirt with the wire pulling the cuff closed, or like sewing up a torn garment, except the garment is electrified and might zap me if I touch it.

I'll be doing this all while perched on the end of the cobbled-together robotic arm, my human arms fully extended, and so far from the safety of the airlock that I'm not 100 percent sure I'll be able to get back in the event of a spacesuit problem. This scenario isn't at all inconceivable given the instability of my perch, the high voltage running through the array, and the possibility of encountering a sharp edge that can tear a life-threatening hole in my suit. In addition, since the current in the solar panels can't be turned off, everything that has exposed metal has to be wrapped in nonconductive Kapton tape, including the metal rings on my spacewalking suit. But sometimes you just have to accept a higher degree of risk for a much higher reward.

I know it's going to be a restless night, camping out with Wheels one last time in the airlock as we begin to purge the nitrogen from our bodies in preparation for "going to vacuum" tomorrow. But instead of watching *Caddyshack*, as we'd done the night before our last EVA together, we run through the timeline two or three extra times. We triple-check our tools already staged for the big event, then drift off into our own thoughts.

I can't really toss and turn in my snug sleeping bag, but if I could, I would. An army of brilliant NASA rocket scientists is sending Wheels and me out tomorrow to suture the space station back together. Back home on Earth I was privileged to be a mentor to many young spacewalkers (on my best days regarded by most as an EVA Jedi Master). But right now I'm feeling about as confident as a clumsy and insecure Jedi apprentice. It all seems like a made-for-TV movie. In a cold sweat, I try to wrap my mind around the new task. My entire career has led up to this one day. All my training, all my flight experiences, everything . . .

We never anticipated this crazy scenario, so we certainly aren't trained, in the traditional sense, to do this repair. Nor do we know exactly what we'll find once I get out to the repair site. We will be reliant upon Team 4's procedures, based on incomplete knowledge of the damage, plus our training and experience. We will also rely on each other: the crew outside, the crew inside, and the crew in Mission Control Houston.

No one knows if I'll be able to get the cuff links installed to span the gaps in the time provided by our spacesuits, before Wheels and I will be forced to retreat to the airlock. But I do know this—we'll have only one chance. There are no do-overs. We have the one chance to fix it, and then we have to pack up and leave whether it gets fixed or not.

And if we have to undock and leave without properly repairing it, we might very well significantly damage or destroy the solar array as we undock, if we haven't already cut it loose at NASA's direction. The solar array is critical to power the *International Space Station*, and I am about to go out and try to fix it with some homemade tools and best-guess procedures.

The plan looks really good, prepared by NASA's best and brightest. But what happens if I totally screw up?

As the night wears on with only winks of sleep, I continue to gnaw over what I can see happening tomorrow. First, the tools.

- I have a *loop pin puller*, designed to remove cotter pins via a small hook at the end. I'll use this tool to pull the solar panel in toward me so I can cut the frayed guide wire and work on installing the cuff links.
- My *hockey stick*, an L-shaped tool about two feet in length, will be doing just the opposite—holding the solar panel at a safe distance so it doesn't come in contact with me or my suit.
- On the tool carrier built into the front of my suit I'll also have a borrowed *Russian EVA cutter* designed for snipping cables.
- My *helmet cam* will be recording everything, and it's important to transmit clear photos of the damage and the ongoing repair effort so NASA can track what we're doing and advise us as needed.
- Wheels will be there at the base of the array, perhaps thirty feet below, watching and photographing the effort. He'll also have the critical task of controlling the cable as it retracts onto a spool after I cut the guide wire, using a jury-rigged *Vise-Grip* that will allow him to apply some braking force.
- Perhaps most important, I'll have five of the *cuff links* to install across the damage site.
- And the *exterior cameras*—and the people monitoring them from inside the space station and Mission Control—will be watching, not to mention beaming live video out to the world. I didn't register it at the time, but millions of people will be following along.

We have had about a day and half of prep time as a crew, including two or three videoconferences with Derek, Dina, Sarmad, and members of Team 4.

I watched the animation video the amazing Virtual Reality Lab folks sent up, holding my breath along with our entire crew, stuffed into the airlock module and crowded around a laptop screen. The sped-up clip showed the outrageous, lengthy trajectory the robotic system will take to get out to the very tip of the station, with a rendering of a spacewalker on the end. Me.

If a pin could actually drop in the weightlessness of space, I'm pretty sure I would've heard it right then as a thundering roar. I think I was the first to speak, in an exhale: "Whoa! Play that again!"

But in these final hours tonight my training will be all in my head, seeing myself getting the job done well and overcoming obstacles along the way. I know it isn't the same as physically carrying out the training suited up with the actual tools in the training water-tank environment, but I am so used to previsualization that it seems almost as real as actually being in the pool with the divers around me, with our EVA instructors up on deck directing the action. In my head I'm there, in space, working the problem with my team.

I'm so focused on what I'll have to do outside tomorrow that when a brief doubt floats in my head, I almost ignore it. I push it away because I don't need any new fears or worries. I have plenty of work to do before dawn and not much time. But it comes back. If I were to come directly into contact with the live solar array or if sparks arced to something metal on my suit, could that possibly induce spontaneous combustion? After all, it happened in the rockumentary known as *Spinal Tap*. And perhaps even more insidious, can stray current cause some sort of problem with my spacesuit, or my heart, with the CardioSEAL patch deep inside? Or, even worse, I've already been through one stroke. What if I have another for some strange reason, out on the edge of the cobbled-together robotic arm? Last time I'd lost part of my vision, but what if it happens again and I go blind altogether? Or worse?

Although this isn't a productive train of thought, Pambo, Wheels, and I have already talked through some of these issues with our NASA flight surgeon on the ground, and we have a plan if I become shocked or incapacitated for some reason. The robotic arm would get me from the repair site back to the space station truss in about forty-five minutes. And since Wheels will be at the bottom of the array, he could get me out of the foot restraints and body-drag me back to the airlock to get medical help in perhaps another fifteen minutes. All low-probability stuff, but it is good to have a contingency plan just in case.

I breathe deep, moving my shoulders around to release some tension, and think about my family. Luke, Jenna, Mom, Dad, Gail. They've been with me through all my missions, cheering me on and supporting me, seeing me off and welcoming me home. I know they are all relieved this is my last mission to space. Not to be melodramatic, but I don't want to let them down by not coming home, and I also want to make them proud of me, knowing that I've done my job and I did it well. I have to do this perfectly and carefully, taking no undue chances. I have to be as quick as I can and still be safe. We have a finite but sufficient amount of oxygen, carbon dioxide scrubbing capability, and battery power to get the job done if everything goes per plan.

I want to do it for my family, for the crew, for the hardworking folks on the ground at NASA, and for the citizens of the international community who have supported the building of the *International Space Station*. I don't want to let anyone down, especially since everyone else involved in this repair has done their job up until this eleventh hour to the very highest standard. Now it is up to Wheels and me, along with our watchful crew inside *Discovery* and Mission Control, to finish the job.

Morning finally comes, no alarm needed. But we get the traditional shuttle crew wake-up call anyway, with the music this special day dedicated to me by my awesome son, Luke. It is due to be an epic day with me leading this spacewalk, so it really boosts my spirits when the CAPCOM, Shannon Lucid, voices up to us that they'll be playing his request, the theme to *Star Wars*. I smile and think about my young Skywalker just then, knowing that he'll be in Mission Control this very early morning watching, along with his mom and a couple of his best friends and their dads.

The choreography on the morning of a spacewalk is truly frenetic. Since we'd been camping out in the airlock last night to begin to remove the nitrogen in our systems and prevent the bends, in order to take a quick trip to the space potty we have to open the hatch that communicates with the rest of the ISS, wearing a face mask and breathing 100 percent oxygen, and drag a very long umbilical behind us.

Zambo floats by the airlock as he's done on all three prior spacewalks of the mission to give me a good luck fist bump. "Hey, it's gonna be another great day out there!"

For the first time in my career I don't have a good feel for the eventual outcome. I give a half-hearted "Right on, Zamboni" through my oxygen mask, but I just don't know for sure.

After breakfast and coffee have been delivered to the airlock, and two of our Intravehicular Activity (IVA) crewmembers (the crew staying inside) have floated in with us, we begin the long process of depressurizing the airlock.

With the hatch to the main portion of the station now shut and my oxygen mask off, I put on a game face, eat a quick breakfast, and quip to Wheels: "Time to MAG up!" in reference to the large-capacity diapers (known as Maximum Absorbency Garments) that would accompany us on the walk.

Paolo and Peggy help us finish suiting up, complete with our SAFER jet backpacks and our tools. For the most part, we're pretty quiet and obediently follow instructions as we get buttoned up into our suits. As if I didn't have it already committed to memory, backward and forward, I study the procedures cheat sheet I'll be carrying on my left forearm.

They stuff us into the small external airlock together, with our suits plugged into umbilicals to provide oxygen, power, and cooling until we've depressurized the airlock and are ready to go to suit power. It reminds me of the Barnum & Bailey circus; how many clowns, along with their boxes and bags, can you fit into a tiny clown car? There is absolutely no way for me to even stretch my legs without hitting Wheels in the visor or kicking the airlock control panel, which is kinda important. Moving slowly and deliberately, communicating what I am doing to open the hatch, I am able to swing it up and out of the way without drop-kicking my EVA partner.

Floating out the hatch, I don't even glance at the Earth view as I'm totally in the flow now. Instead, I focus on efficiently moving down the long space station truss to meet up with the end of the robotic booms—the space station arm grappled to the Space Shuttle's inspection boom—where I'll be posted for the next several hours.

Wheels helps secure my boots in the foot restraint and then works his way to the end of the truss, perching himself at the base of the solar array where it attaches to the space station. He will then need to keep a careful eye on me, the ungainly robotic arm flying in close proximity to other solar panels, and the damaged solar panel. Engineers have warned us that contact with the panel can cause it to move in a wavelike pattern, between five to six feet in and out.

Inside the space station, Robeau and Boichi will be on controls of the robotic arm, under the watchful eye of Robotics Officer Sarmad Aziz on the ground. Pambo will be on the comm loop directing me and confirming my actions as I call them out to her and Houston. Derek Hassmann will be in charge of the entire repair effort as Flight Director down at Mission Control, with Dina Contella's oversight of all things EVA, and astronaut Steve "Swanny" Swanson serving as our prime CAPCOM. It is definitely a Dream Team, and this is the gold medal round.

Our goal is to carry out the full repairs, including a major ride on the robotic arm to the repair site and back, within six and a half or seven hours. I don't care about the lack of food or bathroom breaks—I'm fully equipped to manage the latter—but if we attempt to stay much longer, the EVA suit will be close to draining the tanks to empty. In terms of consumables like oxygen, carbon dioxide scrubbing, and battery power, no one wants to cut it too close.

My feet are now locked into the foot restraint on the boom, which in turn is attached to Canadarm2 (I hope those bolts Hadfield and I installed are still just as tight as the day we put them in), and the arm starts moving slowly. The views are staggering, unlike anything any other human being had ever seen before.

I am positioned on top of a space cherry picker, well above the ISS and *Discovery* and our pale blue dot of a home planet. There's no way to do this experience justice; all I can mutter is a markedly uninspired "Wow, that's the most incredible sight I've ever seen!"

I continue flying out toward the end of the solar array, Steph and Dan taking good care of me, but I feel like a tiny worm dangling on the end of a fishing line cast out in slow motion. I am minuscule against the great blackness of space.

I have some prep work to do on this utterly unique commute to work, but I do notice Wheels making good progress out to the tip of the station, back-dropped by an orbital sunset. The sky is below, with the Earth's atmosphere so thin, a beautiful blue skin around the pulsing, glowing blue, green, and rich brown beauty of the planet. Clouds of every color and shape and configuration float inside the bluish atmospheric bubble, sometimes pierced by brilliant streaks of lightning.

I look for edges of continents, and for places I've traveled to and places I still want to go. I see Everest rearing her magnificent snowy head above her sisters, the great chain of the Himalayas. I smile. Maybe someday I'll go there and climb it, and possibly even see the space station fly overhead.

Paolo suddenly interrupts my sightseeing, wanting to run through the cautions and warnings involved in working on the solar panel. He begins rattling off a litany of "no touch" zones, along with a dire warning that I may actually experience current arcing from the damaged panel to my spacesuit. I thank him for his important words of counsel and he replies, "Wait, I'm only halfway done!"

I bend back at my knees as far as they'll take me, since the robotic maneuver has mostly kept the ISS at my back, out of my field of view. I finally see our destination and my heart begins to race. Reverie interrupted, it's time to work.

I go into my hyperfocused state and survey the damage. "The steel metal braid wire is frayed and tangled in front of me, like a hair ball." It looked like the size of a ping-pong ball. "There's several strands of wires all grouped together there," I report.

"I'm sure that's causing shudders on the ground somewhere," says Pambo.

"You have some surgery to do, Dr. Parazynski," she adds.

"I think so." Her voice makes me feel safe. I know she's crouched up in the window with a set of binoculars, tracking my every move.

But wait. I can't quite reach the site.

The arm is stretched out as far as it can go and I can practically feel everyone listening, holding their collective breath. Now it is up to Wheels and me, Stephanie and Dan on the arm, and the rest of the watchful crew inside *Discovery*, the ISS, and Mission Control to get the job done. I ask the robotic arm crew if they can reorient me to allow me another couple feet of reach. Dan replies that he can do so, but it will take some time to pull me back and reorient the arm to make another pass. On the ground, Sarmad confirms, "I can't give him any more." Meanwhile, Swanny calls up and informs us that we're already running short on time, with about an hour and a half before we have to wrap it up.

We haven't even begun the actual repair and we're already short on time. *Dammit!* But I stretch, my long arms extending out fully, and with the pin puller tool I can just barely reach the panel. I pull it gently toward me.

Wheels is watching below. "Looking good, Spike."

Finally, I truly get to work. First we have to cut the hair ball out, allowing the cable to retract toward Wheels, with him controlling it with his modified Vise-Grip.

For the next bit, I need to be even closer, close enough to push a cuff link tab into a hole that had been used to keep the solar panel aligned during its launch. I'm juggling my three tools, using the pin puller to pull in the wing, maneuvering the cuff link into and through the hole with the taped-up wire following it in, and using the hockey stick to keep the wing from getting in contact with my suit. I could really use an extra hand, but that's not gonna happen.

"Heads up!" It's Wheels, and I tell him I see the wave coming. I hear Pam breathe in hard as I lean back a bit and grapple with the hockey stick, using it to push the billowing wing away from me. Then I quickly get back to work.

After that, with the technique and the pattern established, it's just a delicate suture job, and time flows as I concentrate on the tools, the wing, and the work.

Finally, it's done. Hair ball removed. Five sutures in, five homemade cuff links and wires holding it together, spanning two rips. Over six hours have gone by, and we still need to deploy the panel and get home. I stow my tools, stop for a moment, and breathe. I straighten up and try to give my body a quick break, consciously relaxing clenched, tired muscles. I open and close my hands, fighting the pressurized gloves.

"*Discovery*, Houston," Swanny says from the ground. "We are happy with the current config, and we are ready for you to back off and get ready for the deploy." Wheels and I monitor the slow, segmented extension of the balky panel, and soon realize that it's all going to work.

It's a triumphant moment when we hear the panel is fully extended, cheers audible on the communication loop from Mission Control. Our work here is done. And somehow I know it's the best day on the job I will ever have.

"All right," I say, trying not to sound too excited. As if this is just another day in the training pool. "That's how you do it!"

"Excellent," says Pam. Her voice is guarded, though. She still has to get me back inside. "You know there aren't many people in the office who could do what you just did there."

"I hope they don't have to!" I say. Relief washes over me. "That was a beautiful day in space right there."

As I fly back toward the airlock, my stomach growls and my beat-up knuckles sting with blisters. I'm exhausted but overjoyed. As I fly through space this one last time, I'm grateful. I can't believe we all did it. And I can't believe I got to be a part of it. I look once again, drunk with the beauty of the Earth and the thin blue line below.

I think of the team, the hundreds of brilliant and hard-working people who came together for this, one of NASA's finest moments. We did it.

CHAPTER TWENTY-FIVE

The Goddess

Climb high, don't die.

—*Bob "Bobo" Lowry*

EVEREST, 2008

The celebrations start when Wheels and I open the internal airlock hatch after that triumphant spacewalk, even before we get out of our EVA suits. Relief, exhaustion, and elation are all wrapped together. I feel a bit verklempt, choked up with both the amazing success of what had just happened and the fact that I'd probably never float out a hatch again on a spacewalk. I've been so fortunate to serve as an astronaut all these years, living out my boyhood dreams, and am even more overwhelmed to have the chance to end on such a euphoric note.

We land safely back at the Cape on November 7, 2007, ending my twenty-three-million-mile career. A few days later we have a formal ceremony at Space Center Houston, where our crew thanks those who made our epic mission so successful. We give out awards to honor key contributors, including those who'd supported what turned into a heroic effort to save the solar array. In a time-honored Mission Control tradition, we also participate in the plaque-hanging ceremony in the flight control room. To no one's surprise, the mission's EVA flight control team is chosen for the high honor of hanging the mission patch.

Later, we hold a very special awards ceremony at Kevin Pehr's house. By this time he is terminally ill with malignant melanoma and not in a condition to go in to work anymore, but Wheels and I want to celebrate and recognize his work, and in particular to recognize his help inventing the cuff links we used for the repair. I present him with a Silver Snoopy, a special pin representing Snoopy in a bubble helmet and backpack. Charles Schulz had been a big friend of the space program early on. Silver Snoopy pins are made from a piece of space-flown silver, considered the highest honor for an individual in the NASA workforce, and can only be presented by an astronaut. The entire solar-array team is there to celebrate Kevin and the collective team's amazing accomplishments.

As the team settles back into life on Earth, Wheels-turned-Tike-turned-Cupcake becomes almost famous when a photo he snapped of me out on the robotic arm makes it onto the cover of *Aviation Week and Space Technology*.

"Check it out, Wheels. Look who's on the cover." I smirk, waving the magazine.

He grabs it away from me, opens it up, and starts reading about the daring repair and the dangerous spacewalk. After a few minutes, he glances at the cover photo credits. The byline reads *Photo courtesy of NASA*. His face falls. "Oh, man, I took that photo!"

"I'll make it up to you, Tike," I say, grabbing it back. "How about going with me to Everest?"

"What? You're crazy. I've never climbed a mountain in my life."

"You're coming with me. And you won't even have to build a bonfire."

I'd actually formulated my Everest plans months ago during an EVA simulation for our mission, and I already have it all set up for Wheels. One of our EVA instructors running the session, the effervescent Sabrina Singh, starts talking about wanting to lead a trek to the Himalayas, maybe even to Everest Base Camp, in a few months. My eyes light up with disbelief. "You have GOT to time your trip for next spring when I'm going to take a shot at the summit!" It is an uncanny coincidence meshing with my evolving, tentative plans to travel to Nepal, but I take it as an omen that the time for Everest will indeed be the spring of 2008.

Gail isn't overly excited about the money part, or the time I'll spend away from the kids, now eleven and eight years old. The tragedy of *Columbia* had brought us a bit closer together, and we'd tried marriage counseling again. For my part, the all-consuming nature of my job sometimes takes my focus away from working on our marriage, and the situation is still strained, although we are trying our best to hold things together for the kids. We are such different people, seeing our marriage and each other in dramatically different ways. But I'll be the first to admit that going off to climb Everest might not be the best decision for our marriage at the moment. Nevertheless, it is an opportunity to fulfill a childhood dream, and I selfishly can't resist.

In the closing days of March 2008, after exhaustive planning, intense training, and a home equity loan for $40K, I fly to Kathmandu to kick off my attempt to become the first astronaut to summit Mount Everest. All goes well for the first several weeks of acclimatization. The process of climbing Everest is slow and outrageously taxing on the mind and body. After reaching Everest Base Camp (EBC) at 17,500 feet above sea level, we make progressively higher forays up the mountain to build our fitness and speed up the route, along with additional red blood cells to extract oxygen from the progressively thinner air up high. A trip and a night up at Camp 1 at 19,500 feet are followed by several days' rest back at EBC. Then we'll journey up to Camp 2 at 21,500 feet for a couple nights' restless sleep, and then another week of rest at EBC. The final rotation before our summit push will involve a night at Camp 3 without supplemental oxygen, the wind and penetrating cold making it one of the most miserable in any climber's quest for the summit of Everest.

Listening to avalanches on the slopes around Base Camp heightens the feeling of being alone in a very alien environment. For comfort, I surround myself with photos of my family, but the physical and mental challenge is unrelenting and emotional. I feel like attempting to climb Everest is by far the hardest thing I've ever done. I am not sure I have the endurance to keep going, and I realize I am just going to have to take it one day at a time.

Sabrina's trekking group, including Wheels and Jeff "Bones" Ashby (from STS-100), visits me at Base Camp just before our summit push in early May. The NASA team's rugged hike doubles as a wedding-honeymoon trip for Sabrina and her new husband, Adam Gilmore, making them definitely one of the coolest, most adventurous couples I know. The team's arrival is such a huge boost to stave off the homesickness and rigors of those long days and nights on the side of the mountain, and it reenergizes me for the summit climb ahead.

Finally, after more acclimatization, our team gets the go-ahead to try for the summit.[32] The route is established much of the way to the summit, our high camps are stocked, and the weather forecasts are favorable. It feels much like the night before the solar-array repair, but with one huge difference. I'm suffering excruciating back pain here in my tent at Camp 3, on the fifty-ninth day of my climb. It comes on ferociously, and I'm forced to make a critical, life-and-death decision. Tylenol and a strategically placed bag of snow in my sleeping bag are my only hopes of sleeping the pain off. But at sunup, with the summit pyramid clearly in sight, I'm in absolute anguish as I consider my options.

Finally, after getting ready and staggering less than twenty faltering paces on my official summit attempt, I know I have but one choice. There's no way I can make it. I know if I go forward in my condition—whatever it is that's wrong with me—I'll be jeopardizing the success of my friend Adam Janikowski and the rest of the team. And not only will I be preventing my teammates from reaching the summit, if I'm unable to move at some point and can't get back down, I might put us all into a desperate situation. It's a high-stakes decision.

"I'm done," I say, my voice weak and shaking with both the pain and the intense disappointment and sorrow.

As I watch the team leave camp and begin the climb up to Camp 4 and then the summit, heavy tears surge into my eyes. Adam, in his bright yellow down suit, turns back to look at me several times. I can imagine the anguish he feels at leaving a teammate behind. But we'd already agreed long ago that if one of us had to turn back, as long as the other was safe and could descend with his Sherpa sidekick, then the other must continue on.

I know I need to get down the mountain and get help but I'm not sure exactly how that is going to happen. Kami Sherpa stays behind with me and removes the bulk of my backpack load while I lie directly on the snow, using the world's largest ice pack to numb my back. With the pain blunted a bit and my back spasms quiet for a brief moment, we start slowly down the face of the mountain, and I'm able to traverse my way back to the near-vertical route. Then we begin an interminable series of arm-wrap rappels—wrapping the fixed line around my arms and behind my back to create controlled friction—for over 2,500 feet of blue-ice descent.

My buddy Bob Lowry is coming down with us. He'd run out of steam by the time he reached Camp 3, nagged by a "Khumbu cough" that hinders many high-altitude climbers in this region of Nepal. He, too, made the difficult decision to turn around, hoping to try again some future season. Kami and Bob are both practically saints, stopping patiently every twenty or thirty minutes as I repeat the ice and stretch protocol.

Bob, or Bobo the Clown, as I call him, is full of one-liners that distract me from the pity I am wallowing in. I cannot move at more than a snail's pace, trying to guard my back from frequently locking up with muscle spasms as I set up for the inexorable number of rappels down the steep Lhotse Face. I'll never know the pain of childbirth, and I have much respect for moms the world over, but this is about as much as I can handle. Sadly, I am not able to offer much in the way of distraction for the self-pity Bobo himself might be feeling, but he never once lets it show. Bobo holds five black belts, and being a physical trainer on top of his day job in investment banking, he knows what he's doing when he stretches out my back for five or ten minutes at each rest stop.

About halfway down the face we meet up with my teammates Jaroslaw, Justin, and Dean on their way up in the next summit wave. They are winded but full of energy and enthusiasm. The contrast is stark. I'm nearing the end of my frayed and tattered rope, both physically and emotionally spent. Ashen with exhaustion and seething with pain and disappointment, I'm not sure which hurts more—my crippled back or the knowledge that I'm heading away from my goal and don't know if I'll ever return. Although I know these guys well, I can't hold a conversation with them without getting choked up, so I spit out a quick "Good luck" without any further explanation. I'm moving slowly but with resolve, and ultimately, I make it down to Camp 2 at 21,500 feet above sea level. I have plenty of time to brood.

As we descend, I think of the 250 souls who have died on the mountain. As much as I love adventure, I know that's one adventure I'm not yet ready for. I have a lot of respect for this great mountain. Mountaineers harbor a strong sense of superstition about Everest, with people treating the mountain as if it has a spirit or intelligence not to be trifled with. The Tibetan locals call the mountain Chomolungma, or "Goddess Mother of the Earth," and once considered it a holy place off-limits to humans. It wasn't until European explorers came calling that the Sherpas, the native residents of the region known for hard work and a natural ability to handle high-altitude climbing, began to spend time on Everest. They still consider it a holy place, and most mountaineers honor their faith by visiting shrines, offering prayers, and observing age-old rituals.

Everest doesn't let its guard down easily. Fewer than one in three summit aspirants actually make the round-trip to the top and back, and the risk of perishing on the mountain is very similar to the risk faced by astronauts launching aboard a shuttle. On both counts, I'm one of the lucky ones.[33] During the night at Camp 2, I'm shaken awake well before the sun's first light to make a house call for my friend Monty, who has developed a severe, bilateral nosebleed in the cold, dry air of the mountain. He and his climbing partner had planned to launch their bid for the top the following day, but I know in an instant his summit chances are zero.

Upon seeing his pale skin, along with a Nalgene bottle full of blood and a tent full of bloody toilet paper, I am not even confident of Monty's short-term survival. Working in a tent that is straight out of a horror film, with limited supplies, a headlamp, and a crippled back, I manage to get his nostrils packed and stop the bleeding. Monty is a stoic survivor, having narrowly survived a previous summit trip to another of the world's eight-thousand-meter peaks, Shishapangma, where he suffered severe frostbite with the loss of the tips of a few toes and a finger. We form a freak show procession and limp on down to Base Camp together later in the day.

Even though I know I could not have made the summit in my current condition, I am sorely disappointed after a lifetime of dreaming. I know I've just had the adventure of a lifetime, but I fall into a funk as I slowly pick my way down the Khumbu Icefall one last time. I am also physically at my most vulnerable: it's nearing midday, with the sun beating down on us between towering seracs, and I am moving in super slow-mo. When I finally stagger into Base Camp, moving with the grace of a zombie, I let my thoughts turn toward the problem of getting back to the airport in Kathmandu. Can I make the long thirty-six-mile trek out? The doc at the Himalayan Rescue Association clinic, fondly known as Everest ER, concurs with my recommendation to request a helicopter evacuation for Monty out of Base Camp. As his "personal physician," I am grateful for an open seat on said helicopter.

Although I had been looking forward to the walk (or now, more likely, the limp) through the beautiful countryside, watching for baby yaks and the beautiful wild rhododendrons coming into springtime bloom, it's the flight of a lifetime for a pilot and mountaineer like me. The weather isn't ideal, but the front-seat ride in the French-built Cheetah helicopter piloted by the Nepalese Air Force is one I'll never forget.

We skim treetops by mere feet with enormous valleys opening up underneath us. Most of the Himalayan giants are shrouded in clouds during the ninety-minute flight, but I marvel at the raging rivers, tiny villages, and tenuous suspension bridges flashing by below. Soon, I'll be home in Houston reuniting with family, resting up, and finding out what's really wrong with my back. It's got to be something bad, and I'm not looking forward to finding out. I know significant bed rest is in my future, along with an MRI and possible surgery, but I'm hoping and praying my symptoms simply evaporate when I get back to home and family.

Right before I leave Kathmandu, Monty and I visit the famous Rum Doodle bar and restaurant. It's bittersweet, because we cannot yet sign the wall behind the bar where the signatures of Everest legends like Ed Hillary, Tenzing Norgay Sherpa, Jim Whittaker, Tom Hornbein, Willi Unsoeld, Naomi Uemura, Doug Scott, Dougal Haston, Reinhold Messner, Chris Bonington, Ang Rita Sherpa, Ed Viesturs, Babu Chiri Sherpa, Rob Hall, and many more decorate the walls. We nurse our Everest-labeled local beer and our injuries, wondering what it would've been like to actually summit. We are not yet worthy, but we both hope to one day get another chance at adding our names to the wall.

After a long series of coach flights home, it's time for a diagnosis and healing. It's so great to spend time at home with the kids, and I rest, hoping to regain the twenty-five pounds I'd lost. I am also hoping my back will stop hurting. But nothing I do gets rid of the discomfort, and I start to experience numbness in my left leg. I go in for an MRI and sure enough, it's bad news. I have a small ruptured disc in my low back requiring surgical repair. My intervertebral disc, which serves as the cushion between the L2 and L3 vertebrae, is like a jelly donut squashed by a car tire and it's pressing on the nerves feeding my left leg. If I don't immediately do something about it, I could lose the sensation and motor function in my leg. It's possible I might not even be able to walk. As a result, I'm put on the OR schedule first thing the following week.

While back problems are a known hazard of space travel, astronauts also face an increased loss of bone and muscle mass, visual-acuity problems, cataracts, and a slight increase in various kinds of cancer due to exposure to radiation. The pressures and demands of the astronaut corps can also lead to mental health issues. I think of, and feel bad for, astronaut Lisa Nowak, who drove from Texas to Florida to inappropriately confront a romantic rival. She was arrested, and the high-profile case opened her up to much ridicule in the media. Although we weren't close friends, I'd sat right next to her in our STS-118 crew office for a year and a half, well before this awful event. I knew her to be a very competent, bright professional who was also a doting mom. Although a bit serious by nature, she had a very kind heart, propagating *Columbia* astronaut Laurel Clark's iris flowers and sharing them with others who wanted to keep them in memory of Laurel. Lisa's crisis taught me the importance of compassion and that mental illness can happen to anyone, regardless of background or perceived success.

Another common challenge for astronauts can be the most painful—the toll on relationships. The notoriety that comes with flying in space, along with the single-minded focus and time and energy required, has seriously strained many marriages, including mine. John Glenn was a wonderful exception, married to his childhood sweetheart, Annie, for well over seventy years.

So even though my bulging disc is repaired via surgery that summer in a microscope-aided procedure called a microdiscectomy, my marriage is not as easy to fix. Gail and I are struggling, still holding things together for the kids, but not seeing eye to eye on many things, including the idea of a return trip to Everest to try for the summit again the following year. Ultimately we agree it would be far better to go for it again while I am still young, rather than take on much greater risk as a sixty-plus-year-old climber.

The decision I'd made up high on Everest during my first summit attempt was the right one. Mountaineering is about personal accomplishment to some extent, and triumphing over the challenges. But it's also very much about the team. You have to put your teammates first and know what's best and safest for the whole. I'd felt summit fever and I was able to resist. The picture of my ruptured disk on the MRI reinforces the difficult decision I'd made on the mountain to quit. I had failed, but I'd also won.

I have another important decision to make, knowing I'd flown my fifth and final mission on STS-120. I begin thinking about hanging up my spacesuit and retiring from NASA, although my energy level and my mortgage mean I won't be retiring from the workplace, probably ever. I've done all I had dreamt of doing as an astronaut, save for perhaps a long-duration mission, but that meant being away for many months on end, and with kids still at home that didn't sound good at all. Moreover, I've used up all my accrued vacation on the Everest climb this year, and I won't be able to take out yet another home equity loan to go back next year, either. For a second Everest attempt, I'll need to find sponsors, and doing so will be especially tough while still a government employee.

With a month to go until I return to Everest in April 2009, I take a job with a NASA contractor, Wyle Integrated Science and Engineering Group in Houston. I join Wyle to support human health and performance services for the federal government, NASA and otherwise. The hook for me is the potential to eventually serve as the Medical Director for Wyle's bid to run medical support for the US Antarctic Program, managed by the National Science Foundation. Antarctica has been the source of many of my childhood dreams of exploration, and near the top of my bucket list.

I look forward to my second time on Everest—Chomolungma and I have some unfinished business. And this time, courtesy of Neil Armstrong and the historic Apollo 11 Mission, I'll be taking along a moon rock from the Sea of Tranquility. If all goes well and my body and my back hold up, I will stand on the summit of the world's tallest mountain and enjoy an orbital sunrise.

My wife and parents have mostly come to terms with the idea of a second attempt, and at my core, I am eager to summit, albeit with a few lingering worries. What if my back gives out on me again? Or something else as serious, or worse, happens and I become one of the Everest casualties?

But I feel as if a powerful force is drawing me back there. I can't really put it into words. It is just something I have to do.

CHAPTER TWENTY-SIX

Rare Air

Success consists of going from failure to failure
without loss of enthusiasm.

—*Winston Churchill*

EVEREST, 2009

As I interval train to exhaustion and pack with purpose for my second Everest attempt in the spring of 2009, I put together a collection of important items I want to carry to the top of the mountain. One special item is a Space Shuttle mission STS-51F patch in memory of astronaut Karl Henize, the only other astronaut so far to attempt Everest.

Back when I was a newbie astronaut, I had the chance to meet Karl when he lectured our ASCAN class on astronomy and space science. He'd already left the astronaut corps, having returned to scientific pursuits elsewhere at NASA. This allowed him to pursue his dream of summiting Everest, just as I did when I departed fifteen years later.

Karl was invited to participate on an expedition to the mountain's north side (via Tibet, in 1993), including testing of a radiation dosimeter that would also be used aboard the Space Shuttle. By report, he succumbed to high-altitude pulmonary edema at Advanced Base Camp, 21,300 feet above sea level. Unfortunately, he never had the chance to stand on the summit or to return home. My route will not take me by his final resting place, but I do want to honor him and his family by taking his shuttle mission patch to the top. Taking special things up to the summit is symbolic, a way to remember and honor causes and people close to your heart.

I've also made a special set of Tibetan prayer flags to honor astronauts and cosmonauts who had fallen in the line of duty. The likenesses of the Apollo 1, *Challenger*, *Columbia*, *Soyuz 1*, and *Soyuz 11* crews are depicted on a pair of flags that I will tie off on top of the world. Tibetans place their multicolored prayer flags on the highest peaks and mountain passes, where the wind, sun, snow, and ice slowly absorb them, launching goodwill into space. I can't think of a better way to pay homage to those who made the ultimate sacrifice.

My collection of summit items also includes several patches on my down suit, with an autism puzzle piece for Jenna, a Challenger Center logo (an educational organization on whose board I serve), and the US flag from my spacesuit used in the solar-array repair. I also have photos of my loved ones, a special Star Wars patch for Luke, an Explorers Club flag, and other tchotchkes I'd been given for summit photos.

I've been hoping to return and climb the mountain with my friends Bobo and Rohan Freeman, who were with me on Everest the year before. Bobo's job and finances aren't in sync with that plan, unfortunately. Rohan ends up getting a more favorable rate with a smaller team, so happily I'll see him in Base Camp and elsewhere on the mountain.

Conversely, and perhaps most important, I'll be back with my Sherpa buddies from the International Mountain Guides (IMG) team, climbing with arguably the strongest climber on the mountain, Danuru Sherpa from Phortse. Danuru is a family man with a gentle nature and a ready smile, and I am honored to be able to rope up with him. He is the Usain Bolt of the Himalayas, getting stronger and faster the higher he goes.

I wouldn't be able to even consider going back to Everest this year if it hadn't been for a chance encounter with my multitalented buddy Miles O'Brien, who is in between gigs at CNN and PBS. Over Christmas break I'd met Miles for lunch in New York City. Although I've been marching forward with grand ambition to return to the mountain, I have no real way of paying the $40,000 or so I need. Another home equity loan is out of the question; I'll need sponsorships, and Miles is the best pep-talker and strategizer I've ever known. We set forth on a plan of education outreach, along with mutual friend Keith Cowing, in the form of broadcasts from Nepal on behalf of the Challenger Center for Space Science Education.

Miles is tech savvy and a leading media authority in all things aerospace. A third-generation private pilot, he had been tapped to become the first journalist to fly on a Space Shuttle, although the opportunity evaporated with the loss of *Columbia*. Base Camp won't make up for the loss of his chance at a shuttle flight, but Everest will be an incredible, shared adventure.

I know I'll be forever grateful for Miles's star power and introductions, leading to a sponsorship from SPOT, a satellite messenger device to track my progress to the top of the planet. I've also been asked to serve as team physician for the Discovery Channel's third season of a television show called *Everest: Beyond the Limit*. This time around, somehow I've managed to find a way to go to Everest and actually make money rather than lose it.

Our friend Keith Cowing, an astrobiologist and former NASA employee, is the voice behind a widely read NASA watchdog blog called *NASA Watch*. Although sometimes critical of NASA's direction—he uses the term "snarky"—he is a passionate advocate of spaceflight, first and foremost, and is often able to hold the agency accountable to its mission. Keith is also the catalyst of a plot to take a very special item to the top of Everest: an Apollo 11 moon rock.

Moon rocks are very hard to come by and they're kept closely guarded in repositories where availability is generally limited to scientific inquiry. Occasionally, if you apply and have a really good reason, a moon rock is lent out. Technically, a moon rock shouldn't be taken out of the country or transported someplace like Mount Everest where it could possibly be lost, confiscated, or dropped into a crevasse or into China. But Keith and I decide to try, and we submit an application to a committee of top-level geologists and meteorite specialists. Somehow, permission is granted, and we promise NASA the rock will be returned. I may have even signed something in blood, but I can't quite remember (I'll blame high-altitude exposure).

I leave for Kathmandu in late March without the moon rock, but Keith and I are hoping it will arrive in time for his departure, a few weeks later. The day before he leaves, Keith goes out at five in the morning to retrieve his Sunday paper and trips over a box from FedEx lying there on the porch. He grabs the box, opens it up, and there it is. A piece of the moon.

Actually, it is four tiny rock pieces embedded in a small Lucite dome, like a miniature snow globe. Ecstatic, he immediately dubs it "the nugget" and keeps it safe in his pocket during the long journey to Kathmandu and Base Camp.

Meanwhile, Miles's independent production work had started to pick up, and he won't be able to travel to Nepal as we'd all hoped. Instead, he will run a Mission Control of sorts from his laundry room in Manhattan, distributing streaming video from Everest over Hulu and other means to huge numbers of schoolkids and armchair mountaineers around the world. Keith will operate from Base Camp and titles himself the resident "News Sherpa"; their tag team approach promises to be incredibly successful.

My journey back to the Khumbu of Nepal feels like a huge homecoming, reconnecting with many Sherpa and Western climbing friends from the year before, and reimmersing myself in the culture and rugged beauty of the place. I tell everyone about going under the knife to get my lumbar disc slurped out; I don't think they expected me back quite so soon.

I settle into the well-known routine of "climb-high-sleep-low" rotations up the mountain for the six-plus weeks of preparation required in order to have a fighting chance for the summit. It feels like returning to space on a second shuttle flight, with many of the rookie-season unknowns and uncertainties replaced with knowledge and confidence. Only the summit climb is still veiled in mystery for me, but I know there will be plenty of sweat and suffering before that final day.

After twelve days of trekking through the Khumbu Valley, Keith and the nugget arrive safely at Base Camp. One of the first things we do together is visit the Sherpa dining tent to show them the moon rocks and hand out photos of Everest I snapped while on orbit during my first mission, STS-66. We want to honor and thank the Sherpas for their extraordinary courage and accomplishments. Their eyes light up at the photos, and they each hold the lunar sample to their foreheads in reverence. The Sherpas' strength, humility, and character astonish me.

One afternoon at lunch in the mess tent, I raise my fear of loss and litigation to Keith. What if I accidentally drop the nugget while on the summit? It is entirely possible that I could get to the top, completely exhausted, and accidentally drop it down the vertical slopes with zero likelihood of being able to retrieve it. I'll have a helluva time explaining to NASA what happened to their priceless lunar sample. Suddenly I notice, scattered around us in the detritus of the carb-laden junk food eaten by mountaineers, numerous cans of Pringles potato chips. For some reason, Pringles are a ubiquitous sight wherever climbers congregate in Nepal.

In a flash, I grab two Pringles lids, my Leatherman tool, and a roll of duct tape. I cut a small central hole in one of the transparent, flexible plastic Pringles lids, then sandwich the moon rock in between the two lids, securing it all together via a ring of duct tape while Keith holds it all together. From a distance it looks like a proper, well-engineered enclosure that will be much easier to hold on to with big climbing mitts on. That night, and every night thereafter as I ascend the mountain, I sleep with the "Nugget Containment Device" (NCD) in a zippered fleece pocket directly over my heart, the safest place in such a harsh environment.

After Keith arrives, we begin to transmit with Miles back in his laundry lair. I also throw myself into the now-familiar acclimatization climbs up and down the mountain, spending many nights at progressively higher camps, tossing and turning in my tent with nervous energy. The frequent avalanches, extreme cold, and physical exertion near the edge of human performance are reminiscent of last year's painful attempt. I had forgotten, however, the way the jet stream screams overhead. The whooshing, turbulent airflow often dips down to greet us in the Western Cwm, rustling our tents like an out-of-control freight train.

Over a month into the expedition and I'm at Camp 3, roughly 24,500 feet above sea level. One of my climbing partners, a French Canadian ultramarathoner named Rejean, and I experience a truly awful night, with the tent imploding around us as the jet stream hammers Everest. Around midnight, we feel the full brunt, with our tent walls compressing and flapping as if to take flight. The noise is deafening, like a rock concert drum solo without rhythm. I'm wearing my down suit, and I can probably quickly don the rest of my gear if necessary to work my way down the fixed lines to the safety of Camp 2. But for now, the safest place I can be is right here.

Dawa, Rejean's Sherpa sidekick, pops his head in our tent at 5:35 in the morning with directions from our sirdar (the IMG Base Camp boss), Ang Jangbu Sherpa, to break down the tents and descend as quickly as we can, due to the weather. Rejean and I pack, harness up, and are ready by six. We head down in punishing winds, and once back in the relative protection and safety of the upper Western Cwm, I'm blown around by even stronger gusts, and I have to dig in and stabilize myself with my ice axe. Occasionally I have to sit down to keep from being blown away. But at least the sun is shining and we're less than an hour away from Camp 2, our Advanced Base Camp. And I know the fierce weather will soon abate. We're almost ready for our summit push.

It's hard to describe the excitement welling within as I prepare for my summit bid on the highest mountain in the world. Years of dreaming, reading, and training have led up to this point in my life—a chance to overcome the summit that overcame me last season. I feel joy in the middle of the pain. But May 7 turns out to be a major false start for us, with a tragic outcome.

My core climbing team of six heading for the summit includes Danuru Sherpa, Rejean and his sidekick Dawa Sherpa, as well as Ed Wardle, a proud Scotsman and extreme cameraman for Discovery Channel, and his partner Sanduck Sherpa. We leave Base Camp in the early morning hours to get through the icefall before "sun-hit," with the goal of making Camp 2 later in the morning. If all goes well, we'll be standing on top in just a few days' time.

Danuru and I are in fine rhythm and moving fast, anxious to get the suffering of the Western Cwm behind us before the heat of the midday sun. Meanwhile Rejean and Dawa are moving a bit slower, still about twenty minutes away from Camp 1, when I get a call on the radio asking, "Do you have any aspirin?" Rejean has developed some chest pressure just below camp. Acclimatizing to high altitude often results in sludge-like blood, and climbers have experienced heart attacks and strokes as a result of vascular blockages. I immediately send down aspirin and request some oxygen be sent from Camp 1 to help him down the icefall. I'm worried for my friend, sorry for his loss of the summit, and sad to lose a summit companion.

Rejean is able to hydrate and feels better, so he and Dawa begin their descent but the time of day could not be worse. A massive avalanche from the west shoulder of Everest decides to let loose onto the icefall, nearly burying Rejean and Dawa for eternity. The pair frees themselves, but with the descent route now in complete disarray, they rush to the aid of three nearby climbers in the middle of the icefall who have been completely buried. Dawa heroically leads a pickup team of rescue climbers to aid other groups caught in the avalanche, valiantly trying to save their lives. One life is lost; RIP, brother Lhapka Nuru Sherpa. I never had the chance to meet him, as he was with another climbing team. Married with three children, Lhapka is never found.

It is time to stand down and reflect.

CHAPTER TWENTY-SEVEN

The Sky Below

If you think you can do a thing or
think you can't do a thing, you're right.

—*Henry Ford*

EVEREST, 2009

I've already had some incredible experiences on this great mountain, including the lifelong comradeship that comes from the shared struggle of climbing as a team. But Rejean's medical emergency and the fatal avalanche shake me, as do the near misses of other climbers I've personally treated for high-altitude pulmonary edema. No one ever conquers Everest. You merely make peace with it for a very short while.

On the balance sheet, I am as fit as I'll ever be, and I know the mountain and my skilled companions well. A five-day favorable weather window is in the forecast, and the route to the top has been established, as have our high camps. The odds of a successful summit and return are as high as they could ever be, but elements beyond my control can still result in failure to summit, or even failure to return. But by this point I am committed to making a summit attempt, armed with the knowledge and experience of last year; if it doesn't look right, or if conditions turn, I will again do the right thing and turn around. The mountain will always be there.

DAY 56: I wake up in the middle of the night and look at my watch. It's 1:51 a.m. Too early. I toss and turn and finally get up at 3:50 and put on my clothing and gear. I'm on the trail to Crampon Point by 4:32 in another typical day of preparing for the summit push from Base Camp. Danuru, Ed Wardle, Sanduck Sherpa, and I have an uneventful climb through the icefall and Western Cwm to Camp 2. Although I am throttling back to preserve energy for the actual summit push, I have a personal best time-to-camp. The final slog into upper Camp 2 is still pure misery, but I do it with less internal whining than before.

DAY 57: I rest and picture myself like a space station solar cell, soaking up every shred of energy for the summit push. Many teams are in position, some already on the move on this ideal summit day. I hope it holds. Having had one prior false start on the summit a week earlier, my bags are more or less already packed for Camps 3 and 4. Thankfully I didn't try for the summit on May 11, as the handful of compatriots who did were hammered by bad weather; they even had to lower an injured teammate down the Lhotse Face in whiteout conditions. The spartan living and cooking conditions of Camp 2 mean less-than-ideal food, but I love ramen noodles. I thought Spam only existed in Monty Python skits, but the canned meat product somehow makes its way into our kitchen and our stomachs.

The documentary film crew corners us, asking about our feelings on climbing to the summit in the days ahead. Not bashful, I admit I am scared and uncertain. As I always advised my friend Rejean (while he was still with us on the mountain), "It's gonna hurt!" An early morning ascent to Camp 3 is planned. I'll be wearing my full down suit and don't want to get caught in direct sunlight high on the Lhotse Face.

DAY 58: I am not a morning person, much preferring a warm bed and a slow transition to vertical, but Everest doesn't allow for this. Instead, I wriggle into my down suit while still mostly in my sleeping bag, then quickly unzip, put on my mountaineering boots, and shuffle to the cook tent, stiff from the uncomfortable night I've just shivered through. A couple of cups of Sherpa tea help wash down a pair of ultra-fried eggs; then it's time to put on my harness and crampons. Steam from my breath and my teacup compete with visibility. Many others are now alongside me: three female Singaporean climbers, plus Ed, Jaime, Dawes (sixty-six years old and one of the oldest men ever to attempt Everest), Chris, Mike, Louie, and Paul, all awake and in final preparations for ascent to Camp 3.

The slope above Camp 2 starts out gently enough, and the Bergschrund (the point where the mountain separates from the glacier we are climbing) seems almost close enough to touch, judging by the string of headlamps already there at this early hour. Twenty minutes into the climb it seems as if we are no closer, and the glacier has grown dramatically steeper.

I lead the fixed lines all the way up the Lhotse Face in quick tempo, thankful for much better kicked-in steps than on our first trip up to Camp 3. Danuru and I pass everyone we come across in our four-and-a-half-hour climb. Once in camp, I feel great after snacks and half a liter of black tea with sugar. My back is holding up, the nugget is safe in my breast pocket, and I think I can do this!

Regrettably, that afternoon Paul from the UK develops significant shortness of breath at rest, and I diagnose high-altitude pulmonary edema. The only assured treatment is descent, so we very sadly send him back down on oxygen. His expedition has unexpectedly ended on its fifty-eighth day—almost identical to the timing of my turnaround in 2008. Paul is a great guy with enormous strength and potential on this mountain, but for him the summit is not to be.

Ed and I share an oxygen bottle overnight (one liter/minute between the two of us). I smile as I see the Sharpie mark *120* on the cylinder. That's a good number for me. An omen for the great day ahead. With the sun up and warming us inside our tent, the system works perfectly well. But as the night chill falls, our exhaled breath condenses within our masks, making a slobbery mess every time we turn from side to side. I eventually tie a bandana on my chin to sop up the moisture, but even this becomes wet and miserable.

DAY 59: We venture into terra incognita up to Camp 4. We have a head start to get back on the face, as IMG's Camp 3 is perched above all others, carved into the Lhotse Face just below a set of enormous ice towers. An early start limits the exposure to falling debris from other climbers. While Danuru and I both wear climbing helmets, a plastic "brain bucket" can only protect you so much.

Once again I lead out on the face, and we make quick time up to the limestone feature known as the Yellow Band, the broad traverse above, and the slate of the Geneva Spur. Crossing the Yellow Band and Geneva Spur entails some brief, steep mixed climbing (snow, rock, and ice). Careful crampon placement on sloping rock slabs allows us to pass without incident.

Strangely enough, the higher we get, the stronger I feel. By making it to the Yellow Band, I have set a personal altitude record, and our cadence and stride enable us to pass a number of Sherpas also heading to Camp 4 that day. I begin to think I might actually summit this beast.

On top of the Geneva Spur I continue for ten or fifteen minutes along some rolling rises, surmounting the eight-thousand-meter mark—the so-called Death Zone, above which the body can no longer sustain itself for any prolonged period—and am finally treated to a full view of the Triangular Face and the southeast ridge. Descending slightly, I finally round the corner and see a huge boulder my teammate John Golden had told me about. That means the South Col and Camp 4 are very near!

Feeling reasonably strong on two liters of supplemental oxygen a minute, I explore the wasteland that is the South Col before settling in. The area is rocky and windswept, about the size of two or three football fields side by side. Primus fuel canisters, tent poles, and random garbage from expeditions long since past are underfoot. I had been led to believe that earlier environmental cleanup expeditions had brought down all the mess, but it turns out these groups primarily brought down oxygen bottles because these have commercial value. For the most part, the Nepalese side of Everest is quite clean, but Camp 4 is certainly an exception.

I assemble a tripod a short distance from camp and mount our GigaPan camera for operations. The GigaPan is a robotic camera mount we're using to hopefully acquire a 360-degree, high-resolution panorama of the South Col. The NASA-developed technology is similar to that used on Mars Landers and other robotic spacecraft. Keith and I will process the billions of pixels of imagery once we return to the United States and provide a link to this remarkable photographic scene. We are certain that it will be the highest such image ever taken.

As at Camp 3, rest is paramount at Camp 4. Moreover, I only have a few short hours to recharge my internal battery. May 20, 2009, is The Day and I want to be a leader, not a follower. I don't want to get caught in a conga line of climbers, so I plan to leave at 11:00 p.m. the night before. But as the sun sets and summit fever begins to stir in neighboring tents, I can't help but keep pace. My fresh oxygen cylinder is in my backpack, my harness on, my hot water in the proper containers, and I am mentally prepared to depart camp at 8:00 p.m.! My goal has always been to see an orbital sunrise from the top of the mountain, which will occur sometime around 4:15 a.m.

The Singapore team has previously been the slow-and-steady group and, per plan, leaves just after 8:15 p.m. Quickly developing a new strategy (we call this "strategery" down where I come from in Texas), I think the Singaporeans might make very good pacesetters and keep me ahead of the traffic jam that could potentially develop in the hours to follow.

Danuru and I leave camp at 8:17 p.m. in the wake of the Singapore team, with Ed and Sanduck in trail, our headlamps illuminating a six-to-eight-foot sphere of influence around each of us. Our crampons scratch the unstable, grapefruit-sized, snow-dusted rocks of the Col near our tents, but soon we're on packed snow and ice. With little warning, the terrain steepens, and much of the slope is unconsolidated snow. Two steps up, sink in, then one step back. Unrelenting, miserable, and disheartening. Worse, it's straight up, and a blowing snow makes me question whether we've chosen the correct weather window.

For a spell, Danuru and I end up in front of a large undulating snake of headlamps on the Triangular Face, but I relinquish our lead to Singaporean teammates Li Hui and Ester as quickly as I can. I knew I'd have the tendency to push myself too hard too soon and possibly fail to make the summit, or arrive far too early to see the orbital sunrise I dream of. What I don't realize is the truly impressive pace Li Hui sets for a pitch-black summit arrival!

Toward the top of the Triangular Face we cross several rock bands. These bands are often close to vertical and are tricky to ascend while covered in loose snow and wearing crampons. I hope the Balcony is near, but when I ask Danuru how far, he will only say, "Pretty soon, ten minutes."

Several prior seasons' worth of tattered, fixed ropes remain as we crest each tier of exposed rock. Each time I see these ropes I re-inquire: "Balcony?"

"Pretty soon, ten minutes."

This refrain becomes disheartening as hell, and I begin to question whether I will make it, especially when we hit another section of really loose snow. It's very difficult to keep my breathing in check when every step is a struggle. The little voices in my head start to tell me to go back down, but just as I think about crying uncle, I hit solid snow again, where I can get back into my rhythm, called the rest step. I kick in a step, lock my knee for a brief respite, *breathe*, then rock forward to kick in the next.

Three and a half hours into the ascent, we arrive at the Balcony. The Balcony is a jink in the road to the top, about the size of a basketball key, just enough room for a few of us to swap out oxygen tanks and then press on to the summit. I'm pretty exhausted and thankful for a small ledge to sit down on, and Danuru helps me swap tanks. A swig of warm water and a double espresso–flavored Gu help me kick it back into gear.

By this time, the frozen condensate from my oxygen mask has formed a shield of ice down the front of my down suit. I see that my zipper is encrusted. My digital camera is lodged in the inside front pocket, but I can't worry about summit photos just yet.

Our next waypoint is the South Summit, and I lead off with Danuru following close behind. My thick mountaineering mitts can barely fit through the handle of my ascender device, but thankfully I modified my down suit to clip the mittens onto the suit. At each anchor point—there are hundreds—I remove one outer mitten (I have glove liners underneath) and relocate my safety carabiner above the anchor, followed by my ascender.

The going is very steep, and on at least two pitches below the South Summit the terrain is quite technical, with upward traverses on featureless, snow-dusted slabby rock while under tension from my ascender. Occasionally, Li Hui and Ester, who are immediately in front of me on this tough terrain, come to a halt, but generally the pace is very crisp. By the time I get to the South Summit at 2:35 a.m. I know I am well ahead of schedule.

I sit on the sub-peak under a thin crescent moon and try to visualize the route ahead. My headlamp provides no cues, and my eyes can't adjust enough to see the enormous summit I know remains ahead. As Dawes and Mingma Chirring Sherpa arrive on the South Summit, Danuru and I saddle up and continue along the thin ridgeline, guided by the fixed line stretching off in front of us.

Beneath me is a narrow path of snow, rock, and ice. To my right is a snowy cornice and to my left pure blackness. Later I will see down into this void, a pure drop of several thousand feet into Nepal. Just over the corniced ridge is a similar vertiginous drop down the Kangshung Face into Tibet.

The Hillary Step is one of the most famous landmarks in all of mountaineering. The roughly forty-foot vertical pitch begins as a dihedral. The first few feet are covered in snow and ice, making it straightforward for a tall guy like me to work my way up. At the top of the step, you traverse a few feet to the left and around a large block of exposed rock. It feels like a fairly unintimidating rock climbing move, at least from what I can see with my headlamp, but during daylight descent the enormous exposure will look much more intense.

My heart races because within minutes, the summit can be mine. Topping one of several false summits, I see Li Hui's stationary headlamp up on the summit, with Ester's close by. Off in the distance to the south, I see flashes of lightning, and I wonder if they will have any bearing on the weather for my descent. By that point it doesn't even matter, though, because I have no intention of diverting from the summit.

At 4:00 a.m. local Nepal time, I proudly step onto the summit, a dining-room-table-sized snow platform with sloping sides, and carefully sit down on a mat of wind-weathered Tibetan prayer flags. After catching my breath and giving Danuru a double fist bump, I begin to see a faint orange glow on the horizon. It's going to happen. I'm going to see the equivalent of an orbital sunrise from the summit of Everest!

The sun begins to peek over the horizon, and it reminds me of my first shuttle launch. I loved those moments, when I was able to clearly see the curvature of the Earth and the full spectrum of light behind the horizon, but they only lasted perhaps thirty seconds. Here atop Everest, the orbital sunrise stretches to perhaps thirty minutes, and I will soak it all in, reveling in the light and the suggestion of warmth. I know I will never forget these all too short moments at the top of the world.

I report to IMG base on my handheld radio, thanking the Sherpas in particular for all they've done for us in the preceding weeks. Before I can forget, I struggle with the ice but prevail, unzipping my jacket and digging into my inner fleece-jacket liner for the moon rock. It's an ancient piece of the solar system, and thanks to the Apollo 11 astronauts, it's traveled so far to get here. I hold it up above my head with a sliver of the moon shining down from above and think of my boyhood dream of flying into space.

Thin, graying, and diminutive in stature, Dawes is a resilient Energizer Bunny of a man. He soon joins me on the summit, becoming the oldest American to ever reach the summit. I'm thrilled for his amazing accomplishment.[34]

I look down at my jacket and think of Luke, Jenna, Gail, Mom, and Dad, and so many others I love who have cheered me on, helped me, and encouraged me to explore and take on seemingly impossible challenges. They are each here with me in spirit. Then I tie off those special prayer flags I'd made to honor my spaceflight heroes.

I look out again at the snow-glazed peaks surrounding me, and I honestly feel as if I'm getting some sort of sneak peek at heaven or eternity—seeing a place that humans weren't really meant to see until much later. The scale of the scene seems to defy the laws of nature and physics. Then it's time to go. Every summit has a descent and it's time for mine.

Coming down the Hillary Step in the light, I see it for what it really is—a jaw-dropping knife's edge where other climbers have fallen and died. I am beginning to feel like a zombie, exhausted and at risk of stumbling down steep, hard ice. As the day warms up, I sink deeper in the snow at times and have to pull myself out. I feel like I'm in a trance, pulling my boots up and out of the steep slope, clipping and unclipping from fixed lines in an endless procession. I know I can't let my guard down. That's when people trip and fall.

At Camp 4 I rehydrate, collect my belongings, and continue on to Camp 3. By now I'm almost completely spent, but all of our team tents are occupied for the night. We have to continue downward, via the Lhotse Face, one last time. It's a dangerous spot, and I take my time at each transition, clipping my safety carabiner below the next anchor before I release the carabiner from above. I can tell I'm starting to move slower and become more and more sloppy. *Focus!*

When I finally make it to Camp 2, it's been a full twenty hours on the go. Jaime from the Discovery film crew catches our elation and exhaustion on tape as the cook staff greets us with warm orange Tang and clanking pots and pans. I feel as if I'd just crossed the finish line of the Olympic marathon to take the gold, one of the most jubilant moments of my life.

I thank my good friend Danuru, our Sherpa team, and IMG once again for the experience of a lifetime. I look over to see my climbing partner crashed outside the dining tent and, for the first time, every bit as wiped out as I am. I have nothing more to give, but the memory of my brief time at the top is playing in my head in an endless loop as I climb into my bag, pat the moon rock in my pocket, now joined by a fistful of Everest summit rocks, and instantly fall asleep.

The things in life that come to us the hardest mean the most. Everest has challenged me to the core and nearly broke my back the year before, but I returned, persevered, and made a round-trip to the top. Whenever I find myself down or struggling to solve a problem, my mind goes back to that triumphant moment, and I pick up the pace again.

CHAPTER TWENTY-EIGHT

Moonstruck

You cannot look up at the night sky on the Planet Earth
and not wonder what it's like to be up there amongst the stars.
And I always look up at the moon and see it as the single most
romantic place within the cosmos.

—*Tom Hanks*

HOUSTON, 2011

In stark contrast to my summit success, the excitement and sense of accomplishment at finally climbing Mount Everest are tempered by the situation at home in Houston. Things are just as difficult as ever, but try as I might there aren't any solutions to our marriage that involve us staying together. There's no warmth on either side, and whatever bonds we once had are now gone. I recognize that I have not been anywhere near the ideal husband, with my pursuit of exploration and adventure a huge stressor for Gail. While it's clearly time for us to go our separate ways, and has been for a while, I'm devastated as we begin to work through the painful details of how to parent the kids from two separate households, as well as a myriad of other plans that need to be made. It's going to take a while to figure it all out.

As I continue to grieve the end of my marriage and feel guilty for my contribution to it, I compensate by throwing myself into my new job. It feels strange not to be walking the halls at NASA anymore. Although I keep up with the space program and what's going on with launches, EVAs, landings, and other developments, I guess I'm feeling the loss of my duties as an astronaut, too. I barely remember what it's like not to head to NASA every day or be preparing for a mission with countless hours in the training pool. I lived and breathed and loved my job, and I will miss it.

I spend as much time as I can with the kids and set up a very small but happy home for us three. The hardest thing about my Everest trips was being apart from them for two months at a time. I certainly respect and admire our long-duration ISS astronauts, who spend almost half of their time away from family in the two years leading up to their six-plus-month missions, but I realize I'm not built for that. I love playing basketball and tennis with Luke and swimming with Jenna as often as we can. It's a time of transition, but I wouldn't trade away any of those beautiful mornings driving Jenna to school, waving our arms and singing off-key like nobody's business. She has always been my precious daughter, but she becomes the greatest joy in my life. Those moments when she surprises me with a big hug, a kiss, and an enthusiastic "I love you" are moments I treasure in the deepest part of my heart. She is spontaneous and unfiltered and she expresses emotions as they come. I'm trying to learn how to live my life as unfettered as she does.

I also begin to stay in touch with my many NASA friends and coworkers on Facebook, where many of them hang out. One day, I get a strange message from someone I've never heard of.

> You don't know me, but how was your climb, and where's my moon rock?

Whoops. With everything that's been going on, I haven't given much thought to the moon rock. For a while it's been lying on my shelf, snug inside the rigged Pringles lid. Those rocks have been to places most people will never get the chance to go, and I can only imagine what their beginnings had been like. I tap out a quick message in reply.

> I'm sorry. Who's asking?
>
> Sorry! I'm Meenakshi Wadhwa, and I know a thing or two about the rock. How did your trip go? Did you make it to the top? And where's the moon rock?

Uh oh. It's now closing in on a year after my Everest expedition, and I hate to break it to her—truthfully I have no plans to ever return it.

Somewhere along the way, during those months of preparing for my return to Mount Everest and deciding what patches and flags I wanted to take to the top to honor my heroes and my loved ones, I'd come up with an idea for what to do with the moon rock when I got back home. And right at the very moment I hear from Meenakshi, big plans for the nugget's next epic journey are afoot.

At my request, NASA recently granted permission for the moon rock to be mounted onto a special plaque along with a summit rock I brought back from the top of Everest. When finished, the plaque will be flown up to the *International Space Station* by my friend and former STS-120 crewmate George "Zambo" Zamka, now promoted to Commander of an upcoming shuttle mission (STS-130).

Zambo will be installing the plaque in the *Tranquility* cupola, a panoramic control tower on the ISS with seven windows for observation. One of the windows is thirty-one inches, the largest window ever used in space, providing a glass-bottom boat's perspective on planet Earth below. There, the precious fragments from the lunar Sea of Tranquility and the not-so-tranquil summit of Everest will continue their journey at 17,500 miles per hour as they orbit the planet. Those little samples were collected worlds apart. Perhaps someday they'll be carried by explorers to other new worlds.

I tap out a quick reply to Meenakshi and discover why she is so concerned about the moon rock. She's a cosmochemist—a chemist who studies space rocks—and her current job is Director of the Center for Meteorite Studies at Arizona State University's School of Earth and Space Exploration. But she had also been the Chair of CAPTEM, or Curation and Analysis Planning Team for

Extraterrestrial Materials, when our application for the moon rock came across her desk.

CAPTEM is a NASA advisory committee comprised of prominent members of the scientific community who typically receive requests from research scientists who want to analyze moon rocks or other astromaterials from the federal government's vast collection. Since Keith originally petitioned the committee for the Apollo 11 moon rocks with my name and the Everest expedition on the application, there had been no direct interaction between me and the committee, or Meenakshi. But even though she thought our request to take the moon rock to Everest was unusual at best, she and the committee decided it might be good PR for NASA, and moreover might help inspire children around the world to follow their dreams of adventure and exploration. She and the committee had made the call to let us borrow the lunar sample, but it sounds like she had expected to eventually get it back.

Wondering if she is a little perturbed that I haven't immediately returned the rock, and feeling like a kid who has kept out a library book way too long, I message her back to tell her about the successful Everest expedition and the nugget's journey to the top of the world. My enthusiasm for the 3.7-ish-billion-year-old Apollo 11 moon fragments[35] and their future destination must have satisfied her, and she doesn't give me too much of a hard time. It's a pleasant exchange, so I tell her if she's ever in Houston to let me know and I'll buy her coffee as a thank-you for the favorable moon rock allocation.

Meanwhile, I'm already making my transition back into the health care and technology worlds, getting back to my roots in medical innovation, and beginning to invent and commercialize a number of consumer products. I have really big ideas and solutions that I hope will eventually benefit many lives around the world. But closer to home I am still coming to terms with being separated, and trying to be the very best dad I can despite the new world order. When I have the kids, my time is all theirs, but I feel tremendous loneliness when they aren't with me in my new homey, but tiny, apartment.

Enter the Wolf Pack, a group of pretty random guys who already were or will become really close friends through the common denominator of divorce. Wheels is already like a brother to me, but our impromptu self-help group grows with the addition of Lil' John and Tomcat. John Michels, also known as LJ, is anything but lil'. He's a six-foot-seven former NFL great with two Super Bowl rings from his two seasons on the Green Bay Packers. Career-ending injuries sent him back to school and a successful medical career. I'd met him when I was Chief Technologist at a medical research institute in Houston, and we hit it off immediately. Tomcat (Tom Edman) is a hysterically funny chemical salesman and alter ego to Wheels—aren't all chemical salesmen funny?—who could easily make Amy Schumer blush. I don't realize it at the time, but my Wolf Pack (and other close friends) will help me weather the storm of divorce, and I am glad to step up for them during some of their lowest of lows.

Time passes and I begin to get comfortable as a single dad with a new purpose in life. Almost as if on cue, I get a message from Meenakshi (who goes by Mini) before she arrived in town for an annual conference. She is ready to collect on that coffee I owe her. She also asks if I can recommend a yoga studio; she is in training for a triathlon and needs a flexibility workout after sitting under fluorescent lights and listening to presentations all week.

I haven't done much yoga—I am more of a running, climbing, and weights guy—but I'm open to new fitness challenges, so I volunteer to go along. Little do I know what I'm getting myself into. Mini chooses a class featuring Bikram hot yoga, where they heat the studio to a cool 108 degrees. I also don't know she is the real deal, a yogi with a genetic advantage in the art. While I'm not the most graceful or flexible person in the convection oven–like room, I am a quick study at savasana, also known as the corpse pose. I refuse to quit, and I sweat my way through it.

Afterward we go for barbecue, perhaps somewhat incongruous to that sort of healthy workout, but I need something more than coffee to replace those burned-off calories. Then we talk. And we talk. Something magical begins to happen. She isn't what I expected. She is breathtakingly beautiful, warm, smart, athletic, and adventurous, and she likes to laugh.

Mini was born and raised in India. Her father, Jawahar, had been an officer in the Indian Air Force, who moved the family around every couple of years, so she was a third culture kid, too, learning to speak five different languages in the process. She knows what it is like to uproot and make new friends every few years. "I was a little different from the other girls growing up," she says. "I always wanted to climb trees with the boys, and I still have lots of scars on my knees."

At one point she lived in a house surrounded by mango groves. Her mom, Asha, cautioned her to be patient and let the mangoes ripen, but Mini couldn't wait. She'd climb the trees and bite into the mangoes, then show up with a nasty rash on her face the next day. She is an innately warm-hearted, loving person, too, frequently adopting street dogs into her family home, much to her parents' consternation.

Mini's parents encouraged her and her younger sister, Vandana, to pursue their chosen paths through life, rather than accept the traditional female roles and arranged marriages characteristic of the time—and that exist to a degree even to this day. Both remarkable women eventually earned their PhDs in the United States. Sadly, their gorgeous and loving mother, Asha, who looked like the Indian incarnation of Sophia Loren, died of breast cancer when Mini was just fifteen. Through this devastating loss, she had to take on greater responsibilities for her sister and her dad, but it also reinforced a passion for life.

Part of her youth was spent in Chandigarh, in the foothills of the Himalayas. Looking at the mountains, and feeling like she wanted to understand the mystical forces behind their formation, she was inspired to major in geology. Eventually, she earned her PhD in Earth and planetary sciences at Washington University in St. Louis and stayed in the academic world in the United States, teaching, conducting research, and mentoring other scientists.

By the end of our barbecue lunch, I am absolutely in awe of this kindred spirit who seems to love exploration and extremes as much as me. I feel like I'm sitting there with my mouth open in wonder, with a premonition my life will never be the same. Plus, she laughs at my jokes. She leaves the table, and the city of Houston, way too soon, and I can't wait to see her again. We begin to correspond and see each other whenever we can. During one conversation, we discover another strange point of connection—one of the lost *Columbia* astronauts I knew well, Kalpana Chawla, had been a childhood friend of Mini's.

Kalpana's family lived in Karnal, a small town between Delhi and Chandigarh. Mini was fascinated and inspired when Kalpana entered aeronautical engineering at the University of Texas, a very unusual career choice for a woman from India in those days. When *Columbia* failed to return home, Mini felt the enormity of the loss of a woman who had been a hero to her and to so many other young women. I had worked closely with Kalpana, known to many pronunciation-challenged American colleagues as just KC, at NASA, and we had even shared an office for about eighteen months. KC and I had been almost incapable of having a serious conversation, as it would always rapidly deteriorate into teasing or pranking each other. I share my favorite memories of Kalpana with Mini, and with it the pain I'd felt in the aftermath of STS-107.

I wouldn't learn it until much later, but we have yet another uncanny overlap of worlds through my good friend and EVA instructor Sabrina Singh Gilmore. Sabrina's treks to Everest Base Camp both years I was on the mountain included her mother, Manjeet. Mini's uncle Suren was Manjeet's "Rakhi brother," a tradition in India wherein young people form a close bond of friendship, almost like being siblings. Was it just incredible karma or destiny that in KC and Sabrina we had two such points of connection, with over 1.2 billion people in all of India?

Mini is as fascinated by Mars as I am and had become an expert on Mars meteorites. She tells me about using a massive, specialized mass spectrometer she calls the Beast to look at the exact chemical makeup of these little pieces of the Red Planet after they'd fallen to Earth. "I'd love to have actual rocks picked up from the surface of Mars to look at in my lab," she tells me. I wonder if maybe someday I'll have the opportunity to personally bring those rocks back to her. Or maybe we can go collect them together? Mars rocks for moon rocks? Seems like a fair trade.

CHAPTER TWENTY-NINE

Ice and Heat

To love and be loved is to feel the sun from both sides.

—*David Viscott*

ANTARCTICA, 2012

Now that I'm closer to sea level, my sights turn from Everest and moon rocks to Antarctica, the coldest, highest, driest, and most remote environment on Earth. Back in high school in Greece, I once entered a competition to travel to our most extreme continent via the Boy Scouts' Antarctic Scientific Program. I filled out the extensive application and mailed it off, fingers crossed, but didn't make the final cut. But decades later, I still have not been there, and I am still enthralled by our seventh, polar continent.

I pick up some rumblings that University of Texas Medical Branch (UTMB) in Galveston will become the new medical contractor for the US Antarctic Program. UTMB had been involved in extreme environments for years, including telemedicine support for the Space Shuttle Program and the *International Space Station*.

There are three year-round American stations on the coldest continent: Palmer, McMurdo, and Amundsen-Scott at the geographic South Pole. All three stations conduct important scientific research, including astrophysics, particle physics, atmospheric science, marine biology, glaciology, geology, geophysics, astrobiology, and many other unique study areas. These stations, along with several summer field camps, are populated by hundreds of scientific and support employees who need medical care. Moreover, all employees headed to Antarctica need careful medical screening, because while the research stations do basic first aid and primary medical intervention, there are no operating rooms or intensive care units. In a true medical emergency, evacuation would be the desired protocol, but in the middle of the Antarctic winter (stretching almost nine months at the South Pole Station), no one can fly in or out.

Antarctic deployment is an incredible analog environment for future long-duration missions to Mars and places beyond. A major occupational challenge is interpersonal conflict and associated mental health issues: the stations are small, closed communities, making for stressful work conditions as the employees work and live with the same people day in and day out. Equally disorienting, the sun is out twenty-four hours a day in the summer, and it's dark twenty-four hours a day in the winter. Depression and alcohol excess are also common problems during the long winter's night there.

I am incredibly excited to hear that a colleague has recommended me to serve as the Founding Director and Chief Medical Officer of the Center for Polar Medical Operations. The fancy title notwithstanding, I'll basically be screening future Antarctic participants, and then supporting them "on ice" using telemedicine and by hiring medical professionals to staff the clinics there. A welcome perk of the job will be visiting my staff and conducting site visits to the three stations and some of the field camps.

After I take the job, I travel to Antarctica and have the opportunity to marvel at glaciers calving enormous chunks of bluish-green ice into the polar waters, stand among great colonies of penguins, and float alongside breaching whales. I camp on the ice shelf, fly in a helicopter over a venting Mount Erebus, the southernmost active volcano in the world, and crunch through the snow at the South Pole Station. The extreme weather outside the stations reminds me of Everest, although it is much colder.

My relationship with Mini grows exponentially as we spend more time together. I realize she is the most extraordinary woman I've ever met, and also my perfect match. I love her, my parents love her, and my kids think she is pretty great, too. She, too, has struggled through unhappiness leading to a divorce. We begin to talk about making a life together, and I feel like we have everything in common except the color of our skin. We even have Antarctica in common!

As a grad student, Mini had been there as part of the Antarctic Search for Meteorites (ANSMET). Funded by NASA and the NSF, field teams traveled to Antarctica each austral summer (Southern Hemisphere summer) to hunt blue ice fields that essentially concentrate meteorites. Meteorites are easier to spot there because terrestrial rocks are generally buried; if you see a dark rock, there is a high probability it is a space rock. The finds were rich enough to make up for the difficult conditions, with ANSMET teams typically bringing home several hundred meteorites in a field season.

As a senior faculty member and world-class meteorite expert, Mini has recently been invited back to Antarctica for a two-month expedition. As good fortune would have it, I also have a scheduled business trip to Antarctica coming up. If all goes according to my ever-evolving plan, I might just be able to meet up with Mini at McMurdo Station[36] when she returns with her team after her six-week expedition out on the ice. Our meeting isn't assured, given potential weather delays and frequent equipment problems. The best we can hope for is about forty-eight hours of overlap before I am scheduled to depart McMurdo Station to fly north on a ski-equipped US Air National Guard LC-130 aircraft.

Before long, Mini leaves for her expedition to the subzero Antarctic plateau, at an altitude above ten thousand feet, with a team of seven other people. She drives the blue ice fields on a snowmobile searching for meteorites. We are able to connect a handful of times by satellite phone, and I can tell she is in her element. She tells me the team has collected over three hundred meteorites, an awesome trip by any measure.

I fly into McMurdo and do my work, and the night Mini is due to return, I'm up waiting anxiously for her. Lying on the upper bunk in my dorm room, I have a view out the snow-blown window as I watch for her silhouette. I'm getting tired, my eyes wanting to close. It's nearing 4:00 a.m. local, but there's perpetual daylight, and I shake my head to stay awake. People come and go, even at this hour.

Eventually, I see four people shouldering heavy duffel bags, all in red parkas, walking down the dirt road toward the dorm. I just know it's her and her teammates, so I hurriedly throw on my matching red jacket and head outside. It's just begun to snow, unusual for this time of the Antarctic summer. The snow is pristine and beautiful, the sky gray and cloudy. I can't wait to see her. It's been way too long.

Mini sees me, stops, drops her bags, and starts running toward me. I do the same, accelerating toward her; you can almost hear Tchaikovsky's "Romeo and Juliet, Fantasy Overture" in the background. When we meet, I grab her up into a big bear hug. She's been out in the field for weeks, surviving on sponge baths, but she looks radiantly beautiful. Her eyes tell me how much she's missed me, too. She tells me their plane had been overloaded with equipment and they'd had delays. She'd been worried we'd miss each other. But it's so good to see her. I never want to be apart from her that long again.

The next day, we're invited to a special dedication at nearby Scott Base, a Kiwi research station, with the visiting Prime Minister of New Zealand in attendance. Equally unusual, the Google street cam is on the scene but mounted on a backpacker!

We have so much to talk about and so much in common. I've missed everything about her, from her smile to her laugh, and I don't want the day to end.

"Let's go for a walk before bed."

"Oh, I don't know."

"Why don't we take a walk to Scott's Hut?" Also known as Discovery Hut, Scott's Hut is a major McMurdo landmark built by British explorer Robert Falcon Scott when he established a base there in 1902.

"Are you sure? It's really late." She's yawning, practically rubbing her eyes.

"Come on, we have to!"

She's game, and we trudge out to the old wooden hut, about a mile and a half hike to the tip of a peninsula over a soft, crunching blanket of fresh fallen snow. The cold air wakes Mini up, and we hold hands, laugh, and toss snowballs at each other. At the end of the trail, we stop to gaze out at the horizon, trying to see the sun through the clouds. The ice is starting to melt out on the Sound and the water is opening up.

Then, as I get down on one knee, I watch her eyes widen. I pull out a blue Tiffany's box tied with a white ribbon.

I pour out my heart to the most remarkable woman I've ever met. I thought soul mates only existed in Meg Ryan movies, but here is a woman who shares my great passions in life, accepts my weaknesses, and who brings out my very best. We are dreamers who never dreamed we'd find each other. Somehow, the universe brought us together through Earth, space, and ice. And I am never going to let her go.

"I love you to infinity and back. Will you marry me?"

Huge tears well in her deeply intelligent, beautiful eyes. "Yes!"

She was in Antarctica for rocks and she found them. But she hadn't expected this kind of rock.

Much later, Mini and I are married back in the States in the presence of family and many of our closest friends, codifying our deep love, intense passion, and uncanny friendship. It still amazes me that she can almost always read my most complex emotions from across a crowded room and that I can pick the one thing out of a twenty-page menu that she would enjoy the most.

We get each other to the core, perhaps because of remarkably similar-yet-dissimilar third culture upbringings and our innate drive as explorers, even though we were literally born worlds apart. Every once in a while I look over at Mini, her warmth and radiant beauty casually filling the room, and I realize that I still have an overwhelming crush on her after so long.

At night, cupping her stunning face in both my hands, I stare deeply into those brilliant eyes as we lie face-to-face and have the most important conversation of each and every day. Whether we actually utter the actual words or not, we're able to communicate volumes in each long glance. I consider myself the luckiest man in the known universe, and I think of the moon rock that brought us together, floating somewhere high above, as we hold hands and drift off to sleep.

AFTERWORD

The Flight Path Ahead

We are all . . . children of this universe. Not just Earth, or Mars, or this System, but the whole grand fireworks.

—*Ray Bradbury*

MASAYA VOLCANO, NICARAGUA, 2016

Will I ever climb down a ladder and plant my boots into the dust of the Red Planet? There's a far-off, minuscule chance—ideally with Mini by my side. Regardless, those first boot prints I dreamed of will more likely be created by some young person who has probably already been born and may already be hard at work to make those dreams come true. I'm okay with that, because I've been able to help set the stage for their triumph through my career, at least in some small way, and I firmly believe our nation is still capable of such great things. It will happen whether it's us or some future Rocket Boys and Rocket Girls who blast off to Mars for the expedition of a generation.

While it wasn't Mars, I did recently fly to Nicaragua to descend into level zero of an active lava lake. This very book's delivery was delayed to my patient publisher when my friend and fellow explorer Sam Cossman called to ask me to join his team of scientists and filmmakers for an extraordinary expedition to a volcano called Masaya. I've come to know firsthand that exploration is a team sport and NASA is a champion. After all, most of an astronaut's time is spent on the ground, supporting other missions and crews. No explorer operates alone, at least not for very long, and I've been privileged to be a part of a team for virtually every single adventure of my life.

On the crater rim, as I strap on my helmet, headlamp, GoPro camera, and chest harness, adjust the full-face filtration mask, and climb into a fire-retardant suit, I feel like I'll be descending into hell. Or at least a literal lake of fire. A blast of warm, opaque, sulfur dioxide–laden wind surges over me, but my mind wanders back to my home team; I always think about my family at momentous times like this.

Even though this is an exhilarating place, I now realize there is no greater joy than embracing life's many simple pleasures with Luke and Jenna and Mini at my side. My kids truly inspire me, and Mini's love empowers me. Luke is doing incredibly well, a business major at Baylor University, and I savor every moment I can get with him. He's grown into a wonderful young man, with empathy born out of his special relationship with his sister. Our Jenna says and does what comes to her without caring what other people think. People might look at her and think there's something odd about her, but there's absolutely nothing wrong with her. She acts out her happiness, and should never be judged for that. She's taught us true joy by transcending her challenges and frustrations and, by and large, choosing to be happy. She has shaped our thinking as we learn unique coping strategies from her. With her ability to program any electronic device, she's taken over as the tech guru of our home. Along with studying individuals with elite abilities, what can we learn from those with intellectual and physical challenges that can benefit the rest of us? This is a life mission I have embraced. These are some of the new peaks I want to climb.

Before I clip into the zip line on Masaya, I check and recheck my gear and heft the emergency self-contained breathing apparatus (SCBA) backpack onto my back. This is more than a thrill ride; we'll be installing an extensive sensor network to monitor sulfuric gases, temperature, pressure, and carbon dioxide around the caldera and all the way down to the floor of the lava lake, with the goal of ultimately generating predictive models of eruptive activity to protect the local population of the capital city, Managua. I've learned adventure is hollow without a greater purpose. Floating in space and looking back home changed my perspective. I looked down at the sky below and realized all of humankind is in the frame, living and breathing and moving inside that paper-thin atmosphere.

When I step into the void beyond the crater's edge, a steel braid takes my weight as I slowly slide down the cable under tension from a rope above. I stare down into the otherworldly bubbling lava through my face mask's visor, and the long-ago memory of the boy with the machine gun comes back to me. Whatever became of that shivering kid-soldier in Tehran? Why was I so fortunate to be able to leave while he had to stay and freeze in his thin uniform, carrying a heavy gun instead of a football or a basketball? How did I warrant the good luck to be able to chase my dreams and make some of them come true? Sam and I are about to set the very first (crazy) human boot prints in as hostile, beautiful, and extraordinary a place as I've ever been. Caught up in the moment, I feel a deep sense of gratitude for the amazing gifts in my life, and an obligation to steward that gift with every shred of passion and ingenuity I have.

At the bottom, Sam and I hike for thirty minutes over the jumbled, rocky terrain, dodging fumaroles and intermittent lava bombs. Finally, we approach the lava shoreline, keeping a close eye on the molten surf. While I belay Sam over for an even closer look, I think about what lies ahead, the long view. There is just one precious and beautiful planet to care for, and the more I explore this planet and the space around it, the more I love it and want to take care of it. Although I've hung up my spacesuit, there is still much of our planet and solar system yet to be discovered. Whether we visit these places for the first time—much of our ocean floors have yet to be mapped in any great detail—or revisit them with substantially better sensors, the power of big-data analytics, or human-robotic collaboration, there is still much to be learned.

Regrettably I don't look much like Doogie anymore, but I'm still a wide-eyed dreamer. Maybe you are, too. Dreams aren't unusual—they're an essential part of the human existence, as common as three-leaf clovers and bunny rabbits. But repeatedly pursuing and attaining one's dreams is an exceptional rarity, like a jackalope chomping on a field of four-leafers. Most dreams are left on the pillowcase, unfulfilled. Dreams without a plan and a purpose get left behind in the rush of daily life. I get it; I have many dreams still on the shelf, and I learned early on that the pathway to success is long and arduous, and giving up can be tempting as hell.

But I have learned how to dream big and then set course to make it happen. I've learned the essentials: keeping laser focused, visualizing the path to success, maintaining a strong support network, training for success but preparing for failures along the way, and having confidence tempered by humility and a dose of luck. If you are ready for the call of opportunity when it rings, and you are willing to put in the work required, it's remarkable how dreamlets emerge, tangible, from the fog of unrealized dreams. It's really not all that hard if you aren't afraid to stumble every once in a while and then get back up. And back up. And back up again. The summits and calderas and skywalks and other bold life challenges are out there, waiting for you to dust off your dream. Everything is possible until proven impossible, and then you just need to become more creative.

The sky is not the limit. And it never will be.

ACKNOWLEDGMENTS

This book started modestly as a trickle, a slow electronic recounting of a few memorable life experiences onto my laptop over many months. My family and friends had repeatedly encouraged me to share my adventures in life, but only through candid conversations with deeply respected authors Homer Hickam, Bob Vera, and Andy Chaikin did my loose collection of unconnected stories emerge as a rudimentary book proposal. And only through Bob's very kind introduction to his agent, Chip MacGregor of MacGregor Literary, did the book really take root. I'm deeply grateful to Chip for his steadfast support of *The Sky Below*, and for connecting me to my amazing collaborative author, Susy Flory, and then to my visionary editor, Barry Harbaugh of Little A.

I think Susy must have been a world-renowned psychiatrist in another life, as her penetrating questions on motivations, emotions, and failures led me to examine my life from a much deeper perspective than I could have ever achieved on my own. Explorers, inventors, dreamers, and geeks are generally not that introspective, and I'm a card-carrying member of all of these communities. I can't thank her enough for helping me make this story as impactful as possible, for doing the vast majority of the background interviews and the base structuring of the book, and for helping me truly develop my writer's voice. Moreover, Susy's beta readers faithfully offered tremendous constructive feedback as the book took form.

Barry's excitement for the story and his skill as an editor then took the book to an entirely new level as he encouraged us to share the major events of my life in first person present tense. Although I was uncertain and skeptical at first, it was his urging that made *The Sky Below* as fast-paced and page-turning as can be. Moreover, I am so appreciative of having Little A and Amazon Publishing give my memoir a huge soapbox upon which to stand.

One of the perks of the added attention granted by the "John Glenn Mission" (STS-95) was getting to meet a Pulitzer Prize–winning photojournalist by the name of David Hume Kennerly. He'd come to Houston to take snaps of John, and the rest of the crew if we happened to be in the frame, too. As a kid, I vividly remember reading David's book *Shooter*, detailing his work during the Vietnam War in particular, and strongly considering photojournalism as an adventurous vocation. We swapped stories and quickly became friends. My thanks to David for taking the back-cover photo, not to mention the profound images of the world he's shared with all of us over the years.

In a sense, this book is one big thank-you to the many people who have shaped and supported my life's work and passions. I'll never be able to acknowledge each and every star in my constellation loud enough to do them all justice, but it all started with my family. My parents and grandparents never dissuaded me from biting off more than I could chew, although they secretly might've preferred it if I'd pursued a passion for chess or something lower impact than luge or skywalking. My sincere gratitude to Gail for my two kids, Luke and Jenna, who have shown me what's most important in life. My wonderful Mini's deep love ultimately gave me the strength and encouragement to write this memoir. Without my family, I'd be in perpetual writer's block.

There are so many people who helped shape my spaceflight career, but none more than my spacewalking instructors and the divers of the Neutral Buoyancy Lab. Through all of my seven walks in the void of space, I could almost feel their presence just beyond my peripheral view. As I was retiring from NASA in 2009, they organized a last-day-in-the-pool ceremony that I'll never forget. I became the very first astronaut to join the NBL divers' One-Thousand-Hour Club, entitling me to a coveted shirt embroidered with both my name and record-setting hours. But as I was about to ditch my scuba gear and get out of the pool, the divers ripped off my mask and smeared my face in O-ring grease, their longstanding farewell tradition. I'm still trying to get the grease out of my pores, but I'll always be grateful for them teaching me how to really walk the walk, the ultimate experiences of my life.

Sadly, this book goes to print after the passing of one of my greatest heroes, a man who even became both a crewmate and a friend. I was so fortunate to have been able to rub shoulders with John Glenn in outer space, and to see his grace and statesmanship firsthand. It was a real treat for Pinto (Steve Lindsey) and me to fly out to Washington, DC, to attend his senate retirement party, held at the Smithsonian National Air and Space Museum. Standing shoulder to shoulder with him, we peered into his *Friendship 7* capsule with John recounting the tense moments of his launch, orbital flight, and reentry. He'd even marked up the instrument panel way back when, allowable since it was a one-time vehicle, and it had undisputedly been his on February 20, 1962. When he departed the pattern on December 8, 2016, America lost one of its true patriots, and left us a deep void in national leadership.

Two other special heroes lit my path through life. I did try to return that red knit cap of Captain Cousteau's I had taken into space on STS-66. After a wonderful celebration in Paris to formally present it back to him, once the cameras were off, he remarkably said to me: "From one explorer to another, I want you to keep it." And years later my tribute to Neil Armstrong and Ed Hillary atop Mount Everest would lead to a wonderful exchange with Neil in his later years, when he kindly wrote: "It's been a good life. I've left you much to do." I am so thankful for their inspiration, even to this day.

People often ask me what fuels my resolve, and what was more difficult, the rigors of spaceflight or those of scaling Everest? Simply put, the struggle to get back and attempt Everest a second time was the toughest mental, physical, and logistical challenge I've ever faced. Knowing that I was able to overcome so many obstacles and ultimately achieve that mystical summit I'd dreamt of since childhood has given me the strength to take on many other daunting challenges since, both personally and professionally. I'll always be indebted to my friends Keith Cowing and Miles O'Brien for getting me to the mountain and supporting me there, and especially to Danuru Sherpa of Phortse, my steadfast companion on the mountain, who belongs in his own Stan Lee superhero movie.

Mountain struggles forge friendships for life, and I'm also thankful that I had the chance to both climb and survive with Monty Smith on Everest in 2008. He was exceptionally bright and gregarious, a lover of life, his family, and the high mountains. Regrettably, Monty never made it back to try Everest again; in January 2010, he took his own life for reasons I will never know. I think of his energy and the opportunities lost. Like all of his many devoted friends, I wish

I'd stayed in closer touch and could have redirected history. If you're struggling, please reach out to a friend. If you see a friend struggling, please reach out . . .

My many other lifelong compatriots, from grade school to college, and from NASA to the present day, have also supported me through many wonderful triumphs and inevitable periods of sadness, and it amazes me that we can still pick up a conversation from a decade ago as if it were just yesterday. I wish I had the page count to thank all of my friends, climbing partners, instructors, crewmates, NBL divers, flight surgeons, co-pilots, co-inventors, and mentors in the way they so richly deserve, but know for certain that you are in these pages and in my heart. I'm so fortunate to have your positive influences in my life, and I humbly aspire to be that in return for you.

Onward and upward . . .

NOTES

1 A. Schultz et al., "Loads on the Lumbar Spine. Validation of a Biomechanical Analysis by Measurements of Intradiscal Pressures and Myoelectric Signals," *Journal of Bone & Joint Surgery* 64, no. 5 (1982): 713–20.

2 The process of high-altitude acclimatization takes several weeks of progressively higher and higher forays up the mountain, resulting in the body's adaptation to the thinning atmosphere. A wide array of biochemical and physiologic adaptations occurs, including the body producing more red blood cells to capture the limited oxygen molecules in the air a climber takes in with each inspiration.

3 Cheyne-Stokes respiration is also known as periodic respiration, with increasingly deeper, then shallower cycles of respiration, along with possible periods of apnea.

4 Also known as a chockstone.

5 The tragic loss of the Apollo 1 crew during a dress rehearsal for Apollo's maiden voyage was as a result of an electrical short. Because the capsule was pressurized with 100 percent oxygen and as a result of an inwardly opening hatch, the crew had no possibility of exiting.

6 Aluminum tanks with eighty cubic feet of air.

7 NASA loves acronyms, and TFNG is one of my personal favorites.

8 Aimee Berg, "OLYMPICS; Astronaut's Adventure on Earth: Luge," *New York Times*, November 6, 1998.

9 S. E. Parazynski et al., "Transcapillary Fluid Shifts in Tissues of the Head and Neck During and After Simulated Microgravity," *Journal of Applied Physiology* 71, no. 6 (1991): 2469–2475.

10 Mark Springel, "The Human Body in Space: Distinguishing Fact from Fiction," *Science in the News* (blog), July 30, 2013, http://sitn.hms.harvard.edu/flash/2013/space-human-body/.

11 Tracy Kidder, *Mountains Beyond Mountains: The Quest of Dr. Paul Farmer, a Man Who Would Cure the World* (New York: Random House, 2004).

12 You can enjoy your own NASA simulation here: http://www.nasa.gov/multimedia/3d_resources/station_spacewalk_game.html.

13 While the Soviets can boast the first female cosmonaut and first spacewalker, Valentina Tereshkova and Svetlana Savitskaya respectively, they've only flown four female cosmonauts in total over their entire fifty-five-year history of spaceflight. Since Sally Ride's pioneering flight in 1983, over forty American women have flown in space. The most recent NASA ASCAN (2013) class was the first with gender parity: four men and four women.

14 One of the most interesting relics of the early space program is a small shrine of sorts, housed within the men's locker room: Yuri Gagarin's locker is on display behind Lexan, revealing his tennis gear as he'd left it, just prior to perishing in a jet aircraft training flight in 1968.

15 Nikhil Swaminathan, "Fact or Fiction?: Babies Exposed to Classical Music End Up Smarter," *Scientific American*, September 13, 2007, https://www.scientificamerican.com/article/fact-or-fiction-babies-ex/.

16 Poyekhali (meaning "Let's go!") as uttered by Yuri Gagarin when clearing his launch tower.

17 Mark Lee and Carl Madee flew an earlier engineering version of SAFER on STS-64.

18 "Mercury 6: Phase 1: Launch," Spacelog.org, accessed May 25, 2017, http://mercury6.spacelog.org/page/ and "Launch of Mercury-Atlas 6 (Friendship 7)," YouTube, posted March 17, 2010, https://www.youtube.com/watch?v=38deOWJPiFk.

19 Prior life science–dedicated shuttle missions had previously flown this same gear, but who knew how an almost-eighty-year-old would fare with the stressors of spaceflight?

20 The CAPCOM is traditionally a US astronaut or a member of the US astronaut corps who serves in the Mission Operations Control Room (MOCR) as liaison with the astronauts in space.

21 NASA uses NOLS expeditions on a regular basis to train astronauts in team-building and problem-solving in extreme environments like mountaineering or sea kayaking.

22 Jonathan Clark, "Remembering the Columbia Crew, One Day at a Time," *Space Safety Magazine*, January 26, 2015, http://www.spacesafetymagazine.com/space-disasters/columbia-disaster/.

23 An extremophile, from the Latin extremus, meaning "extreme," and the Greek philia, meaning "love," is an organism that thrives in physically or geochemically extreme conditions inhospitable to complex organisms, which includes most life on Earth.

24 "Patent Foramen Ovale," Diseases and Conditions, Mayo Clinic.org, posted July 16, 2015, http://www.mayoclinic.org/diseases-conditions/patent-foramen-ovale/basics/definition/con-20028729.

25 Dan was an American (NASA) astronaut, but also one of the "Ichi Brothers" given his Japanese descent, along with Koichi Wakata and Soichi Noguchi of the Japan Aerospace Exploration Agency. Much to Dan's concern, a senior NASA official responsible for approving flight assignments once confused Dan for a Japanese astronaut while exercising alongside him in the astronaut gym. They were watching a news broadcast demonstrating congressional dysfunction when the senior NASA guy asked him, "Do they have problems like this in your country, too?" Boichi, as he became known to us, was convinced he'd never get a flight assignment!

26 As of January 2017, 224 people from 18 countries have lived on or visited the space station.

27 To see when the ISS is flying over your hometown, visit https://spotthestation.nasa.gov.

28 Joel W. Powell and Lee Robert Brandon-Cremer, *The Space Shuttle Almanac: A Comprehensive Overview of 40 Years of Space Shuttle Development* (Calgary: Microgravity Productions, 2011).

29 The ISS wasn't going to fall out of the sky if the *Harmony* module wasn't installed on schedule, but it was a ticking clock most every NASA employee working on the program was focused on, and likely led to being a bit more cavalier when considering the risks of foam coming off of the external tank. External tank foam shedding was a problem even before the *Columbia* disaster, but experts reasoned that since foam had come off in the past and hadn't been a "major" problem, it wasn't anything to worry about now, especially with the rush to completion.

30 To get a feel for the swarm of Micrometeoroid and Orbital Debris (MMOD) activity above us, visit https://orbitaldebris.jsc.nasa.gov/faq.html.

31 The seventh manned mission in the Apollo space program launched on April 11, 1970, but the lunar landing was aborted after an oxygen tank exploded two days

later, crippling the spacecraft. It seemed like a disaster unfolding, with astronauts Jim Lovell, Jack Swigert, and Fred Haise suffering limited power, loss of cabin heat, shortage of potable water, loss of oxygen, and a failing carbon dioxide removal system. Mission Control was forced to cancel the planned moon landing, and the astronauts moved to the Lunar Module in order to save power that was going to be needed later for reentry. But the problem was the Lunar Module was not designed to support three people for ninety-six hours, and the scrubbers that cleared the carbon dioxide from the air couldn't keep up. The astronauts were in danger of asphyxiation and hypothermia, to mention just a couple of issues. It was the ultimate MacGyver moment, with three men's lives hanging in the balance. Yet back on Earth, Mission Control's Team 4, led by legendary Flight Director Gene Kranz, came up with an incredible hack using random materials available on Apollo. After following a precise set of Mission Control instructions, using materials at hand such as a bungee cord, socks, duct tape, and even the paper cover to the Apollo 13 flight plan, the crew carried out repairs and returned safely to Earth on April 17, 1970.

32 The beginning of the 2008 season on Everest was notable for Chinese political control of access to the upper reaches of the mountain, above Camp 2, as well as severely limiting communications from the Nepalese side of the mountain. A Chinese national team planned an Olympic torch relay to the summit via the northeastern ridge, the most common approach from China. An armed Nepalese team was posted at Camp 2 with orders to shoot to kill any climber heading higher, for fear there might be some form of "Free Tibet" rally on top of the world, interfering with their Beijing Olympic celebrations. Thankfully their team summited on May 8, 2008, and we were able to continue our expedition higher.

33 R. P Ocampo and D. M. Klaus, "Comparing the Relative Risk of Spaceflight to Terrestrial Modes of Transportation and Adventure Sport Activities," *New Space* 4, no. 3 (2016): 190–197.

34 Sadly, he held this American record for just two days, when a sixty-seven-year-old Californian narrowly edged him out.

35 L. B. Ronca, "The Ages of the Lunar Seas," *Proceedings of the National Academy of Sciences of the United States of America* 68, no. 6 (1971): 1188–1189.

36 Capable of housing over 1,200 residents, McMurdo is the largest community in Antarctica. The station was named after Lieutenant Archibald McMurdo of HMS *Terror*, the British ship that first explored and charted the area in 1841.

ABOUT THE AUTHORS

Photo © 2017 David Hume Kennerly

Scott Parazynski was inducted into the Astronaut Hall of Fame in 2016 and is the recipient of many prestigious awards, including five NASA Space Fight Medals, two NASA Distinguished Service Medals, two NASA Exceptional Service Medals, the *Aviation Week* Laureate Award, the Antarctica Service Medal, the National Eagle Scout Association's Outstanding Eagle Scout Award, and the Lowell Thomas Award from the Explorers Club. Now a tech start-up CEO and a prolific inventor, he ventures into some of the world's most extreme environments in the name of exploration and innovation. Scott and his wife, Mini Wadhwa, a renowned planetary scientist, divide their time between Houston and Phoenix. His most important role to date is serving as a doting husband and father of two children.

Susy Flory (coauthor) is the *New York Times* bestselling author or coauthor of twelve books. She is a member of the Authors Guild and was recently named director of a San Francisco Bay Area writers' conference. A breast cancer survivor, Susy celebrates life by riding a crazy ex-racehorse named Stetson, hiking in the High Sierras, and skiing black diamond runs whenever she can.

23336884R00167

Printed in Great Britain
by Amazon